EXAM ESSENTIALS PRACTICE TESTS

Cambridge English: First (FCE)

1

Charles Osbourne
with new material by Helen Chilton
and Helen Tiliouine

Australia • Brazil • Japan • Korea • Mexico • Singapore • Spain • United Kingdom • United States

Exam Essentials Practice Tests 1
Cambridge English: First (FCE) (with key)

Charles Osbourne, with some new material by Helen Chilton, Carol Nuttall and Helen Tiliouine

Publisher: Gavin McLean

Publishing Consultant: Karen Spiller

Editorial Project Manager: Stephanie Parker

Development Editor: Debra Emmett

Strategic Marketing Manager: Charlotte Ellis

Project Editor: Tom Relf

Manufacturing Buyer: Eyvett Davis

Cover design: Oliver Hutton

Compositor: Cenveo® Publisher Services

National Geographic Liaison: Wesley Della Volla

Audio: Martin Williamson, Prolingua Productions

DVD-ROM: Tom, Dick and Debbie Ltd

Contributing writer: Elaine Hodgson (video materials)

ISBN: 978-1-285-74492-6

National Geographic Learning
Cheriton House, North Way, Andover, Hampshire, SP10 5BE
United Kingdom

Cengage Learning is a leading provider of customised learning solutions with office locations around the globe, including Singapore, the United Kingdom, Australia, Mexico, Brazil and Japan. Locate our local office at **international.cengage.com/region**

Cengage Learning products are represented in Canada by Nelson Education Ltd.

Visit National Geographic Learning online at **ngl.cengage.com**
Visit our corporate website at **www.cengage.com**

Photos
The publisher would like to thank the following sources for permission to reproduce their copyright protected photographs:

159 t (Getty Images), 159 b (Waldteufel/Fotolia), 160 t (Andreu Dalmau/Epa/Corbis UK Ltd), 160 b (Redferns/Getty Images), 162 t (Shutterstock), 163 t (BE&W Agencja Fotograficzna Sp. z o.o./Alamy), 163 b (David Fischer/Getty Images), 165 t (Getty Images), 165 b (Shutterstock), 166 t (Transtock Inc./Alamy), 166 b (Motoring Picture Library/Alamy), 168 t (Getty Images), 168 b (Shutterstock), 169 t (Shutterstock), 169 b (Yuri Arcurs/Fotolia), 171 t (Shutterstock), 171 b (Getty Images), 172 t (Blend Images/Alamy), 172 b (Purestock/Alamy), 174 t (Mar Photographics/Alamy), 174 b (Andrew Rubtsov/Alamy), 175 t (Bilderbox/Fotolia), 175 b (Shutterstock), 177 t (Getty Images), 177 b (UpperCut Images/Alamy), 178 t (Frans Lemmens/Alamy), 178 b (Paul Weston/Alamy), 180 t (Shutterstock), 180 b (Arthur Tilley/Getty Images), 181 t (Christine Osborne Pictures /Alamy), 181 b (Alexandre Zveiger/Fotolia).

Text
The publishers would like to thank the following for permission to use copyright material:

Page 12: Adapted from 'Wrestling with demons' by Simon Hattenstone, The Guardian, 21 July 2003, Copyright Guardian News & Media Ltd 2003. Page 32: Adapted from 'How I came to envy the country mice' by Diana Athill, The Guardian, 17 December 2003, Copyright Guardian News & Media Ltd 2003. Page 34: Adapted from 'The Common Hand' by Carl Zimmer, http://ngm.nationageographic.com/2012/05/hands/zimmer-text. Page 52: Adapted from 'In Search of an Old Romantic' by John Walsh, First appeared in The Independent. © 2004. Copyright The Independent, reproduced with permission. Page 70: Adapted from 'Travel's Frenemy: Noise' by Daisann McLane, http://travel.nationalgeographic.com/travel/traveler-magazine/real-travel/noise/. Page 72: Adapted from 'Mountains in the Sea' by Gregory S. Stone, http://ngm.nationalgeographic.com/2012/09/seamounts/stone-text. Page 88: Adapted from 'Photo Research' by Jim Richardson, http://photography.nationalgeographic.com/photography/photo-tips/photo-research-richardson/#page=2. Page 106: Adapted from 'Miracle Above Manhattan' by Paul Goldberger, http://ngm.nationalgeographic.com/2011/04/ny-high-line/goldberger-text. Page 142: Adapted from Barrington Irving, from http://www.nationalgeographic.com/explorers/bios/barrington-irving/, copyright © National Geographic.

Although every effort has been made to contact copyright holders before publication, this has not always been possible. If notified, the publisher will undertake to rectify any errors or omissions at the earliest opportunity. Note that the sample answer sheets in the Practice tests are not the updated official answer sheets provided by Cambridge as these were not available at the time of publication.

Printed in China by RR Donnelley
1 2 3 4 5 6 7 8 9 10 – 18 17 16 15 14

Contents

CAMBRIDGE ENGLISH: First (FCE)

Paper 1: READING AND USE OF ENGLISH (1 hour 15 minutes)

Part	Task type and focus	Number of questions	Task format
1	**Multiple-choice cloze** Task focus: vocabulary	8	A multiple-choice cloze text with eight gaps, followed by eight four-option questions.
2	**Open cloze** Task focus: grammar and some vocabulary	8	A modified cloze text with eight gaps which you must fill with the appropriate word.
3	**Word formation** Task focus: vocabulary	8	A text with eight gaps. You are asked to complete the text by making an appropriate word from the word prompt you are given for each gap.
4	**Key word transformations** Task focus: grammar and vocabulary	6	This task consists of six discrete key word transformations. You are asked to complete a sentence which means the same as the given sentence using the key word.
5	**Multiple choice** Task focus: reading for detailed understanding of a text, gist, opinion, attitude, tone, purpose, main idea, meaning from context, implication, text organisation features	6	You answer six four-option multiple-choice questions on a text.
6	**Gapped text** Task focus: reading to understand how a text is structured	6	Six sentences have been removed and placed in jumbled order after a text. You decide from where in the text the sentences have been removed.
7	**Multiple matching** Task focus: reading for specific information in a text, detail, opinion, attitude	10	You match ten questions with different texts or different sections of a text.

Paper 2: WRITING (1 hour 20 minutes)

Part	Task type and focus	Number of questions	Task format
1	**Question 1** Essay	Part 1 is compulsory. 140–190 words	You must write an essay based on a given title and accompanying ideas, including one of your own.
2	**(FIRST candidates)** **Questions 2–4** may include an article, an email/a letter, a report, a review.	You choose one task from a choice of three. 140–190 words	You must carry out a writing task, using the appropriate style and format.
2	**(FIRST FOR SCHOOLS candidates)** **Questions 2–4** may include an article, an email/a letter, a review, a story. **Question 5** is based on the set books. It may be an essay.	You choose one task from a choice of four. 140–190 words	You must carry out a writing task, using the appropriate style and format.

Paper 3: LISTENING (40 minutes approximately)

Part	Task type and focus	Number of questions	Task format
1	**Multiple choice** Task focus: understanding gist, detail, function, purpose, feeling, attitude, opinion, genre, agreement, etc.	8	A series of short unrelated extracts of approximately 30 seconds each, from monologues or exchanges between interacting speakers. There is one three-option question for each extract.
2	**Sentence completion** Task focus: detail, specific information, stated opinion	10	A monologue of 3–4 minutes. The task consists of ten gapped sentences.
3	**Multiple matching** Task focus: understanding gist, detail, function, purpose, feeling, attitude, opinion, genre, agreement, etc.	5	A series of short related extracts, of approximately 30 seconds each, from monologues. The five questions require selection of the correct option from a list of eight.
4	**Multiple choice** Task focus: understanding attitude and opinion, main idea, specific information and gist	7	A text between two speakers of 3–4 minutes. There are seven three-option questions.

Paper 4: SPEAKING (14 minutes approximately)

Part	Task format	Input	Functions
1 **Interview** **2 mins**	The interlocutor asks each candidate to say a little about themselves.	Verbal questions	You must be able to • give personal information. • talk about present circumstances / past experiences. • talk about future plans.
2 **Individual long turn** **4 mins**	Each candidate talks about a pair of photographs for 1 minute, followed by a 30-second response from the second candidate.	Visual stimuli, with verbal and written instructions	You must be able to • give information. • express your opinions. • relate photos to yourself and your own experience.
3 **Two-way collaborative task** **4 mins**	The interlocutor asks candidates to carry out a task based on written prompts.	A written question with written stimuli and verbal instructions	You must be able to • exchange information and opinions. • express and justify opinions. • agree, disagree or partly agree. • suggest and speculate.
4 **Discussion** **4 mins**	The interlocutor asks candidates general opinion questions related to the topic covered in Part 3.	Verbal prompts	You must be able to • exchange information and opinions. • express and justify opinions. • agree, disagree or partly agree.

Exam Essentials Practice Tests is a new series of materials published by National Geographic Learning for students preparing for the following major EFL/ESL examinations: Cambridge English: First (FCE), Cambridge English: Advanced (CAE), and Cambridge English: IELTS (International English Language Testing System). The series is characterised by the close attention each component pays to developing a detailed knowledge of the skills and strategies needed for success in each paper or part of the exams.

Cambridge English: First (FCE) Practice Tests helps learners become aware of the exam requirements for Cambridge English: First (FCE), offers details about the format and language in the exam, and helps learners develop exam skills necessary for success. The book also offers extensive practice in all parts of the exam, using the actual test format.

Taking the exam

Cambridge English: First is one of a series of five Cambridge English exams corresponding to different levels of the Common European Framework of Reference for Languages (CEFR):

• Cambridge English: Key (KET) CEFR Level A2

• Cambridge English: Preliminary (PET) CEFR Level B1

• Cambridge English: First (FCE) CEFR Level B2

• Cambridge English: Advanced (CAE) CEFR Level C1

• Cambridge English: Proficiency (CPE) CEFR Level C2

Cambridge English: First is widely recognised in commerce and industry, and by universities and similar educational institutions, as proof that the holder of this qualification can do office work or take a course of study in English.

The exam can be taken on many dates during a year, and can be taken on paper or on a computer. It consists of four Papers:

Paper 1, Reading and Use of English (1 hour 15 minutes)

Seven parts: four Use of English tasks including cloze tests, word formation and key word transformations focusing on vocabulary and grammar, followed by three reading comprehension tasks. The reading tasks consist of a long text followed by multiple-choice questions, a gapped text with whole sentences removed and a multiple-matching task. The focus in the reading tasks is on understanding gist, main points, detail, attitude, implication, purpose, opinion and text structure as well as deducing the meaning of words and phrases from context.

Paper 2, Writing (1 hour 20 minutes)

Two parts, each requiring you to produce a piece of writing. In Part 1, candidates of both Cambridge English: First and Cambridge English: First for Schools have to write a compulsory essay *in Part 1*.

In Part 2, 'Cambridge English: First' candidates choose one task from a choice of three questions. These may be an informal letter or email, a formal letter or email, an article, a report, or a review written for a given purpose and target reader.

In Part 2, 'Cambridge English: First for Schools' candidates choose one task from a choice of four questions. These may be an informal letter or email, an article, a review, a story, or a question on a set text written for a given purpose and target reader.

Paper 3, Listening (40 minutes approximately)

Four parts with recorded texts and comprehension questions. Tasks include multiple choice, sentence completion and multiple matching. The focus is on understanding gist meaning, main points or specific information, detail, purpose, function, feeling, attitude, opinion, genre and agreement.

Paper 4, Speaking (14 minutes approximately)

Four parts, involving two candidates and two examiners (one examiner asks the questions and the other listens). The Speaking Paper focuses on the candidates' ability to use general interactional and social language, organise a larger unit of discourse (comparing, describing, expressing opinions), sustain an interaction, exchange ideas, express and justify opinions, etc.

Preparing for the exam

In preparing for the four papers, the following points should be taken into account:

Reading and Use of English: To prepare for the **Use of English** (Parts 1, 2, 3 and 4), as well as getting general practice in grammar and vocabulary, you should practise the precise skills necessary for the tasks here: how to use a word or phrase in context, how words with similar meanings are used in different collocations, accuracy with common structures, phrasal verbs and lexical phrases, and the different methods of word formation.

To prepare for the **Reading** (Parts 5, 6 and 7) you need to be familiar with a range of reading materials, such as newspaper articles, advertisements, brochures, guides, manuals and correspondence, as well as with different approaches to reading. It is important be aware that different strategies can be used for different parts of the Reading

Paper. For example, reading to find specific information is the best strategy in Part 7, where candidates have to find out where a certain piece of information is located.

Writing: You must be able to write an essay for Part 1 and an article, email/a letter, essay, report, review, or story for Part 2 (see above for the difference between the content of Cambridge English: First and Cambridge English: First for Schools exams), so practice of these types of writing is essential. You should practise covering all the points provided in the input and your writing must display organisation and coherence, clear layout, appropriate register, control and accuracy of language.

Listening: Practice with pre-listening tasks (focusing on developing an expectation of what might be said) is essential here, as is thorough familiarity with a wide variety of spoken English in terms of discourse types and genres. Listening for different purposes should also be exercised: to get the gist or to find specific information.

Speaking: You need practice in using spoken English effectively, which includes mastery of conversational skills (such as turn taking and the appropriate way to participate in a discussion), providing full but natural answers to questions, requesting clarification and speaking clearly and audibly at all times.

Further information can be obtained from the following website: www.cambridgeenglish.org.

Practice Tests: contents

Cambridge English: First (FCE) in the **Exam Essentials Practice Tests** series prepares candidates for the Cambridge English: First examination by providing **eight full practice tests,** accurately following the latest exam specifications.

There are **two guided tests** at the beginning, which feature **essential tips** to practise exam strategy. These essential tips offer guidance and general strategies for approaching each task. Other tips offer advice relevant to specific questions in the guided tests. These two comprehensive guided tests will help students prepare for each paper in the ways described in the previous section, while the following **six tests (without guidance)** will offer students thorough practice up to and beyond the level of the exam.

The DVD-ROM accompanying the book includes the **audio materials** for Paper 3 (Listening), which have been recorded so as to accurately reflect the audio element of the actual exam. (Please see the DVD-ROM Introduction for more information about the content of this component.)

A **writing bank** includes sample answers for the tasks in Paper 2 (Writing), writing tips in the form of **notes**, and **useful phrases** and **expressions** for the different task types.

Varied **visual materials** for Paper 4 (Speaking) have also been included, while a **language bank** supplies useful phrases and expressions for use in the Speaking Paper when discussing the visual and written stimuli.

There is also a **glossary** at the end of each test, explaining vocabulary from Paper 1 that is likely to be unfamiliar to students.

Clear and straightforward design simplifies use of the book. **Exam overview** tables ensure that key information is readily accessible, while a specially designed menu makes it easy to navigate through the different papers and parts of each practice test.

You will find sample exam answer sheets on pages 156–158 which you can photocopy and use to note down your answers. These will give you practice in using the answer sheets provided in the real exam.

For more practice, there is also an additional book of tests for this exam: *Exam Essentials Practice tests 2, Cambridge English: First (FCE).*

Practice Tests: principles

In writing this book, three guiding principles have been observed:

Firstly, that it should be useful for teachers, and for students whether sitting the Cambridge English: First exam for the first time, or re-sitting the exam, and whether working alone or in a class. Students approaching the exam for the first time would be best advised to work through the book linearly, developing their skills and confidence; those re-sitting the exam can consult the overview tables to concentrate on particular areas for targeted revision. The **without key** edition can be used by students working in a class, while the **with key** edition provides a detailed **answer key** and all the **audio scripts**, ensuring that students working alone can benefit from active support while attempting these tests.

The second principle is that the questions should accurately reflect the whole range of questions found in the Cambridge English: First exam. Thus students obtain guidance concerning the general content and the best way of approaching the tasks from the questions themselves. Seeing the questions in this light – as instructions to the candidate from the examiner, rather than intimidating challenges – also helps students feel less daunted by the whole experience of sitting a major exam like this.

The third principle is that the texts used in the practice tests should not only be fully representative of those used in the exam but also varied and interesting. Everyone finds it easier to learn a skill if the subject matter is relevant to his or her lifestyle and interests. In choosing, editing and creating the texts here, we have done our utmost to ensure that the experience of working with this book is as stimulating and rewarding as possible.

PAPER 1 Reading and Use of English	▶	Part 1
		Part 2
PAPER 2 Writing		Part 3
		Part 4
PAPER 3 Listening		Part 5
		Part 6
PAPER 4 Speaking		Part 7

For questions **1–8**, read the text below and decide which answer (**A, B, C** or **D**) best fits each gap. There is an example at the beginning (**0**).

Mark your answers **on the separate answer sheet**.

Example:

| **0** | **A** idea | **B** view | **C** thought | **D** decision |

| 0 | A | **B** | C | D |

Essential tips

▶ Read the title and the whole text to get the general meaning.

▶ Some of the questions will ask you to choose a word from a set of words with similar meanings.

▶ The word you need may be part of a collocation, an idiom, an expression or fixed phrase. You may need a preposition, which is part of a phrasal verb or a linker.

▶ If you are not sure which of the options fits best, say the sentence to yourself and use the one that sounds best.

▶ When you have finished, read the text again to make sure it makes sense.

Question 3: The gapped word is part of a fixed phrase. Which verb best completes the phrase *when it ... to?*

Question 6: Sisters, brothers, grandparents are all ... of your family.

Question 8: The gapped word is part of a fixed expression. Which verb best completes the phrase *... the best for somebody?*

Working parents

Reliable studies have shown that children of parents who both go out to work have no more problems than children with one parent staying at home. My personal (**0**) .... is that both parents should go out to work if they wish.

Some parents invest so much in a career that they cannot (**1**) .... to give it up. Others have to work because of economic (**2**) ....

There are several options when it (**3**) .... to choosing childcare from child minders to the kind neighbour (**4**) .... the street.

No (**5**) .... how good the childcare may be, some children protest if their parents aren't around. Babies become dependent on parents and close family (**6**) .... , so parents should make sure they allow (**7**) .... time to help their child settle in with their new carer.

Remember: if parents want to (**8**) .... the best for their children, it's not the quantity of time they spend with them, it's the quality that matters.

1	**A** bear	**B** decide	**C** hope	**D** expect
2	**A** reason	**B** duty	**C** necessity	**D** task
3	**A** refers	**B** concerns	**C** turns	**D** comes
4	**A** of	**B** opposite	**C** across	**D** next to
5	**A** way	**B** matter	**C** surprise	**D** exception
6	**A** people	**B** adults	**C** members	**D** grown-ups
7	**A** little	**B** no	**C** lots	**D** plenty of
8	**A** make	**B** give	**C** have	**D** do

PAPER 1 Reading and
         Use of English
PAPER 2 Writing
PAPER 3 Listening
PAPER 4 Speaking

Part 1
Part 2
Part 3
Part 4
Part 5
Part 6
Part 7

For questions **9–16**, read the text below and think of the word which best fits each gap. Use only **one** word in each gap. There is an example at the beginning (**0**).

Write your answers **IN CAPITAL LETTERS on the separate answer sheet.**

Example: 0 B E E N

Daniela: Skateboard champion

I've always (**0**) .... an outdoors kind of girl, and (**9**) .... a kid, I'd get up to all sorts of stuff with my friends – climbing trees and messing about in the woods. As we got older, my friends started doing other things (**10**) .... shopping and listening to music, but I still loved being outside and needed a new challenge.

(**11**) .... was my brother who first got me (**12**) .... skateboarding. I'd seen him practising on his board hour after hour, and to (**13**) .... honest, I used to think it was uncool. But when he showed me some amazing tricks he could do one day, I had to give it a go.

I've got a competitive streak, so I watched loads of skateboarding clips online and got out on my board whenever I could – even (**14**) .... it was dark – in order to compete (**15**) .... my brother. It obviously paid (**16**) .... because I beat him in a competition last month!

Essential tips

▸ Read the whole text to get the general meaning.

▸ Decide what kind of word is needed (verb, pronoun, article, determiner, quantifier, etc.).

▸ Remember you can only use one word in each gap.

▸ You cannot use contracted forms (*I've, he's, they're, mustn't,* etc.) to fill in the gaps.

▸ Say the phrase or sentence to yourself and see which word sounds right in each gap.

▸ Read the text when you have finished and check that it makes sense.

Question 10: Look at the context. The missing word means 'for example', or 'such as'.
Question 12: This gap is part of a phrasal verb that means 'to become interested in' an activity.
Question 13: The missing word helps to complete a common expression. Which verb and form of the verb is needed?

PAPER 1	Reading and Use of English ▶	Part 1
		Part 2
		Part 3
PAPER 2	Writing	Part 4
		Part 5
PAPER 3	Listening	Part 6
PAPER 4	Speaking	Part 7

For questions **17–24**, read the text below. Use the word given in capitals at the end of some of the lines to form a word that fits in the gap **in the same line**. There is an example at the beginning (**0**).

Write your answers **IN CAPITAL LETTERS on the separate answer sheet**.

Example: | 0 | O B S E R V A T I O N |

Essential tips

▸ Read the whole text to get the general meaning.

▸ Decide what type of word (noun, adjective, verb, etc.) you need for each gap.

▸ Look at the context carefully. The word may be negative or positive.

▸ You may need to add a prefix or suffix to the prompt word.

▸ If the word is a noun, check if you need the singular or plural form.

▸ You may need to make two changes to the word (add a prefix and a suffix, add two suffixes, etc.).

▸ Check the spelling of each word carefully.

Question 21: In this gap you are looking for a noun. Read the rest of the sentence. Should the noun be singular or plural?

Question 22: This word describes the noun (*site*), so it must be an adjective. How can you form an adjective from *idea*?

Question 23: In this gap you are looking for an adverb. How many changes do you need to make in order to form an adverb from *surprise*?

The London Eye

The London Eye, the giant (**0**) .... wheel, is one of the most popular attractions in London. The wheel is one of the tallest of its kind, at a (**17**) .... of 135 metres. 1,700 tons of steel were used for its (**18**) .... People make special journeys to see the (**19**) .... wheel. Fifteen thousand visitors can ride on the Eye every day.

OBSERVE

HIGH
CONSTRUCT
EXCITE

The architects, Julia Barfield and her husband David Marks, won the competition to design a Millennium landmark. Their design was the most (**20**) .... of all the projects and the first (**21**) .... of the wheel were made on their kitchen table in 1993. Julia found the (**22**) .... site by drawing a circle round London and finding its centre.

IMAGINE
DRAW
IDEA

Not (**23**) .... , it took about three years to get the wheel built. In (**24**) .... of their work, the couple were awarded the MBE, a special honour that is given in the UK to someone who has achieved something special.

SURPRISE
RECOGNISE

PAPER 1	Reading and	▶	Part 1
	Use of English		Part 2
PAPER 2	Writing		Part 3
			Part 4
PAPER 3	Listening		Part 5
			Part 6
PAPER 4	Speaking		Part 7

For questions **25–30**, complete the second sentence so that it has a similar meaning to the first sentence, using the word given. **Do not change the word given.** You must use between **two** and **five** words, including the word given. Here is an example (**0**).

Example:

0   I'll be very happy when I go on holiday.

   FORWARD

   I'm .... on holiday.

The gap can be filled by the words 'looking forward to going' so you write:

Example: | 0 | LOOKING FORWARD TO GOING |

Write only the missing words **IN CAPITAL LETTERS on the separate answer sheet.**

---

25   Richard asked me how much I had paid for the theatre tickets.

   COST

   Richard wanted to .... the theatre tickets.

26   It wasn't a good idea for you to delete that file.

   SHOULD

   You .... that file.

27   The ferry couldn't sail because the weather was bad.

   DUE

   The ferry couldn't sail .... weather.

28   The teacher told us not to be late on Friday.

   BETTER

   'You .... late on Friday,' the teacher said.

29   There are Spanish and French translations of the book.

   BEEN

   The book .... into Spanish and French.

30   She will only phone if she gets lost.

   UNLESS

   She will .... lost.

Essential tips

▶ You must use between two and five words in the gap. Contractions (*didn't, we're, it's,* etc.) count as two words.

▶ Check that you have used all the information from the first sentence, and that you haven't added any more information.

▶ Make sure you don't change the word given in any way.

▶ Decide what structure you need to use (passive voice, indirect speech, etc.) by looking at what comes before and after the gap.

▶ Remember to check your spelling carefully.

Question 28: What verb is used with *better* to mean 'should'? After it do we use the infinitive with or without *to*? Must this be positive or negative?

Question 29: Here you need to use the passive. Your prompt word is *been.* What tense do you need?

Question 30: *Unless* means 'if not', so what change do you need to make to one of the verbs in this conditional sentence?

PAPER 1	Reading and ▶	Part 1
	Use of English	Part 2
PAPER 2	Writing	Part 3
		Part 4
PAPER 3	Listening	**Part 5**
PAPER 4	Speaking	Part 6
		Part 7

You are going to read an article about a wrestler who became an author. For questions **31–36**, choose the answer (**A**, **B**, **C** or **D**) which you think fits best according to the text.

Mark your answers **on the separate answer sheet**.

The wrestler who became an author

Pete Watson looks like the biggest, sweetest teddy bear you ever saw. It is only when he opens his mouth that you notice the missing front teeth. Watson is a three-time world champion wrestler turned author. He was adored by fans because he was different: while other wrestlers were supreme athletes, he was just a hulk who knew how to take a hit. You could throw as many chairs as you liked at Pete Watson, you could smack him repeatedly, but he wouldn't go down.

After two autobiographies and a series of children's stories, he has just written a brilliant first novel: a work of immense power and subtlety, likely to gain a wide readership. At its simplest, it is about a boy and his dad getting together after a lifetime apart, though there is far more to it than that. Was he inspired by anyone he knew? The father, he says, is based on guys he met on the road – wrestlers, friends of his, who appeared to be leading exciting lives, but deep down were pretty miserable.

line 11 Watson does not come from traditional wrestling stock. He grew up in Long Island, New York. His father was an athletics director with a PhD, his mother a physical education teacher with two master's degrees – one in literature, the other in Russian history. He was a big boy, bullied for his size. One day his neighbour had a go at him, and for the first time Watson realised he could use his weight and size instead of feeling awkward about it. It was a turning point.

At college, he did a degree in communication studies. Meanwhile, he was learning the ropes of professional wrestling. Did his parents try to dissuade him? 'No. They were just really insistent that I finished college. I am pretty sure they thought I'd get hurt and quit wrestling.' But he didn't.

He looks in remarkably good condition for someone who spent 20 years in the ring. His skin is smooth and firm; there are few visible scars. 'It's amazing what retirement can do for you. I looked really rough five years ago, and now I think I look a good deal younger,' he says. People are surprised by the softness of his handshake. 'Yeah, that's the wrestler's handshake,' he says.

Do you have to be a good actor to be a good wrestler? 'I used to really resent the acting label, but it *is* acting. When it's really good, when you're feeling it and letting that real emotion fly, it comes closer to being real.' What did his children think when they saw him getting hurt? 'Well, they used to think I never got hurt because that's what I told them. When they got old enough to realise I did, they stopped enjoying it. That was, in part, what led to my decision to get out.'

Nowadays, his time is dedicated to family and books – his next novel is about boy wrestlers living on the same block, and he is also writing more children's stories. He does not think this life is so different from wrestling. 'Wrestling is all about characters,' he says. 'So when my fans hear I've written a novel, I don't get the sense that they feel I've abandoned them.'

- Read the text first to get the general meaning. Don't worry about individual words that you don't know.

- The questions follow the same order as the relevant information in the text.

- Underline the key words in each question and in the four options.

- Look in the text for information that supports one of these options, but don't expect to find exactly the same words.

Question 31: Look at option A. It consists of two parts: he frequently lost and he was not aggressive. If an option consists of two parts, it is correct only if both parts are correct. For example, it is true that Pete was not aggressive, but as he didn't frequently lose, option A is not correct.

Question 33: This is a question about vocabulary. If you don't know the meaning of the words (in this case *stock*), you can answer the question by looking at the context. The sentences after *traditional wrestling stock* are about his parents' professions. What is the correct option?

Question 34: An option is correct only if you can find clear support for it in the text. For instance, option C claims that Pete's parents wanted him to stop wrestling. Can you find support for that in the text? For which of the four options can you find support in the text?

31 What impression do we get of Pete Watson's skills as a wrestler?

A He frequently lost because he was not very aggressive.
B He was too gentle and friendly to be a good wrestler.
C He was injured a lot because he didn't fight back.
D His speciality was letting his opponent hit him.

32 It is suggested that Watson's first novel

A is based on his own autobiography.
B will be popular with those who liked his autobiographies.
C will not only appeal to his fans.
D is not much more than a simple story.

33 What does 'traditional wrestling stock' in line 11 refer to?

A Watson's childhood
B Watson's family background
C Watson's educational background
D Watson's background in athletics

34 What did Watson's parents feel about his interest in wrestling?

A They were afraid he would get hurt.
B They insisted that he should have proper training at college.
C They wanted him to give up wrestling.
D They thought he would abandon the sport quite soon.

35 How does Watson regard the idea that wrestling is like acting?

A He resents the suggestion.
B He thinks wrestlers aren't good actors.
C He has come to accept it.
D He doesn't think wrestling can compare to acting.

36 Watson's present life is not so different from his past profession because

A his work is still connected with characters.
B he is writing about wrestling, his previous profession.
C his family are still more important than anything else.
D his fans still follow his career with interest.

For the Glossary see page 27 ▶

PAPER 1 Reading and
          Use of English
PAPER 2 Writing
PAPER 3 Listening
PAPER 4 Speaking

Part 1
Part 2
Part 3
Part 4
Part 5
Part 6
Part 7

You are going to read an article about computer games. Six sentences have been removed from the article. Choose from the sentences **A–G** the one which fits each gap (**37–42**). There is one extra sentence which you do not need to use.

Mark your answers **on the separate answer sheet**.

Films and computer games

In just a few decades the gaming industry has become a lot bigger than the film business. In terms of turnover, what is rather grandly called 'interactive entertainment' makes twice as much money as Hollywood cinema. Which of course leaves people in the film business wondering if they can harvest any of this new income. Is there any way of making films more appealing to people who regularly like to play computer games?

Making a film out of a best-selling computer game can certainly guarantee a large audience. **37** New games have stunning action sequences that rely on fantasy effects, and now films are being released with similar scenes. Gravity is discarded as heroes leap across huge gaps, while slow-motion techniques show bullets moving through the rippling air.

A major segment of the gaming market comprises science-fiction games, and film-makers have started to realise that they could set films in similar sci-fi future worlds. **38** Any attempt to borrow more than the setting from a game is probably doomed.

There are many examples of successful film-game combinations. Rather than making a film using characters and stories from a computer game, the trick seems to be to make a film that has a fast-moving action sequence and then bring out a game based on that sequence. People who enjoyed the film will probably want to buy the game. This clearly creates a new market opportunity for the gaming industry.

Why do gamers feel disappointed by films based on their favourite games? **39** Computer games can show the action from a number of perspectives easily, because everything is computer-generated. But filming a sequence from 20 different cameras would cost a fortune, so it simply isn't done in the film version – leaving the gamers feeling that the film didn't look as real as the computer game.

Cameras matter in another sense, too. In a film the director shows you the action from certain perspectives but makes sure he doesn't show you some things to keep you in suspense. Think of your favourite thriller. **40** In films you are not supposed to have access to all the information. Suspense and mystery are essential elements of film-making.

41 When you play a game, you have to do certain tasks to proceed to the next level. Therefore, you must be able to see everything in order to make your choices, to decide what to do next: which door to open, and so on. You must have access to all the information. You, as the player, are always in control. In the cinema you never control the action. You just sit and watch.

There can be some interaction between films and computer games on a number of different levels, but in the end they fulfil different needs. **42** For all the similarities between technologies and special effects, we shouldn't forget that a story and a game are fundamentally different.

A We go to the cinema to let someone else tell us a story, knowing we can't influence what happens at all.

B You wouldn't be interested in watching the film if you knew the identity of the murderer, for instance.

C This is not true for computer games.

D Its success lies in the use of special effects.

E This usually means that the film has a good chance of being as commercially successful as the game on which it is based.

F One reason is technical.

G However, the difficulty for the producers of Hollywood appears to be knowing where and when to stop.

Essential tips

▸ Look at the text to see what it is about. Even without the missing sentences, you can understand the general meaning.

▸ Read the text before and after each gap. Try to guess what the missing information is.

▸ Go through the gapped sentences. Try to find a link between the text and the gapped sentences.

▸ The text and the gapped sentence will be on the same topic.

▸ Re-read the whole text to make sure it makes sense.

Question 37: The sentence before the gap talks about guaranteeing *a large audience*. If a film has a large audience, what is it? Find an option that defines what it is.

Question 40: What kind of film is a thriller? Which sentence option refers to one?

Question 41: The last sentence of the paragraph before the gap talks about 'essential elements of film-making'. The next paragraph talks about computer games. Which sentence option makes a suitable topic sentence for this paragraph?

For the Glossary see page 27 ▶

You are going to read a magazine article in which four young people talk about how their parents' careers have influenced them. For questions **43–52**, choose from the people (**A–D**). The people may be chosen more than once.

Mark your answers **on the separate answer sheet**.

Essential tips

▸ Skim through the whole text to get a general idea.

▸ Read the questions and underline the key words. Make sure you understand the exact meaning of each question.

▸ Look quickly through the text for information about the key words in each question. Remember that the key words might not be in the text at all, but there will be other words or expressions with that meaning.

▸ If you find a text where the key words are mentioned, look through the other texts as well to make sure you have got the correct answer.

Question 43: This person thinks their parent's job is *boring*. What is the key word and what are synonyms for it?

Question 48: If someone comes from *a long line* of people in a certain profession, who else was in that profession?

Question 52: There are different ways to say that something is *rewarding*. In which text can you find reference to this?

Which person

thinks his or her parent's job is boring?	**43** ☐
was discouraged from following the same profession?	**44** ☐
changed his or her mind about a future career?	**45** ☐
experienced pressure to follow the same profession?	**46** ☐
feels he or she has not been influenced in choosing a career?	**47** ☐
comes from a long line of people in this profession?	**48** ☐
thinks the profession in question offers few opportunities?	**49** ☐
is concerned his or her choice will cause an argument?	**50** ☐
thinks that success in his or her parent's profession is difficult?	**51** ☐
thinks his or her parent's profession is rewarding?	**52** ☐

For the Glossary see page 27 ▶

A chip off the old block

How much are children influenced in their choice of profession by their parents' jobs?
We asked four young people about their experience.

A Graham Button

My dad is a self-employed builder, like his father and his grandfather, and that means he was often out working in the evenings or at weekends when I was a child. I think he was proud of doing a 'real' job, something with his hands, which is perhaps why he always tried to push me into taking up the same profession. And of course he had his own business, which he wanted me to continue after he retired. When I was in high school, I decided that I really didn't want to go into the family business, so at the moment I'm studying history. My father probably thinks I'm going to become a partner in his firm after I graduate, so I do worry that we might have a big fight about this some time in the future.

B Sue Smith

My mother's a nuclear physicist, which sounds very exciting. The truth is it's a pretty tough profession. And I just don't think it's a very interesting job. Of course it's important, but as far as I can see, you spend most of the day at a desk doing hundreds of calculations, and then checking and rechecking them. My mother did try to motivate me to take an interest in science subjects when I was about 14 or 15, and I think she'd be secretly pleased if I wanted to be a scientist, but she's never put any sort of pressure on me. But I know she also thinks – as I do – that there aren't so many jobs available in pure research, which is what she does.

C Barry Porter

When people find out my mother's an actress, they always ask what Hollywood films she's been in, and I have to explain that she's only ever worked in provincial theatres. She's hardly ever been on television, which is why not many people know her. That's one of the problems with the theatre: very few people get to the top of the profession, and you have to be extremely lucky just to make a living from it. Actors often worry about where the next job's coming from. Even if I had any talent for acting, I'd be put off by that side of it. As you can gather, I really don't think my future is in the theatre, and in any case my mother has always tried to steer me away from taking up the profession.

D Ruth Lawrence

My father teaches maths at high school, which definitely used to come in handy when we had a maths test the next day! I think in the back of his mind he expected me to be good at maths because he was always there to explain it. The truth is I've always been terrible at the subject. He also used to tell me about the satisfaction you can get from teaching, and I do think he's right about that. I used to think I wanted to be a teacher, but then I began to think of the disadvantages. The profession's changed and these days teachers have to work a lot in the holidays and prepare a lot at home. In the end I decided to go into accounting, and I don't really think my dad's job affected my decision at all.

You **must** answer this question. Write your answer in **140–190** words in an appropriate style.

1   In your English class you have been talking about the value of learning a foreign language. Now, your English teacher has asked you to write an essay.

Write an essay using **all** the notes and give reasons for your point of view.

Is it worth learning a foreign language?

Notes
Write about:

1. using a foreign language for work
2. using a foreign language for travel
3. .... (your own idea)

Essential tips

Part 1

▶ Decide whether you think it is worth learning a foreign language and state your opinion clearly in the introduction.

▶ In the body of your essay you need to give reasons to support your argument. Use all of the topics in the notes and put each idea in a separate paragraph. Give examples of why you think (or why you don't think) it is important to learn a foreign language for the purposes of work or travel. You could also consider other people's points of view.

▶ Make sure you include **your own idea** on a third, related topic and use it to support your opinion. For example, you could say that learning a foreign language is also useful for communicating with friends of other nationalities.

▶ Summarise your overall opinion in the final paragraph.

▶ Check the length of your essay, your grammar, spelling and punctuation.

PAPER 1 Reading and
         Use of English

PAPER 2 Writing   ▶ Part 1

PAPER 3 Listening   Part 2

PAPER 4 Speaking

Write an answer to **one** of the questions 2–5 in this part. Write your answer in **140–190** words in an appropriate style.

2   You see this notice on your school/college noticeboard:

What is your favourite possession?

Write an article for our student magazine about your favourite possession and say why it is special to you.

We'll publish the most interesting articles in our magazine.

Write your **article**.

3   You have received this email from your English-speaking friend, Maria.

From: Maria
Subject: English course – activities

Hi!

I'm looking forward to the English course we've decided to do! There are classes in the morning and activities in the afternoon. We need to decide whether we do indoor activities, like swimming, or outdoor activities, like horse riding. What do you think we should choose? What kind of activities do you like best?

See you soon!

Maria

Write your **email**.

Essential tips

Part 2

▶ Decide which question you can answer best. Do you have ideas and vocabulary for any of the questions?

▶ Underline the key words in the instructions.

▶ Plan the different sections of your answer and decide on the main point of each paragraph.

▶ Spend some time making notes about each paragraph.

▶ Make sure your ideas are clearly organised. Every paragraph should be on one topic.

▶ Check the length of your answer, your grammar, spelling and punctuation.

Question 2
Use a neutral style. In your introduction you should say briefly what you are going to write about. Make sure you answer the question. Describe your possession in detail. Give some background information to explain what makes it special to you.

Question 3
Use an informal style. Thank Maria for her email and say that you're also looking forward to the English course. In the main body of your email, answer Maria's questions. You could ask Maria some questions, too, for example, does she agree with your choice? In your conclusion, say that you hope to hear from Maria soon. Should you use an informal or formal way to end your email?

Continued on next page ▶

4   You see this notice in a popular English-language magazine called *Cinema News*:

> Have you seen any good films lately? If you have, write a review for
> our magazine! Include information on the plot and the characters, and
> say why you think the film is worth seeing.
>
> We will publish the best reviews in next month's issue.

Write your **review**.

5   (*for FIRST FOR SCHOOLS candidates only*)

Answer the following question based on your reading of **one** of the set books.

If the book you have read were made into a film, which character would be the
most interesting? Write a **letter** to an English penfriend who has read the same
book, saying which character you imagine would be most interesting in a film
and explaining why. Do not write any addresses.

Essential tips

Question 4
You are writing for a popular
magazine, so the style of your review
could be semi-formal. Organise your
ideas in paragraphs and make sure
you answer all parts of the question.
In the introduction, you could describe
the film in general terms (What is the
film called? What kind of film is it?
Who directed it? Who acts in it?). The
main body could consist of two or
more paragraphs in which you should
describe and comment on the plot and
the characters. In the conclusion say
why you think the film is worth seeing.

**Question 5 (*for FIRST FOR SCHOOLS
candidates only*)**

The question asks you to think of an
interesting character. You don't have
to write about the main character. Your
letter should be informal.

Essential tips

▶ Look carefully at the question for each listening text and underline the key words.

▶ Read the three options and think of words that are associated with them.

▶ The listening texts are dialogues and monologues. The answer may come at the beginning, in the middle or at the end of the listening text.

▶ Don't worry about understanding every word you hear. Listen for the general meaning.

▶ If you hear a word or phrase from an answer, do not assume that this is the correct answer.

▶ Decide on an option after the first listening. Use the second listening to check your answers.

Question 3: All three options may be discussed in the listening text. You need to decide which of them both speakers say.

Question 6: The question asks what the speaker is doing. You will need to listen to the whole text to understand this, rather than hearing the answer in a single sentence.

Question 7: You need to know how the speaker is feeling. The listening text may not use the same words, so listen carefully for synonyms.

🎧 **Track 1**

You will hear people talking in eight different situations. For questions **1–8**, choose the best answer (**A**, **B** or **C**).

1 You hear a student talking about her college course.
   What does she say about it?
   A She enjoys seeing how things work in practice.
   B She is sure she'd like to work in a related field.
   C She wants to know more about an aspect of the course.

2 You hear a conversation between a customer and a florist.
   What does the customer decide to do?
   A take the florist's advice
   B research a new species of rose
   C buy an expensive bunch of flowers

3 You hear two students discussing their maths class.
   What do they agree about?
   A how helpful their maths teacher is
   B how useful the maths phone app is
   C how difficult the maths topic is

4 You hear a weather forecast on the radio.
   Where are violent storms expected?
   A the south coast
   B the east coast
   C the west coast

5 You hear a woman leaving a message for a plumber.
   The woman wants him to
   A correct an error he has made.
   B call her when he finishes work.
   C discover the source of a problem.

6 You hear a man talking about his travel plans.
   What is he doing?
   A complaining about train timetables
   B confirming a hotel reservation
   C making a request of someone

7 You hear two friends talking about the football team they support.
   How does the man feel?
   A optimistic about the team's prospects
   B annoyed by the referee's decision-making
   C surprised by the goalkeeper's ability

8 You hear part of an interview with a student who wants to become a volunteer.
   What does the student say about it?
   A He is keen to pass on his knowledge.
   B He wants to repay the people who helped him.
   C He regrets not getting involved earlier.

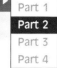 **Track 2**

You will hear part of a talk by a man called James Edwards, who is the director of a museum association called **Museums for All**. For questions **9–18**, complete the sentences with a word or short phrase.

Museums for All

The association Museums for All was started

(**9**) .... years ago.

James says the task of Museums for All is to change people's

(**10**) .... of museum visits.

James worked for a big (**11**) .... company

before he was offered his current position.

James believes that museums should be more

(**12**) .... in the way they attract visitors.

James says that traditional museums used to be aimed at people with a good

standard of (**13**) ....

To raise interest in museums, James would like museums to have good

(**14**) .... with local schools.

James wants museums to be friendly, in the same way that

(**15**) .... are.

James says that a trip to the museum can be (**16**) ....

for some people.

James feels that it is the role of the (**17**) .... to invest

in rebuilding museums.

The Museum Festival next year will be held in

(**18**) ....

Essential tips

▶ Read the instructions and think about the topic before you listen.

▶ Go through the questions carefully and think about the sort of information that is missing.

▶ Remember that the questions follow the order of the text.

▶ You will hear the word or words you need for each question, but the rest of the sentence will be slightly different.

Question 9: What kind of information is missing? The reason why Museums for All was started, the time that it was started or the people who started it?

Question 12: Are you listening for a noun or adjective for this gap?

Question 18: Look at the context. The missing information must be a place or a time.

PAPER 1 Reading and
         Use of English

PAPER 2 Writing

PAPER 3 Listening ▶

PAPER 4 Speaking

Part 1
Part 2
Part 3
Part 4

🎧 **Track 3**

You will hear five short extracts in which people are talking about school trips they went on when they were younger. For questions **19–23**, choose from the list (**A–H**) what each speaker says. Use the letters only once. There are three extra letters which you do not need to use.

A I made some new friends.

B I had some communication problems.

Speaker 1 [ ] **19**

C I would like to go back to the area soon.

Speaker 2 [ ] **20**

D I went on similar trips over the next few years.

Speaker 3 [ ] **21**

E I wasn't properly prepared for the trip.

Speaker 4 [ ] **22**

F I thought the trip was good value for money.

Speaker 5 [ ] **23**

G I thought the trip was too long.

H I would have liked more independence.

Essential tips

▶ Read the instructions carefully to identify what the speakers will be talking about.

▶ Before you listen, look at each option and think of how these ideas can be expressed.

▶ If a speaker mentions a word from the options, think carefully before you choose that option; it may be that the word is used in a different meaning.

▶ All the speakers will be talking about the same topic. You need to focus on the differences between the speakers.

Option D: If one of the speakers says that he or she *wanted* to go on more trips, or *intended* to do this, does it mean that he or she really did go on more trips?

Option E: The key word here is *prepared*. You can get prepared for a journey in a number of ways: you can start by making plans, getting information or doing some shopping. What else could it mean?

Option H: The key word here is *independence*. What are the synonyms of this word? How else could this be phrased?

Track 4

You will hear a radio interview with Julia Emerson, a young writer. For questions 24–30, choose the best answer (**A**, **B** or **C**).

24 According to Julia, nowadays Hollywood producers
  A usually think of ideas for films themselves.
  B write screenplays and contact stars.
  C contact agents to find writers for them.

25 Julia says that she
  A has written a number of successful screenplays for studios.
  B was lucky enough to have her first screenplay accepted.
  C was not discouraged by the lack of response from studios.

26 Julia began writing in her spare time when she
  A published some articles in a magazine.
  B had an idea for a TV series.
  C came first in a short-story competition.

27 Julia says that
  A she would like to write a version of a classic film.
  B there is a danger she might imitate other films.
  C creative people should think a lot about films.

28 Julia's screenplay is about two sisters who
  A set out to try living in the jungle.
  B find themselves in a difficult situation.
  C end up hating each other.

29 The theme of the story is
  A how our emotions about our family can change.
  B Julia's relationship with her brothers and sisters.
  C about the importance of having a family.

30 It appears that the film based on Julia's screenplay
  A must be made within the next few months.
  B will be made when the studio has paid Julia.
  C might never be made.

Essential tips

▶ Read the questions or question stems carefully.

▶ Read the options carefully and underline the key words.

▶ Be careful: an option may include words or phrases from the recording, but this does not necessarily mean that the option is correct.

▶ The questions follow the order of the text.

Question 24: Who do you expect writes the screenplay for a film? Is this the same person who thinks of the idea for a film? The correct answer may be different from what you think, so listen carefully.

Question 26: Aspects of all the options are heard in the listening text, but only one option completes the stem correctly.

Question 28: The correct answer summarises the story of the film. Which option does that?

Part 1 (2 minutes)

The examiner (interlocutor) will ask each of you to speak briefly in turn and to give personal information about yourselves. You can expect a variety of questions, such as:

Can you describe the area where you live?
What do you like and dislike about this area? (Why?)
How do you think the area could be improved?
Where else would you like to live? (Why?)

Part 2 (4 minutes)

You will each be asked to talk for a minute without interruption. You will each be given two different photographs in turn to talk about. After your partner has finished speaking, you will be asked a brief question connected with your partner's photographs.

1 Places to live

Look at the two photographs on page 159 which show different types of accommodation.

Candidate A, compare the photographs, and say why you think people have chosen to live in these places.

Candidate B, which of these would you prefer to live in? (Why?)

2 Audiences

Look at the two photographs on page 160 which show people at concerts.

Candidate B, compare the photographs, and say how you think the people are feeling.

Candidate A, which of these events would you prefer to go to? (Why?)

Essential tips

Part 1

▸ Try to sound natural. Don't learn a speech off by heart.

▸ Avoid one- or two-word answers or answers that are long and complicated.

▸ You can prepare for this part of the interview by making sure you can talk about yourself, your home, your family, your hobbies, etc.

▸ Listen carefully to the question and answer exactly what is asked.

Part 2

▸ In this part you must compare the two colour photographs you are given. When you compare them say what the two photographs have in common and how they are different.

▸ Listen carefully to what the examiner asks you to do. After comparing the photographs the examiner will ask you to comment and give your personal reaction to them.

▸ You are supposed to speak for a full minute. Practise speaking for a minute, so you know how this feels.

▸ The examiner will ask you to comment on your partner's photographs. You have about 30 seconds for this.

▸ Don't interrupt when your partner is speaking. Use a few sentences to answer the question you are asked after your partner has spoken.

PAPER 1 Reading and
Use of English

PAPER 2 Writing

PAPER 3 Listening

PAPER 4 Speaking ▶
Part 1
Part 2
Part 3
Part 4

Part 3 (4 minutes)

You will be asked to discuss something together without interruption by the examiner. You will have a page of ideas and a question to help you.

A camping trip

Imagine you're going on a camping trip to the mountains. Turn to page 161 which shows ideas for items you could take with you and a question for you to discuss. Talk to each other about how each item could be useful during the trip. Then decide which **two** of these items you would take on your camping trip.

Part 4 (4 minutes)

The examiner will encourage you to develop the topic of your discussion in Part 3 by asking questions, such as:

Would you enjoy a camping holiday? (Why? / Why not?)
What other type of holiday would you enjoy? (Why?)
Would you prefer to go on holiday with your family or with a group of friends? (Why? / Why not?)
What is the best time of year to go on a holiday? (Why?)
Is it usual for people in your country to visit other countries on holiday?
What's a typical kind of holiday for someone in your country?

Essential tips

Part 3

▶ Work together with your partner. Discuss the question and the ideas and decide on an answer together.

▶ Involve your partner in the discussion. Your contribution and your partner's contribution to the discussion should be equal.

▶ Practise expressions used for giving your opinion and agreeing/disagreeing, such as *in my opinion, I'm afraid I don't agree*, etc.

▶ Don't make a decision too quickly. Look at the ideas first, give your opinion about them, ask your partner's opinion and then make a decision.

▶ Remember you don't have to agree with your partner. What is more important is reaching a decision.

Part 4

▶ Don't interrupt when your partner is speaking, but be ready to give your opinion after your partner has finished.

▶ It doesn't matter if you agree or disagree with your partner, but it is important to give reasons for your opinion.

PAPER 1 Reading and Use of English

▶▶ PART 5

adore (v) to like very much, to love deeply

supreme (adj) the greatest, the best

hulk (n) something or someone large and awkward

take a hit (phr) to be hit by someone

smack (v) to hit with force

immense (adj) extremely large

subtlety (n) the quality of not being noticeable or obvious in any way

gain (v) to achieve

readership (n) the people who read a certain newspaper, people who regularly buy a magazine

stock (n) one's parents, grandparents and other older or past relatives, sometimes including an entire race

bully (v) to force others to do things

turning point (n) the point at which a very significant change occurs, a decisive moment

the ropes (phr) all the things one needs to know in order to do a job or deal with something

dissuade (v) to persuade someone not to do something

insistent (adj) demanding over and over again that something should happen

quit (v) to give up an activity

resent (v) to feel anger at something, to feel hurt about something

abandon (v) to leave someone or something when you should stay with them and look after them

▶▶ PART 6

turnover (n) the amount of annual business

grandly (adv) suggesting that something or someone has great importance

interactive (adj) describes a system or computer program designed to involve the user in the exchange of information

harvest (v) to collect or receive the benefits of something

stunning (adj) very beautiful, very surprising

sequence (n) a part of a film that shows a particular event or a related series of events

gravity (n) a natural force pulling objects to the ground

discard (v) to throw away, to dispose of

leap (v) to jump, to bound

rippling (adj) moving in small waves

segment (n) a separate piece, a section of something

comprise (v) to include, to contain

set (v) if a film is set in a place or period of time, it happens there or at that time

doom (v) to send to an unhappy, inescapable end (failure, ruin, destruction, etc.)

perspective (n) a way of seeing things, a point of view

fulfil (v) to satisfy, to accomplish

fundamentally (adv) basically, essentially

▶▶ PART 7

chip off the old block (phr) a child whose appearance or character closely resembles that of one or the other parent

self-employed (adj) working for yourself and not employed by a single company

take up (phr v) to enter into a profession or business

retire (v) to leave the work force and stop working

tough (adj) difficult, demanding

motivate (v) to encourage, to stimulate

research (n) a study of something

provincial (adj) relating to an area which is governed as part of a country or an empire

put off (phr v) to annoy or disgust

steer (v) to guide someone by gently pushing or leading

come in handy (phr) to be useful

PAPER 1 Reading and	Part 1
Use of English	Part 2
PAPER 2 Writing	Part 3
	Part 4
PAPER 3 Listening	Part 5
PAPER 4 Speaking	Part 6
	Part 7

For questions **1–8**, read the text below and decide which answer (**A, B, C or D**) best fits each gap. There is an example at the beginning (**0**).

Mark your answers **on the separate answer sheet**.

Example:

0 **A** quantity   **B** piece   **C** unit   **D** part

| 0 | A | B | C | D |

Essential tips

Question 2: Which of the four verbs collocates with *weight*?

Question 5: Look at the context. Is it a good thing that diets don't work for most people? Does the missing word have a positive or negative meaning?

Question 6: Which of the four nouns can be followed by the preposition *to* and a gerund?

Going on a diet

A calorie is a (**0**) .... for measuring the amount of energy food will produce. The average person needs about 1,800 calories per day to stay healthy. Without energy, the heart cannot (**1**) .... blood through blood vessels and the organs cannot function.

You (**2**) .... weight because you consume more calories a day than your body requires. The only way to lose weight is to (**3**) .... the number of calories you consume. This is the basic (**4**) .... behind most diets.

(**5**) .... , diets don't work for most people. It's not that they don't lose weight: they do, but when they go off the diet, the kilos creep back. The (**6**) .... to losing weight and maintaining weight loss is a sensible diet and exercise plan. You need to work out how to eat fewer calories than you (**7**) .... consume. You should also exercise daily so you can use up calories. Burning 250 or 500 calories per day can (**8**) .... a big difference.

1	**A** pump	**B** pull	**C** drag	**D** force
2	**A** make	**B** increase	**C** gain	**D** put
3	**A** shrink	**B** take	**C** remove	**D** reduce
4	**A** way	**B** principle	**C** method	**D** kind
5	**A** Similarly	**B** Though	**C** Unfortunately	**D** Although
6	**A** key	**B** secret	**C** way	**D** idea
7	**A** preferably	**B** actually	**C** consistently	**D** eventually
8	**A** have	**B** do	**C** make	**D** give

For questions **9–16**, read the text below and think of the word which best fits each gap. Use only **one** word in each gap. There is an example at the beginning (**0**).

Write your answers **IN CAPITAL LETTERS on the separate answer sheet**.

Example: | 0 | M | A | N | Y | | | | | | | | | | | | | | | |

I'm not superstitious, honestly!

How (**0**) .... people could truly say they are not superstitious? A recent survey shows that almost 90% of people believe in one sort of superstition (**9**) .... another and say that it influences their lives.

One of the questions people (**10**) .... asked is whether they saw themselves as lucky or unlucky. Their answers turned out to be the most interesting aspect of this survey. Nearly two-thirds (**11**) .... those taking part said they believed that people were naturally lucky or unlucky.

Professor Morgan Howard, (**12**) .... analysed the results of the survey, was fascinated by this finding, so he went a step further and asked these people (**13**) .... kind of superstitions they believed in. (**14**) .... his surprise, he discovered that almost all the people who regarded themselves (**15**) .... lucky believed in positive superstitions. They did things to promote their good luck, such as crossing their fingers. (**16**) .... would appear that people make their own luck by their attitude to life.

Essential tips

Question 10: Is the verb *ask* being used in the active or the passive form here?

Querstion 13: The gap is part of an indirect question about the kind of superstitions people believe in.

Question 15: The gap follows a verb, *regard*, and a reflexive pronoun, *themselves*. What preposition comes after *regard* + object?

PAPER 1 Reading and ▸
         Use of English

PAPER 2 Writing

PAPER 3 Listening

PAPER 4 Speaking

Part 1
Part 2
Part 3
Part 4
Part 5
Part 6
Part 7

For questions **17–24**, read the text below. Use the word given in capitals at the end of some of the lines to form a word that fits in the gap **in the same line**. There is an example at the beginning (**0**).

Write your answers **IN CAPITAL LETTERS on the separate answer sheet**.

Example: | 0 | R | E | C | E | N | T | L | Y | | | | | | | | | |

Essential tips

Question 17: The missing word is a verb. What verb form do you need?

Question 19: The gap is between the auxiliary (*have*) and the main verb (*discovered*), so it must be an adverb.

Question 24: Read the sentence carefully. It says *a large number of*. Do you need the singular or plural form of a noun?

Wild animals

Wild animals have (**0**) .... made an appearance in the back gardens of American suburbs. They have caused havoc and have (**17**) .... domestic pets.

Mountain lions that wander into suburbs are now quite (**18**) .... to attack humans, which is worrying, while bears and wolves have (**19**) .... discovered rubbish bins. If you find the (**20**) .... of your bin scattered all over the garden one morning, there is a distinct (**21**) .... that a bear has been feasting there during the night.

Nobody should be particularly surprised by this development, which was predicted by experts years ago, and it's not (**22**) .... under the circumstances. One cause is the massive expansion of (**23**) .... into areas that were wild and uninhabited not long ago. In addition, over the past few decades a large number of (**24**) .... have been placed on hunting certain animals, allowing their populations to grow. It looks as if humans will simply have to get used to their new neighbours.

RECENT

THREAT

WILL
APPARENT
CONTAIN
POSSIBLE

EXPECT
HOUSE

RESTRICT

PAPER 1 Reading and ▶
        Use of English
PAPER 2 Writing
PAPER 3 Listening
PAPER 4 Speaking

Part 1
Part 2
Part 3
Part 4
Part 5
Part 6
Part 7

For questions **25–30**, complete the second sentence so that it has a similar meaning to the first sentence, using the word given. **Do not change the word given.** You must use between **two** and **five** words, including the word given. Here is an example (**0**).

Example:

0 I'll be very happy when I go on holiday.

  FORWARD

  I'm .... on holiday.

The gap can be filled by the words 'looking forward to going' so you write:

Example: | 0 | LOOKING FORWARD TO GOING |

Write **only** the missing words **IN CAPITAL LETTERS on the separate answer sheet**.

Essential tips

Question 25: What is the opposite of *cheap*? How can 'as' be used with an adjective?

Question 26: If someone didn't do something and you think this was wrong, what modal verb can you use?

Question 29: What structure do we use after *asked* to report a request? How do we report a negative request?

25 The phone was cheaper than I expected.

  AS

  The phone was .... I expected.

26 Why didn't you tell me I was wrong?

  TOLD

  You .... I was wrong.

27 She found the photographs when she was cleaning her room.

  CAME

  She .... when she was cleaning her room.

28 How many portraits did Picasso paint?

  BY

  How many portraits .... Picasso?

29 'Please don't stay out late,' his mother said.

  ASKED

  His mother .... out late.

30 I'd rather not go out this afternoon.

  FEEL

  I .... out this afternoon.

PAPER 1 Reading and
         Use of English
PAPER 2 Writing
PAPER 3 Listening
PAPER 4 Speaking

Part 1
Part 2
Part 3
Part 4
Part 5
Part 6
Part 7

You are going to read an article about life in the countryside. For questions **31–36**, choose the answer (**A**, **B**, **C** or **D**) which you think fits best according to the text.

Mark your answers **on the separate answer sheet**.

How I came to envy the country mice

I have been living in London for more than 60 years, but still, when I'm driving and take some clever back-street short cut, I catch myself thinking: how extraordinary that it is me doing this! For a moment the town mouse I have become is being seen by the country mouse I used to be. And although, given a new start, I would again become a town mouse, when I visit relations in the country, I envy them.

Recently, I stood beside a freshwater lake in Norfolk, made by diverting a small river, near where my brother lives. As he was identifying some of the birds we could see, in came seven swans. They circled, then the haunting sound of their wing beats gave way to silence as they glided down for splashdown.

It is not a 'picturesque' part of the coast, but it has a definite character of line and light and colour. 'You do live in a lovely place,' I said to my brother, and he answered, 'Yes, I do.' There are probably few days when he does not pause to recognise its loveliness as he works with his boats – he teaches sailing – or goes about his many other occupations.

The lake's creator is a local landowner, continuing a tradition whereby the nature of our countryside has been determined by those who own the land. Formerly, landowners would almost certainly have made such changes for their own benefit, but this time it was done to help preserve the wildlife here,
line 15 which is available for any visitor to see, providing they do nothing to disturb the birds. It is evidence of change: country life is changing fast.

One of the biggest changes I have witnessed is that second-homers, together with commuters, have come to be accepted as a vital part of the country scene. And the men and women who service their cars, dig their gardens, lay their carpets and do all the other things they need are vital to modern country life. It is quite likely that the children of today's workers may be moving into the same kind of jobs as the second-homers and the retired. Both the children of a country woman I know are at university, and she herself, now that they have left home, is working towards a university degree.

Much depends, of course, on the part of the countryside you are living in and on personality – your own and that of your neighbours. In my brother's Norfolk village, social life seems dizzying to a Londoner. In addition to dropping in on neighbours, people throw and attend parties far more often than we do. My brother's wife Mary and her friends are always going into Norwich for a concert or to King's Lynn for an exhibition. The boring country life that people from cities talk about is a thing of the past – or perhaps it was always mainly in their minds.

This is very unlike living in a London street for 50 years and only knowing the names of four other residents. In these 50 years I have made only one real friend among them. I do enjoy my life, and Mary says that she sometimes envies it (the grass on the other side of the fence ...); but whenever I go to Norfolk, I end up feeling that the lives of country mice are more admirable than my own.

► After reading the text for general understanding, read each question and see if you can locate the answer in the text. When you locate the answer in the text, underline it. Some questions refer to specific lines in the text (Question 33), while others refer to specific paragraphs (Question 36).

► Look carefully at the key words in the four options. For example, in question 31, option A, the key words are *driving through back streets* and *source of surprise*. This option can only be correct if the writer does drive through back streets and is surprised to find herself doing this.

Question 32: The text refers to the *sound* of the swans landing. Does it say that the sound was very loud, in which case *deafening* would be the correct answer? How is 'haunting' used here?

Question 34: The question asks you what is *suggested* about outsiders. This means the answer is not clearly stated in the text. You need to 'read between the lines' and see what is implied in the text.

Question 36: The answer to this question can be found in the whole of the last paragraph.

31 It is sometimes a source of surprise to the writer

   A to find herself driving through back streets.
   B that she has been in the city for so long.
   C to realise how much she has got used to living in London.
   D that she lives in the city when she prefers the country.

32 The atmosphere created by the writer when she describes the swans is

   A moving.
   B frightening.
   C deafening.
   D disturbing.

33 What does 'It' in line 15 refer to?

   A the lake
   B the fact that the lake belongs to a landowner here
   C the reason for the landowner's action
   D the fact that wildlife now needs to be preserved

34 What is suggested about outsiders who now live in the country?

   A that country people no longer reject them
   B that they often do work like servicing cars and digging gardens
   C that the men and women who work for them are from the city
   D that many of them have been in the countryside for a long time

35 Social life in the country

   A depends completely on where you live.
   B is not as boring as people in cities think it is.
   C is not affected by your neighbours.
   D is always less exciting than life in the city.

36 What do we learn about the writer's attitude to London in the final paragraph?

   A She can't adjust to living in London.
   B She has regretted moving to London.
   C The people in her street are unusually unfriendly.
   D Life there is very different to country life.

For the Glossary see page 47 ►

PAPER 1 Reading and   ▸   Part 1
         Use of English   Part 2
PAPER 2 Writing   Part 3
                             Part 4
PAPER 3 Listening   Part 5
                             Part 6
PAPER 4 Speaking   Part 7

You are going to read an article about the evolution of hands. Six sentences have been removed from the article. Choose from the sentences **A–G** the one which fits each gap (**37–42**). There is one extra sentence which you do not need to use.

Mark your answers **on the separate answer sheet**.

Our amazing hands

The hand is where the mind meets the world. We use our hands to build fires, to steer airplanes, to write. The human brain, with its open-ended creativity, may be the thing that makes our species unique. But without hands, all the grand ideas we think up would come to nothing.

The reason we can use our hands for so many things is their extraordinary anatomy. **37** [ ] Some are connected to bones within the hand, while others snake their way to the arm. The wrist is a floating group of bones and ligaments threaded with blood vessels and nerves. The nerves send branches into each fingertip. The hand can generate fine forces or huge ones. A watchmaker can use his hands to set springs in place under a microscope. A sportsman can use the same anatomy to throw a ball at over 100 kilometres an hour.

Other species have hands too. **38** [ ] In other cases we have to look closer. A bat's wings may look like sheets of skin. But underneath, a bat has the same five fingers as a human, as well as a wrist connected to the same cluster of wrist bones connected to the same long bones of the arm.

In exploring how hands have evolved, researchers over the past 150 years have dug up fossils on every continent. They've compared the anatomy of hands in living animals. They've studied the genes that build hands. It appears that our hands began to evolve at least 380 million years ago from fins – not the flat,

ridged fins of a goldfish but the muscular, stout fins of extinct relatives of today's lungfish. Inside these were a few chunky bones corresponding to the bones in our arms. **39** [ ] The digits later emerged and became separate, allowing the animals to grip underwater vegetation as they clambered through it.

40 [ ] Some species had seven fingers. Others had eight. But by the time vertebrates were walking around on dry land 340 million years ago, the hand had been scaled back to only five fingers. It has retained that number of fingers ever since – for reasons scientists don't yet know.

Nevertheless, there are still many different types of hands in living species, from dolphin flippers to eagle wings to the hanging hooks of sloths. **41** [ ] They can also see that despite the outward differences, all hands start out in much the same way. There is a network of many genes that builds a hand, and all hands are built by variations on that same network. It takes only subtle changes in these genes to make fingers longer or to turn nails into claws.

The discovery of the molecular toolbox for hand building has given scientists a deeper understanding of evolution. **42** [ ] It may just be a little more of one protein here, a little less of another there. In the past, scientists could recognise only the outward signs that hands had evolved from a common ancestor. Today scientists are uncovering the inward signs as well.

A Over time, smaller ones developed that would eventually become wrists and fingers.

B Although a vulture's wing and a lion's paw may appear to have nothing in common, the difference between them may come down to tiny variations.

C They also use them for a number of different purposes.

D No one would doubt that the five fingers at the end of an orangutan's arm are part of anything else.

E By studying these, scientists are beginning to understand the molecular changes that led to such dramatic variations.

F The thumb alone is controlled by nine separate muscles.

G Early hands were more exotic than any hand today.

Essential tips

▸ Read the main text from which paragraphs have been gapped to get the general idea.

▸ Look carefully at the sentences before and after the gap. Are there any words that show you what the missing sentence is about?

▸ There are many ways you can link parts of a text. It could be a contrast, a comparison, an example, etc. Look for linking expressions that connect ideas in a text.

▸ Pay special attention to nouns, pronouns, words like *this* and *that* and any other words or phrases that refer to what has gone before or what comes after them.

Question 37: The sentence before the gap says the hand is amazingly constructed (*their extraordinary anatomy*). The sentence option that fits this gap is an example of this and links with the sentence after the gap.

Question 38: The sentence before the gap mentions other species. Two sentence options refer to other species, but only one links with the sentence after the gap.

Question 41: The sentence before the gap describes different types of *hands*. The sentence option that fits this gap refers to these different types of hands. In the sentence after the gap, who does 'they' refer to?

For the Glossary see page 47 ▶

PAPER 1 Reading and Use of English	Part 1
	Part 2
PAPER 2 Writing	Part 3
	Part 4
PAPER 3 Listening	Part 5
	Part 6
PAPER 4 Speaking	**Part 7**

You are going to read an article about the activities organised by four schools for Environmental Awareness Day. For questions **43–52** choose from the schools (**A–D**). The schools may be chosen more than once.

Mark your answers **on the separate answer sheet**.

Which school

became better known after Environmental Awareness Day? **43**

provided online information about the environment? **44**

asked a specialist to give a talk? **45**

raised money to help an organisation? **46**

organised a trip to study animals by the sea? **47**

is following changes in general weather conditions? **48**

carried out a project about endangered animals and plants? **49**

arranged a talk on pollution and local architecture? **50**

decided to protect a local historical site? **51**

is located in the centre of the city? **52**

Essential tips

▸ Read the questions first, and underline key words. Make sure you understand what the question asks.

▸ Locate the answers in the text and underline them.

▸ When you read the text, look for words/phrases which express similar ideas. Do not look for identical words.

Question 44: How can we provide online information?

Question 46: How can a school raise money? When you try to locate the answer, do not look for the verb *raise*. Look for the idea of *raising money*.

Question 48: Can you find another way of saying *general weather conditions*?

For the Glossary see page 47 ▶

Environmental Awareness Day

A Plumpton High School

This school decided to arrange a variety of activities, some aimed at achieving a better understanding of environmental problems, and others designed to be of practical help. For instance, the school magazine brought out a special edition on the subject, full of articles and stories where pupils expressed their feelings about the threats facing our environment. In another attempt to find out for themselves how serious these threats really are, the pupils decided to study the problem of pollution by making a survey, run by the science department, into air pollution in the local shopping centre. The school also held a sponsored walk and handed over nearly £1000 to the World Wide Fund for Nature. Pupils prepared a campaign to ban cars from the city centre and reduce traffic congestion. They gained a lot of publicity for the school by cycling through the city and handing out brochures about the benefits of cycling and walking.

B Cresswell College

The staff and students at Cresswell College held a meeting and discussed a number of suggestions. The most popular suggestion turned out to be the most practical one; it was decided that the local environment should be brightened up. Teams were sent out to plant flowers and young trees on areas of land in the neighbourhood. Senior students monitored the progress of species threatened with extinction and prepared a report on their findings. It was hoped that this would help publicise the problem. A leading expert on wild birds was invited to come and give a talk about the dangers faced by these creatures. He explained the importance of the food chain and asked people to support local wildlife reserves.

C Grayner Institute

This school had already been involved in some projects connected with the environment, though naturally efforts were increased for Environmental Awareness Day. For the last two years the school had been studying the effects of variations in climatic patterns around the world and how these can affect wildlife. A film about those magnificent marine mammals, whales, which was shown to the whole school as part of Environmental Awareness Day, was received with great enthusiasm by pupils. Meredith Summers was invited to talk about how pollution can destroy buildings in the region. Following that, pupils decided to launch a campaign for the restoration of the medieval square in the city centre and asked local authorities to support them financially.

D Halliwell Academy

The pupils at this inner-city secondary school felt that the best way to mark Environmental Awareness Day would be to help people in the area understand how important the environment is to them. One suggestion that was greeted with enthusiasm was to measure the levels of noise in Stanley Road, a busy local shopping street. The information was then placed on a website that the school had started. In order to give them a chance to see for themselves the problems facing some local species, the school took pupils to the coastal marshes of Easton. Many pupils reported afterwards that they had never realised how terrible the effects of pollution could be on coastal wildlife.

You **must** answer this question. Write your answer in **140–190** words in an appropriate style.

1 In your English class you have been talking about where people shop. Now, your English teacher has asked you to write an essay.

Write an essay using **all** the notes and give reasons for your point of view.

Is it better to shop in small local shops or big supermarkets?

Notes
Write about:

1. goods available
2. prices
3. .... (your own idea)

Essential tips

▸ Decide if you prefer small local shops or big supermarkets and state your opinion clearly in the introduction.

▸ In the body of your essay you need to give reasons for your choice. Remember to use all the topics in the notes. If you prefer local shops even though they do not have the range of goods available in a supermarket, you could say why it isn't necessary for them to have several varieties of each type of item. You could also give examples of things that local shops sell that can't be found in supermarkets.

▸ Make sure you include **another topic** (your own idea) and use it to support your opinion. For example, you could say that local shops are **more convenient** because they are close to people's homes (or if you prefer supermarkets, you could say it's **more convenient** to get everything you need in one place). You could talk about how friendly and helpful **staff** tend to be in the two different types of shops.

▸ Summarise your overall opinion in the final paragraph.

PAPER 1 Reading and
         Use of English
PAPER 2 Writing   ▶ Part 1
                           Part 2
PAPER 3 Listening
PAPER 4 Speaking

Essential tips

Question 2

Think of famous people from your country. It could be a historical figure or someone alive today. Do you know enough relevant vocabulary about one of them to write a good letter?

Think about why this person is famous. Give as many reasons as you can.

Is this person popular or unpopular? Say why people have this opinion of the person.

Question 4 (*for FIRST candidates only*)

Think of different sorts of things that families can do in their spare time: hobbies, sports, going out with friends, etc.

Try to organise this information in a clear way for the reader. How many paragraphs will you need? Think of appropriate headings for each of the paragraphs.

Summarise your findings in the final paragraph and make recommendations for improvements to local facilities.

Write an answer to **one** of the questions **2–5** in this part. Write your answer in **140–190** words in an appropriate style.

---

2   This is part of a letter you receive from Fran, your Australian friend.

> I'm doing a college project on famous people in different countries. Could you tell me about someone famous in your country. Why is this person famous? What do people in your country think about this person?
>
> Thanks!
>
> Fran

Write your **letter**.

3   You see this notice on an English-language website:

> **Reviews wanted   Comedy TV Series**
>
> Write us a review of a TV series that makes people laugh. Your review should include information about the storyline and the characters. Why do people think this TV series is funny? What do you think about the series?

Write your **review**.

4   (*for FIRST candidates only*)

Your college English-language magazine has asked you to write a report on the spare-time activities that are typical of families in your area. Include information on what people do, where they go, and whether local facilities used by families could be improved.

Write your **report**.

Continued on next page ▶

PAPER 1 Reading and
          Use of English

PAPER 2 Writing ▶   Part 1

PAPER 3 Listening   **Part 2**

PAPER 4 Speaking

Essential tips

Question 4 (*for FIRST FOR SCHOOLS candidates only*)

Think of a way to link the content of your story with the title. What kind of noise did Tim hear? What happened when he went outside? Decide on the characters and the setting.

Is your story going to be told in the first person (*I*) or third person (*he*)?

The events in your story should appear in a logical sequence. Use narrative tenses and time expressions to tell your story effectively.

Question 5 (*for FIRST FOR SCHOOLS candidates only*)

If the book is performed as a play, it will have to be much shorter. Could it work with just a few main scenes?

A play can't have too many characters. Think of the characters in the book. Are they intriguing characters? How many of them are there in the book?

A play has to be short and exciting. Are there interesting scenes in the book that could be effective on stage?

4 (*for FIRST FOR SCHOOLS candidates only*)

You see this announcement in an English-language magazine for teenagers.

Stories wanted
Write a story for our short-story competition! Your story must begin with this sentence:
As soon as he heard the noise, Tim ran outside to see what was happening.
Your story must include: • TV cameras   • a surprise

Write your **story**.

5 (*for FIRST FOR SCHOOLS candidates only*)

Answer the following question based on your reading of **one** of the set books.

Your English class is thinking of performing the book or short story you have read as a play. Your English teacher has emailed everyone in your class asking whether you think this is a good idea. Write an **email** to your teacher giving the reasons for your opinion.

Essential tips

▸ If you are listening for numbers or dates, you may not hear the number or date you want, but you will hear some information that will tell you the answer. For example, you may hear: 'My birthday is not in March. It's a month later.' In this case the birthday is in April, but you don't actually hear the word 'April'.

▸ Look carefully at questions that have two parts. In Question 7, for example, you must listen for a road which is blocked, and it must be blocked by a crash. If a road is blocked, but not by a crash, this is not the correct answer.

Question 3: Be careful. The speaker does not say the date, but gives information about it (*two years later*).

Question 5: All three options are mentioned. Which of the three is the correct answer?

Question 7: What other words could you hear instead of *crash* that have the same meaning?

🎧 **Track 5**

You will hear people talking in eight different situations. For questions **1–8**, choose the best answer (**A**, **B** or **C**).

1 You hear a physiotherapist talking to a patient.
   What kind of exercises does she recommend?
   A exercises done while lying on the back
   B exercises done while standing up
   C exercises done while lying on the stomach

2 You hear a woman phoning an Indian restaurant to order a takeaway meal.
   Which curry has rice included?
   A beef
   B lamb
   C chicken

3 You hear a woman in an art gallery talking about a painting.
   What date was it painted?
   A 1848
   B 1884
   C 1888

4 You hear a man giving directions to a football ground.
   What does he say the other person must do at the traffic lights?
   A turn left
   B go straight on
   C turn right

5 You hear two colleagues talking about a character one has invented.
   What animal is this character supposed to be?
   A an elephant
   B a horse
   C a bear

6 You hear a woman talking to a policeman at a police station.
   What is her problem?
   A Her bag has been stolen.
   B Her purse has been stolen.
   C Her camera has been stolen.

7 You hear a radio announcement about traffic.
   Which road has been blocked by a car crash?
   A M63
   B A36
   C B636

8 You hear a woman talking about a slimming diet.
   What does she say about the diet?
   A It can have useful results.
   B It can be extremely harmful.
   C It is scientifically approved.

Part 1
Part 2
Part 3
Part 4

 Track 6

You will hear a woman called Jane Robertson giving a talk about a language called Gaelic. For questions **9–18**, complete the sentences with a word or short phrase.

Essential tips

Questions 10 and 11: The missing information is a number for both questions. Which words in question 11 tell you this?

Question 15: The missing word comes after *more* and is followed by an adjective, so it is likely to be an adjective as well.

Gaelic

Jane is the (**9**) .... of a Gaelic school in Scotland.

Today approximately (**10**) .... people speak Gaelic
in Scotland.

If fewer than (**11**) .... people speak a language,
it is considered dead.

Jane would like to see one-third of people under 25 speaking and
(**12**) .... Gaelic.

If very young children are exposed to a language
(**13**) ...., they can learn it most effectively.

Some parents send their children to Jane's school for
(**14**) .... reasons.

Jane says that two character traits of bilingual children are being more
(**15**) .... and tolerant.

Jane feels very (**16**) .... about the future of Gaelic.

Jane says that what is needed is help from (**17**) ....

With a lot of effort, nowadays 80% of children learn Welsh as a
(**18**) .... language.

PAPER 1 Reading and
Use of English

PAPER 2 Writing

PAPER 3 Listening ▶
Part 1
Part 2
Part 3
Part 4

PAPER 4 Speaking

Essential tips

Option A: A *family tradition* must mean that the speaker's parents or family members have been connected with the sport. The adjective *strong* means that at least two family members were involved in the same sport.

Option B: This option mentions *social life*, which means that the speaker practises it regularly with friends or people he/she knows.

Option H: What adjective would be used to describe a competition or athletic event where people from different countries compete together?

Track 7

You will hear five short extracts in which young people who are outstanding at sports are talking about their lives. For questions **19–23**, choose from the list (**A–H**) the comment each speaker makes about his or her attitude to sport. Use the letters only once. There are three extra letters which you do not need to use.

A This sport is a strong family tradition for me.

B I think of it as part of my social life.

Speaker 1 ☐ 19

C I started off wanting to impress my parents.

Speaker 2 ☐ 20

D It's an investment for my future.

Speaker 3 ☐ 21

E I hope to win a lot of prize money.

Speaker 4 ☐ 22

F I like the thrill of knowing I'm the best.

Speaker 5 ☐ 23

G I'm grateful for a friend's encouragement.

H Representing my country is my greatest ambition.

PAPER 1   Reading and
          Use of English

PAPER 2   Writing

PAPER 3   Listening   ▶
                          Part 1
PAPER 4   Speaking   Part 2
                          Part 3
                          Part 4

Essential tips

▶ Look closely at the
questions before you hear
the recording and mark
the key words, including
adverbs. For example, in
question 24, option B uses
the word *completely*. If the
speaker says that the sport
is *safe*, but not *completely
safe*, option B is not the
correct answer.

▶ If you hear a word that
is in one of the options,
decide whether it is used
in the same way. For
example, in question
25, option B includes
the word *sensations*. On the
recording you will hear the
word *sensation*, but does
that make it the correct
answer?

Question 26: Questions in
Part 4 ask you to interpret
the speaker's feelings. It's
important that you know the
exact meaning of the words
in the options. For instance,
is *accomplished* the feeling
you get when you have
accomplished something?

Question 28: Words can have
different meanings when used
in different structures. For
example, if someone is *anxious
to do something*, does this
mean he or she is worried?

🎧 **Track 8**

You will hear a radio interview with a man called Sam Hall, who is a mountain
climber. For questions **24–30**, choose the best answer (**A**, **B** or **C**).

24 Sam describes mountain climbing as
   A dangerous if people have the wrong attitude.
   B completely safe if people are prepared.
   C a sport with an exciting reputation.

25 For Sam, the attraction of climbing is
   A primarily the excitement.
   B a matter of sensations.
   C hard to describe.

26 How does Sam feel when he reaches the top of a mountain?
   A proud
   B exhausted
   C amazed

27 Sam thinks that we all have a moment in childhood
   A when we know what our ambition is.
   B when we realise we can't do everything we want.
   C when we make plans about our future.

28 What was the attitude of Sam's parents when he took up the sport?
   A They were very anxious.
   B They didn't want to discourage him.
   C They gave him every support.

29 Sam explains that feeling confident
   A is the result of doing many climbs with his friend.
   B is natural after some time.
   C can provoke people to make mistakes.

30 When Sam and his friend were lost on the mountain,
   A they didn't feel lucky.
   B they thought the storm might last for a week.
   C they were sure someone would find them.

Essential tips

Part 1

▸ Make sure you have the necessary vocabulary to give personal information. In this case, you will have to talk about the sports that you enjoy doing. You can say, for example: *I'm very keen on basketball and volleyball* or *I'm not really very interested in sports.*

▸ Listen to your partner's answer. The examiner may ask you if you agree or not.

Part 2

▸ Make sure you address both parts of the instructions. Here you will have to compare the photos but also say why you think the people are working in these different places and how they feel about working there. Give your personal opinion using expressions like *I think ... , It seems to me ... , In my view ... , Personally, I ... ,* etc.

Part 1 (2 minutes)

The examiner (interlocutor) will ask each of you to speak briefly in turn and to give personal information about yourselves. You can expect a variety of questions, such as:

What would you say are the most popular sports in your country?
Which sports do you enjoy playing? (Why?)
What kind of sports do you like watching? (Why?)
Are there any sports you find boring? (Why?)

Part 2 (4 minutes)

You will each be asked to talk for a minute without interruption. You will each be given two different photographs in turn to talk about. After your partner has finished speaking, you will be asked a brief question connected with your partner's photographs.

1 Places to work in

Look at the two photographs on page 162 which show people working in different places.

Candidate A, compare these photographs, and say why you think the people are working in these places.

Candidate B, which of these places would you prefer to work in? (Why?)

2 Family groups

Look at the two photographs on page 163 which show different family groups.

Candidate B, compare these photographs, and say what you think it would feel like to grow up in these families.

Candidate A, do you think it's better to come from a small or a large family? (Why?)

Essential tips

Part 3

▶ Talk about each type of film before you reach a conclusion. Remember that there are no right or wrong answers.

▶ You are being tested on your ability to work together and complete the task. Involve your partner in the discussion using expressions like *Do you agree ... ?, What do you think ... ?, Let's decide which ... ,* etc.

▶ In deciding which type of film would appeal to students, think about students with different interests and students with different personalities. You need to justify your opinion and say why a certain type of film would appeal to the majority of the students.

Part 4

▶ Avoid giving 'yes/no' answers. Give your opinion, justify it and develop your ideas.

▶ Try to keep the conversation going by responding to your partner's answers or by asking your partner questions. You can use expressions like: *Don't you think that ... ?, How do you feel about ... ?, I agree up to a point but ... , I couldn't agree with you more, I'm sorry but I disagree with you on that,* etc.

Part 3 (4 minutes)

You will be asked to discuss something together without interruption by the examiner. You will have a page of ideas with a question to help you.

Film day

Imagine your English class is going to watch a film. Turn to page 164 which has ideas for different types of film and a question for you to discuss. Talk to each other about what type of film would appeal to students in your class. Then decide which type of film your class should watch.

Part 4 (4 minutes)

The examiner will encourage you to develop the topic of your discussion in Part 3 by asking questions such as:

What type of film do you enjoy watching? (Why?)
Do you prefer watching films at home or in the cinema? (Why? / Why not?)
Do you think watching a film in a cinema creates a special atmosphere? (Why? / Why not?)
Why do you think some films are still popular a long time after they were made?
Can you think of any recent films that will still be popular 20 or 30 years from now? (Why?)
Do you think people of different ages enjoy the same types of film? (Why? / Why not?)

PAPER 1 Reading and Use of English

▸▸ **PART 5**

short cut (n) a shorter way to a place than usual

envy (v) to want the same things someone else has

divert (v) to cause something or someone to change direction

give way to (phr) to be replaced by something else

haunting (adj) beautiful, but in a sad way and often in a way which cannot be forgotten

glide (v) to fly through the air without power

splashdown (n) a landing by a spacecraft, etc. in the water

picturesque (adj) like a picture, pleasing to the eye, charming

occupation (n) any activity on which you spend time

landowner (n) a person who owns land, especially undeveloped land or farmland

whereby (adv) by means of which

preserve (v) to guard, to protect from harm or change

commuter (n) a person who travels regularly, especially between home and the workplace

vital (adj) most important, absolutely necessary

lay (v) to put in place

dizzying (adj) very exciting

drop in on (phr v) to make an informal visit without an appointment

▸▸ **PART 6**

open-ended (adj) without limits

creativity (n) the ability to produce new things and ideas

unique (adj) different from everyone and everything else

anatomy (n) the structure of part of the body

snake (v) to move like a snake

ligament (n) what links the bones together

blood vessel (n) a tube through which blood flows in the body

fossil (n) the remains of a plant or animal that has been preserved in rock for a very long time

gene (n) part of a cell that controls a person's characteristics, passed on from parent to child

evolve (v) to develop and change over a long period of time

fin (n) part of a fish used for balance and movement

chunky (adj) small and solid

grip (v) to hold tightly

digit (n) finger

clamber (v) to move and climb with difficulty

vertebrate (n) an animal with a spine

retain (v) to keep

subtle (adj) very small

▸▸ **PART 7**

edition (n) a specific printing of a book or periodical

threat (n) a danger

sponsor (v) to help pay for something like a cultural or sporting event

congestion (n) excessive crowding, heavy traffic

monitor (v) to observe the actions of others

species (n) a grouping of living things

extinction (n) the act of destroying life

food chain (n) a community of organisms where each member is eaten in turn by another member

reserve (n) land kept for a special purpose

mammal (n) a warm-blooded animal, the female of which feeds its own milk to its young

launch (v) to start, to put into operation

restoration (n) making something look like it did when it was new

medieval (adj) connected with the Middle Ages (the period between about 1100 AD and 1500 AD)

PAPER 1 Reading and ▶	**Part 1**
Use of English	Part 2
PAPER 2 Writing	Part 3
	Part 4
PAPER 3 Listening	Part 5
	Part 6
PAPER 4 Speaking	Part 7

For questions **1–8**, read the text below and decide which word (**A, B, C** or **D**) best fits each gap. There is an example at the beginning (**0**).

Mark your answers **on the separate answer sheet**.

Example:

0   **A**   awaited   **B**   waited   **C**   expected   **D**   predicted

| 0 | A | B | C | D |

Vinyl attraction

Nobody ever really (**0**) .... my Uncle Peter to make much money. When he left school, he didn't have any plans for a career, and he got a job in a second-hand record shop. Peter's mother couldn't (**1**) .... over it. Her other children had both (**2**) .... to get places at university, and she was quite (**3**) .... that a young person needed a good education to get on in life. To (**4**) .... things worse, this was the time when vinyl records were being phased out. It looked as though my uncle would soon be looking for (**5**) .... somewhere else.

Then, all of a (**6**) .... Peter's luck changed. He announced he was going to start collecting records and set (**7**) .... a mail order business selling rare records. Nobody really (**8**) .... him seriously at first. Who would be interested in a technology that's out of date? Vinyl records have since become collectors' items, and my uncle is now a very rich man.

1	**A** come	**B** take	**C** get	**D** pass
2	**A** achieved	**B** succeeded	**C** accomplished	**D** managed
3	**A** convinced	**B** persuaded	**C** determined	**D** convicted
4	**A** get	**B** make	**C** bring	**D** drive
5	**A** work	**B** job	**C** career	**D** profession
6	**A** once	**B** moment	**C** sudden	**D** minute
7	**A** up	**B** out	**C** off	**D** in
8	**A** took	**B** believed	**C** thought	**D** gave

PAPER 1 Reading and
Use of English

PAPER 2 Writing

PAPER 3 Listening

PAPER 4 Speaking

Part 1
Part 2
Part 3
Part 4
Part 5
Part 6
Part 7

For questions **9–16,** read the text below and think of the word which best fits each gap. Use only **one** word in each gap. There is an example at the beginning (**0**).

Write your answers **IN CAPITAL LETTERS on the separate answer sheet**.

Example: 0 W H O

Agriculture in ancient Britain

Professor Emma Thomas is an archaeologist (**0**) .... specialises in the study of Ancient Britain and its people. The professor and her colleagues have been involved (**9**) .... the analysis of skeletons to discover more about (**10**) .... way Ancient Britons lived. 'Studying bones can tell us (**11**) .... great deal about our ancestors,' says Professor Thomas. 'We know for a fact that between 9000 and 5200 BC, people ate a seafood diet, while after that people had a preference (**12**) .... plants and animals.

(**13**) .... is still a mystery why people gave up eating fish. One explanation might be the influence of migrants to Britain. 'Britons changed (**14**) .... diet after people from Europe arrived,' says Professor Thomas. 'It was a time of change. Our ancestors stopped hunting and started growing crops. Farming methods (**15**) .... imported from Europe and people no longer relied (**16**) .... wild foods; they could control what they ate.' This marked the beginning of agriculture in Britain.

PAPER 1 Reading and ▶	Part 1
Use of English	Part 2
PAPER 2 Writing	**Part 3**
	Part 4
PAPER 3 Listening	Part 5
	Part 6
PAPER 4 Speaking	Part 7

For questions **17–24,** read the text below. Use the word given in capitals at the end of some of the lines to form a word that fits in the gap **in the same line**. There is an example at the beginning (**0**).

Write your answers **IN CAPITAL LETTERS on the separate answer sheet**.

Example: | 0 | A | N | N | O | U | N | C | E | M | E | N | T | | | | | | |

Sailing away

One Sunday morning our Aunt Emily made an (**0**)	ANNOUNCE
She told us (**17**) .... she was going to take us on a cruise!	HAPPY
I was surprised, knowing how expensive holidays like that	
were. We weren't a (**18**) .... family, but Aunt Emily said	WEALTH
she'd put some money aside over the years, and she	
wanted to use some of her (**19**) .... for the holiday.	SAVE

When the day of our (**20**) .... finally came, we were delighted	DEPART
and thrilled to see how huge and (**21**) .... the ship looked.	LUXURY
Our cruise liner sailed elegantly out to sea and our holiday	
began. But it turned out to be such a (**22**) .... !	DISAPPOINT

There was so little to do on the ship and we were incredibly	
bored. We visited several ports, but we didn't have the (**23**)	FREE
to do what we wanted. We had to follow a very tight schedule of	
guided tours and visits to museums. It was a (**24**) .... holiday!	DISASTER

PAPER 1 Reading and
          Use of English
PAPER 2 Writing
PAPER 3 Listening
PAPER 4 Speaking

Part 1
Part 2
Part 3
Part 4
Part 5
Part 6
Part 7

For questions **25–30**, complete the second sentence so that it has a similar meaning to the first sentence, using the word given. **Do not change the word given.** You must use between **two** and **five** words, including the word given. Here is an example (**0**).

Example:

0   I'll be very happy when I go on holiday.

FORWARD

I'm .... on holiday.

The gap can be filled by the words 'looking forward to going' so you write:

Example: | 0 | LOOKING FORWARD TO GOING

Write **only** the missing words **IN CAPITAL LETTERS on the separate answer sheet.**

---

25   'I'm sorry I'm late again,' he said.

APOLOGISED

He .... again.

26   She looks like my cousin Mary.

REMINDS

She .... my cousin Mary.

27   Someone is going to redecorate the kitchen for us next month.

HAVE

We are going .... next month.

28   Could you speak up because I can't hear you properly?

MIND

Would .... up because I can't hear you properly?

29   We advise customers to buy their tickets in advance.

ADVISED

Customers .... their tickets in advance.

30   It's such a pity I didn't see that film on television last night.

WISH

I .... that film on television last night.

PAPER 1	Reading and ▶	Part 1
	Use of English	Part 2
PAPER 2	Writing	Part 3
		Part 4
PAPER 3	Listening	**Part 5**
PAPER 4	Speaking	Part 6
		Part 7

You are going to read an article about an English poet, William Wordsworth. For questions **31–36**, choose the answer (**A**, **B**, **C** or **D**) which you think fits best according to the text.

Mark your answers **on the separate answer sheet**.

Daffodils everywhere

Two hundred years ago the English poet William Wordsworth wrote 'I wander'd lonely as a cloud', a poem that expresses a basic spirit of early English Romanticism. It was Thursday, 15 April 1802. William and Dorothy Wordsworth, the poet's devoted, journal-writing sister, were walking home to Dove Cottage in the Lake District. The wind was fierce, but the Wordsworth siblings were used to striding long distances in foul weather. They were in the woods close to the water side when they first clapped eyes on a field of daffodils 'fluttering and dancing in the breeze'.

What makes this poem an example of Romantic thinking? It isn't just that Wordsworth chooses to write about a natural scene: it is the way he describes the scene as if it had human emotions. For him, nature is not merely a neutral mixture of scenery, colours, plants, rocks, soil, water and air. It is a living force that feels joy and sadness, shares human pain and even tries to educate us human beings by showing us the beauty of life.

Wordsworth's home, Dove Cottage, is now one of the most popular destinations in the Lake District. You can go on a tour of the garden which William planted with wild flowers and which survived in his backyard even after they disappeared from the area. 'He always said that if he hadn't been a poet, he would have been a terrific landscape gardener,' says Allan King of the Wordsworth Trust, the organisation that looks after the cottage and gardens.

The Lake District in the north-west of England becomes particularly crowded during the summer months with tourists and ramblers eager to enjoy the region's majestic valleys, hills and sparkling lakes. Wordsworth himself was far from keen on tourists, which was quite apparent. He wanted outsiders to admire the local sights he enjoyed so much, but was afraid the district might be 'damaged' by too many visitors. He opposed the coming of the trains, and campaigned in the 1840s against a plan to link the towns in the area – Kendal, Windermere and Keswick – by rail.

line 19

The place near Ullswater, where Wordsworth saw the daffodils, is at the southernmost end of the lake. The lake is wide and calm at this turning point. There's a bay where the trees have had their soil eroded by lake water so that their roots are shockingly exposed. You walk along from tree to tree, hardly daring to breathe, because you are walking in the footprints of William and Dorothy from two centuries ago. The first clumps of daffodils appear, but they aren't tall yellow trumpets proudly swaying in the breeze. They're tiny wild daffodils, most of them still green and unopened, in clumps of six or seven. They're grouped around individual trees rather than collecting together.

But as you look north, from beside a huge ancient oak, you realise this is what delighted the Wordsworths: clump after clump of the things, spread out to left and right but coming together in your vision so that they form a beautiful, pale-yellow carpet. What you're seeing at last is nature transformed by human sight and imagination. For a second, you share that revelation of Dorothy and William Wordsworth's, the glimpse of pantheism, the central mystery of English Romanticism.

31 According to the article, Wordsworth's poem

    A started the Romantic movement.
    B was based on actual experience.
    C was written while he was visiting his sister.
    D was written after he had been lonely.

32 What was Wordsworth's attitude to nature?

    A He believed nature had a character of its own.
    B He felt nature was human.
    C He thought nature could talk to people.
    D He believed that we could influence nature.

33 We are told that Dove Cottage

    A has gardens designed by a landscape gardener.
    B has a wide range of flowers in its garden.
    C receives a lot of visitors.
    D has a very large garden.

34 What does 'which' in line 19 refer to?

    A the number of tourists who come to the Lake District
    B Wordsworth's desire for outsiders to admire the local sights
    C the fact that Wordsworth was keen on tourists from far away
    D Wordsworth's dislike of tourists

35 In what way is the scene different from what Wordsworth described?

    A All the daffodils are green and small.
    B There are no daffodils by the lake.
    C The daffodils are fewer and smaller.
    D There are no daffodils around trees.

36 The writer implies that the poem describes

    A exactly what Wordsworth saw in detail.
    B the effect the daffodils had on Wordsworth.
    C what Wordsworth saw around an ancient oak.
    D clumps of daffodils on the left and on the right.

PAPER 1 Reading and ▶
         Use of English

PAPER 2 Writing

PAPER 3 Listening

PAPER 4 Speaking

Part 1
Part 2
Part 3
Part 4
Part 5
Part 6
Part 7

You are going to read a newspaper article about the benefits of playing computer games. Six sentences have been removed from the article. Choose from the sentences **A–G** the one which fits each gap (**37–42**). There is one extra sentence, which you do not need to use.

Mark your answers **on the separate answer sheet**.

Computer games: not just for kids!

More people than ever are turning to computer games for fun and health benefits

Susie Bullen lines up, swings her arm back, and releases another perfect throw for yet another strike. When the game is over, the 94-year-old has rolled a personal best of 220. But Bullen isn't hanging out in the local bowling alley – she's playing on a popular interactive gaming system that has gained immense popularity with people of all ages.

Bullen, who once competed in leagues but hasn't bowled in nearly 70 years, said the interactive sports games give her the opportunity to reconnect to many of the activities she enjoyed in her formative years. 'I try to play as much as I can,' says Bullen, resident of a peaceful retirement community in Ontario, Canada. **37** Bullen regularly competes against her great-granddaughter, 16-year-old Melanie, on her gaming console.

Bullen is amongst a growing number of older people participating in this kind of pastime, which is helping to bring generations together in a shared activity. 'It's great fun playing against my great-grandma', says Melanie. **38**

According to recent research in the entertainment software sector, the percentage of people over 50 playing computer games has more than doubled since the year 2000, and the number is expected to increase as the popularity and visibility of current computer game platforms continue to grow. **39**

Interactive games have been linked to providing increased mental and physical well-being across the age groups. In addition to boosting mood, playing an 'exer-game' for around half an hour, three times a week, improves balance and leaves players feeling refreshed and energised. **40** Just like traditional forms of exercise, interactive gaming promotes better mental sharpness and hand-eye coordination. And one study has shown that there are some characteristics of gaming that promote visual learning, too – that is, acquiring skills through associating ideas and concepts with images and techniques.

So, what is it that has attracted older people to join in the gaming world? **41** Not only are the most successful platforms those with user-friendly controls, but the best games for the whole family to get involved in together are those which aren't overly-complicated, but still offer plenty in terms of stimulus.

42 A ten-pin bowling game, for example, requires users to swing their arms in the same motion as a bowler, while holding down a button on the controller. When the player is ready to release the ball, he or she simply releases the button. And as he or she does so, the feel-good factor is released along with it!

A In a market flooded with thousands and thousands of games, finding the right fit can be challenging.

B And as computer game usage amongst older people has risen, researchers have conducted studies that have concluded that computer games provide much more than simple entertainment value.

C 'I've always been sports-minded and like watching sports. Playing computer games is a bit of fun and it's great to see how you can do, as well as providing some much-needed exercise.'

D Games which mimic the movements of the sports they represent are particularly popular amongst gamers who not only want to have fun, but want to incorporate a bit of heart-pumping action into their free-time activities as well.

E This includes balance boards that record movements and give feedback on performance. Activities include yoga poses, push-ups, strength, balance and aerobic exercises.

F 'She's a real pro and it's hard for me to keep up! She's a fantastic opponent and we have a lot of laughs.'

G Active game-playing helps people of all ages recognise that exercise can be fun and socially enjoyable, and isn't just about hitting the treadmill at the gym.

PAPER 1 Reading and ▶
          Use of English
PAPER 2 Writing
PAPER 3 Listening
PAPER 4 Speaking

Part 1
Part 2
Part 3
Part 4
Part 5
Part 6
Part 7

You are going to read a magazine article about people who work from home. For questions **43–52**, choose from the people (**A–D**). The people may be chosen more than once.

Mark your answers **on the separate answer sheet**.

Which person

is aware of the importance of conforming to industry requirements?	**43**
understands the health implications of certain types of work?	**44**
compares two different places of work?	**45**
mentions a natural phenomenon that helps her concentrate?	**46**
doesn't think she would take as much pleasure in her work in a different place?	**47**
appreciates the need to feel mentally and physically prepared for work?	**48**
recognises that her current workplace benefits others as well as herself?	**49**
has improved her efficiency by adapting her workplace to her needs?	**50**
has observed a particular effect of where she works on what she creates?	**51**
is grateful that she is able to leave work behind when she's finished for the day?	**52**

Working from home

A Petra Rosso

I'm a student, which means I have to have peace and solitude when I'm trying to get my assignments done for college. There's a great attic room at home which I've been working in. I'm studying creative writing and it's important not only to get into the right frame of mind, but the right surroundings, too, in order for the ideas to flow. The room's flooded with light which helps me stay really focused when I'm writing, and the view from the window is inspiring. In fact, I've done some of my best work since I've been using the room for study purposes. The benefits extend beyond the walls of the room too – once the door's closed, it means I can totally switch off and spend time with my family without the thought of college work interfering.

B Jade Pickett

I share a large apartment with some other young professionals like myself. We get on well together and tend to congregate in the kitchen, which is large and spacious. I like to keep it clean and tidy as I run a catering business from home and it's imperative that I stick to certain standards of cleanliness. I'm always experimenting with new dishes and often prepare meals for my flatmates and our friends who come over. What could be more fun than chilling out with good company and food? I like the sociable atmosphere that cooking can create and without such a lovely space to try things out in, I doubt I'd enjoy what I do even half as much.

C Kara Francis

As an artist, it's vital to have the right working environment. I do have a room at home designated for the purpose, though it's undergoing a bit of renovation work at the moment, so I'm working in the living room for the time being. It's a light, airy space and there are some huge glass doors leading out onto the back of the house, which looks over the fields. It's almost like the countryside spills into the house. I paint portraits and the light there makes it almost as good as working in my studio. The people who sit for me can look out at the greenery while I'm studying them, and it's fascinating what a calming effect this seems to have on them. I've noticed recently that the portraits I've produced lately have a real air of serenity about them.

D Tina Tyford

I work from home and have a home office, which is the ideal place to get my head down and run my business. When I first started working from home, I undertook some research into what makes the best environment for home-workers and that included buying some ergonomic furniture which I had specially designed to suit my needs. Yes, the financial outlay was significant, but it's really increased my performance and output. I know that having a sedentary job can cause physical problems, so making sure I have the right chair to support my back and so on makes an enormous difference. My office is also well lit and all necessary equipment is within easy reach of my desk. It was definitely worth the effort I put in to make the room suitable for my requirements.

You **must** answer this question. Write your answer in **140–190** words in an appropriate style.

1 In your English class you have been comparing using public transport with travelling by car. Now, your teacher has asked you to write an essay.

Write an essay using **all** the notes and give reasons for your point of view.

Do you think it is better to use public transport than travel by car?

Notes
Write about:

1. environmental effects
2. cost
3. .... (your own idea)

Write an answer to **one** of the questions **2–5** in this part. Write your answer in **140–190** words in an appropriate style.

---

2   You have seen this announcement in a magazine called *Sports World Monthly*.

> **SPORTS WORLD MONTHLY**
>
> What is your favourite sport? What kind of clothes and equipment do you need for this sport? Does this sport require any special qualities?
>
> We will publish the best article.

Write your **article**.

3   This is part of a letter you have received from Sam, your English-speaking friend.

> In class we've been talking about how the places we live in change. Can you tell me about how your neighbourhood has changed? Do you think the changes are positive or negative?
>
> See you soon!
>
> Sam

Write your **letter**.

4   You have recently used a good website where you can download music. Write a review of the website for your student magazine. Include information about how the website is better than others of its type, and say what the special features of the website are. Say who you would recommend the website for.

Write your **review**.

5   (*for FIRST FOR SCHOOLS candidates only*)

Answer the following question based on your reading of **one** of the set books.

'A good book always conveys an important message.' Your teacher has asked you to write an **essay**, giving your opinions on this statement with reference to the book or one of the short stories you have read.

PAPER 1 Reading and Use of English

PAPER 2 Writing

PAPER 3 Listening ▶ | Part 1

PAPER 4 Speaking | Part 2 | Part 3 | Part 4

🎧 **Track 9**

You will hear people talking in eight different situations. For questions **1–8**, choose the best answer (**A**, **B** or **C**).

1 You hear a man talking about planting flower seeds in his garden.
When does he expect them to grow?
A June
B May
C April

2 You hear two friends talking about when they last met.
What was the occasion?
A a birthday party
B a wedding
C a Christmas party

3 You hear a woman talking about the kind of book she currently enjoys reading.
What kind of book is it?
A romance
B detective novel
C fairytale

4 You hear two friends discussing the sports they play.
Which sport do they most enjoy playing?
A basketball
B tennis
C volleyball

5 You hear a shop assistant talking to a customer.
What is the customer looking for?
A a shirt
B a suit
C a sweater

6 You hear a man talking about his job as a lighting technician in a theatre.
How does he feel about tonight's performance?
A concerned about making mistakes
B surprised to be so nervous about the experience
C excited about working in live theatre

7 You hear a boy talking about school.
Which subject does he like best?
A maths
B art
C history

8 You hear a travel agent talking about a journey.
What is the customer's final destination?
A Houston
B New York
C Los Angeles

Part 1
Part 2
Part 3
Part 4

🎧 **Track 10**

You will hear a man called Tom Botham giving a talk about newspaper journalism. For questions **9–18**, complete the sentences with a word or short phrase.

Journalism

Tom mentions business, news, sport and (**9**) .... as examples of what journalists write about.

Many journalists have a degree in journalism, though Tom took his in (**10**) ....

Tom says it's important to gain a certificate in reporting, carrying out (**11**) .... and editing.

When applying for a job, Tom says you need to show a selection of (**12**) .... you've written.

Tom got experience of writing by working as a (**13**) .... on a student magazine.

Tom says journalists must have good communication and (**14**) .... skills, in addition to personal characteristics such as motivation.

Tom was able to demonstrate to employers his experience of (**15**) ....

As a junior reporter, Tom was pleased to attend (**16**) .... as well as other local events.

In Tom's present job, he has a range of responsibilities and most enjoys doing (**17**) ....

Tom is currently exploring the idea of working as a (**18**) .... on the paper.

FIRST
TEST 3

PAPER 1 Reading and
         Use of English
PAPER 2 Writing
PAPER 3 Listening ▶
         Part 1
         Part 2
         Part 3
         Part 4

Exam Essentials

 Track 11

You will hear five short extracts in which people are talking about their favourite films. For questions **19–23**, choose from the list (**A–H**) the reason each speaker gives for his or her preference. Use the letters only once. There are three extra letters which you do not need to use.

A   It has a complex storyline.

B   You want to know what happens next.

Speaker 1 | **19** |

C   It is highly amusing.

Speaker 2 | **20** |

D   It has an unexpected ending.

Speaker 3 | **21** |

E   It is very true to life.

Speaker 4 | **22** |

F   The special effects are interesting.

Speaker 5 | **23** |

G   The acting is outstanding.

H   It has an unusual theme.

🎧 **Track 12**

You will hear part of a radio interview with a woman called Alice Barker, who has a rare condition called synaesthesia. For questions **24–30**, choose the best answer (**A, B** or **C**).

24 Alice describes her ability as
    A   connecting emotions and words.
    B   linking colours and emotions.
    C   connecting colours with words.

25 We are told that Alice developed this condition
    A   because it is in her family.
    B   when she was a child.
    C   when she had children.

26. When she was younger, Alice and her brother
    A   used to think they were going mad.
    B   would argue about the colours connected with words.
    C   saw the same colours for certain words.

27 Alice says that this ability
    A   is directly associated with her moods.
    B   can make her feel depressed.
    C   makes her feelings more intense.

28 What is the effect of Alice's condition on her reading?
    A   It makes her read more descriptions of colours.
    B   It can encourage her to reread a sentence.
    C   It makes her avoid sentences with bright descriptions.

29 Alice feels that having this condition
    A   is very unpleasant at times.
    B   is generally not a problem.
    C   is not pleasant at all, on the whole.

30 Doctors used to believe that this condition
    A   made people insane.
    B   only affected the insane.
    C   indicated the person was going mad.

Part 1 (2 minutes)

The examiner (interlocutor) will ask each of you to speak briefly in turn and to give personal information about yourselves. You can expect a variety of questions, such as:

When did you start learning English?
In what ways do you think English is going to be useful for you?
Do you have any plans for a future career?
Will you be able to use foreign languages in the career you choose?

Part 2 (4 minutes)

You will each be asked to talk for a minute without interruption. You will each be given two different photographs in turn to talk about. After your partner has finished speaking, you will be asked a brief question connected with your partner's photographs.

1 Meals

Look at the two photographs on page 165 which show people having different sorts of meals.

Candidate A, compare these photographs, and say how you think the people feel in these situations.

Candidate B, which of these sorts of meals would you enjoy most? (Why?)

2 Cars

Look at the two photographs on page 166 which show different cars.

Candidate B, compare these photographs, and say how you think it would feel to travel in these cars.

Candidate A, which of these cars would you prefer to travel in? (Why?)

Part 3 (4 minutes)

You will be asked to discuss something together without interruption by the examiner. You will have a page of ideas and a question to help you.

Outdoor activities

Imagine you are helping to organise an outdoor activity holiday for a group of teenagers. Turn to page 167 which has ideas for activities and a question for you to discuss. Talk to each other about the advantages and disadvantages of these outdoor activities. Then decide which two activities should be chosen.

Part 4 (4 minutes)

The examiner will encourage you to develop the topic of your discussion in Part 3 by asking questions such as:

What are the most popular sports to watch and play in your country?
Do you prefer team sports or individual sports? (Why?)
What skills do team sports require? (Why?)
Why do you think some people are good at sports and others aren't?
Do you think some sports are too expensive to play? (Why? / Why not?)
Do you think professional sportspeople earn too much money? (Why? / Why not?)

▸▸ PART 5

devoted (adj) giving someone a lot of love and attention

fierce (adj) powerful, intense

sibling (n) a brother or sister

stride (v) to walk strongly with long steps

foul (adj) foul weather is stormy and windy, with rain or snow

clap eyes on someone/something (phr) to see someone/something, especially when you did not expect to

flutter (v) to wave very quickly and lightly

breeze (n) a gentle wind

neutral (adj) neutral language deliberately avoids expressing strong feelings

landscape gardener (n) a skilled worker who designs and works on landscaped areas

rambler (n) someone who goes for long walks for enjoyment

eager (adj) keen and excited

far from (phr) used to say that something different is true

campaign (v) to try to achieve something by persuading people or the government to do something

erode (v) to wear away, to wash away

exposed (adj) not covered

clump (n) a group, mass, or cluster

sway (v) to move back and forth, to rock

transform (v) to change from one shape or appearance to another

revelation (n) an uncovering of something that was hidden, a disclosure

▸▸ PART 6

turn to (v) to start doing something new or different

hang out (v) to spend time somewhere

formative (adj) relating to a period of early development

visibility (n) the capability of being easily observed

platform (n) hardware or software that can be accessed online

well-being (n) when someone is happy, healthy and comfortable

boost (v) to improve or increase something

energise (v) to give energy to

mental sharpness (n) the ability to notice and understand things

hand-eye coordination (n) the coordinated control of hand movement with eye movement

stimulus (n) something that makes something else happen, grow or develop more

flood (v) to enter or fill a place in large numbers or amounts

mimic (v) to copy or imitate closely

incorporate (v) to include something as part of another thing

opponent (n) a person who takes the opposite side in a fight, game, contest, etc.

hit (v) to go to

▸▸ PART 7

solitude (n) being alone

attic (n) a space in a house, just under the roof

frame of mind (n) the way someone feels at a particular time

flow (v) to move in a smooth, continuous way

extend (v) to continue

switch off (v) relax

interfere (v) to intrude

congregate (v) to gather together

spacious (adj) large, with plenty of room

catering (n) providing food and drink for people

imperative (adj) essential

chill out (v) to relax

vital (adj) essential

designate (v) to set aside for a purpose

renovation (n) the act of repairing and redecorating

serenity (n) a feeling of calmness and happiness

get your head down (v) to direct all your efforts to a particular task

undertake (v) to do something, to carry something out

ergonomic (adj) designed to create maximum comfort

outlay (n) cost

output (n) an amount of something produced by a person

sedentary (adj) spending a lot of time sitting down

For questions **1–8**, read the text below and decide which word (**A**, **B**, **C** or **D**) best fits each gap. There is an example at the beginning (**0**).

Mark your answers **on the separate answer sheet**.

Example:

| 0 | **A** informed | **B** told | **C** shown | **D** said |

| 0 | A | B | <u>C</u> | D |

School lunch

Research has (**0**) .... that over half the children in Britain who take their own lunches to school do not eat properly in the middle of the day. In Britain schools have to provide meals at lunchtime. Children can (**1**) .... to bring their own food or have lunch in the school canteen.

One surprising (**2**) .... of this research is that school meals are much healthier than lunches brought in from home. There are strict standards for the preparation of school meals, which have to include fruit, vegetables, meat and a dairy item. Lunchboxes (**3**) .... by researchers contained sweet drinks, crisps and chocolate bars, so the children (**4**) .... an unhealthy amount of sugar at lunchtime.

The research will provide a better (**5**) .... of why the percentage of overweight students in Britain has (**6**) .... in the last decade. Children can easily develop bad eating (**7**) .... at this age, and it's important to try and do something to (**8**) .... it.

1	**A** prefer	**B** manage	**C** want	**D** choose
2	**A** finding	**B** number	**C** figure	**D** factor
3	**A** examined	**B** found	**C** taken	**D** looked
4	**A** take	**B** contain	**C** consume	**D** consist
5	**A** view	**B** knowledge	**C** understanding	**D** opinion
6	**A** expanded	**B** increased	**C** extended	**D** added
7	**A** customs	**B** styles	**C** attitudes	**D** habits
8	**A** prevent	**B** define	**C** decide	**D** delay

For questions **9–16**, read the text below and think of the word which best fits each gap. Use only **one** word in each gap. There is an example at the beginning (**0**).

Write your answers **IN CAPITAL LETTERS on the separate answer sheet**.

Example: | 0 | T | H | E | R | E | | | | | | | | | | | | |

History and storytelling

Over the last few years (**0**) .... has been more interest in the subject of history, perhaps because historical documentaries on television have (**9**) .... attracting large audiences. According to a recent survey, more people are applying (**10**) .... places at university, and the number of those wanting to study history (**11**) .... increased. However, professors of history are (**12**) .... particularly happy about this and have expressed concern about the quality of their students. They claim that most of their first-year students have never read a history book and don't have the skills (**13**) .... study the subject in depth. TV programmes make students think that studying history is as simple as storytelling. Documentaries oversimplify the subject and concentrate (**14**) .... personalities in an attempt to attract audiences.

On the other hand, traditional historians could learn (**15**) .... to tell a story from the makers of such documentaries. Many historians don't have good narrative skills, which is (**16**) .... so many history books are not popular with readers.

PAPER 1 Reading and ▸   Part 1
         Use of English   Part 2
                             Part 3
PAPER 2 Writing   Part 4
                             Part 5
PAPER 3 Listening   Part 6
                             Part 7
PAPER 4 Speaking

For questions **17–24**, read the text below. Use the word given in capitals at the end of some of the lines to form a word that fits in the gap **in the same line**. There is an example at the beginning (**0**).

Write your answers **IN CAPITAL LETTERS on the separate answer sheet**.

Example: | 0 | D | A | N | G | E | R | O | U | S | | | | | | | |

Diving deeper

Free-diving is an extremely (**0**) …….. sport, which is perhaps	**DANGER**
why its (**17**) …….. has grown so fast. Free-divers are attached	**POPULAR**
to a line, and then they have to take a deep breath, dive as	
deep as they can and come up (**18**) …….. .	**IMMEDIATE**

The British free-diver, Tanya Streeter, trains very (**19**) ……..	**CARE**
before each dive to build up her physical (**20**) …….. She never	**FIT**
dives until she's completely confident that she's ready.	

'The danger is caused by the great (**21**) …….. at those depths.	**PRESS**
I think that safety procedures have to be very strict if we	
want to avoid accidents,' Tanya says. Tanya feels that mental	
strength is also very important. She has an emotional response	
to water and feels very calm when she's underwater. Perhaps	
Tanya's greatest asset is her (**22**) …….. to focus. 'In free-diving	**ABLE**
there are no (**23**) …….. around you and there are no cheering	**COMPETE**
spectators to (**24**) …….. you. It's a lonely sport,' says Tanya.	**COURAGE**

For questions **25–30**, complete the second sentence so that it has a similar meaning to the first sentence, using the word given. **Do not change the word given.** You must use between **two** and **five** words, including the word given. Here is an example (**0**).

Example:

0   I'll be very happy when I go on holiday.

FORWARD

I'm .... on holiday.

The gap can be filled by the words 'looking forward to going' so you write:

Example: | 0 | LOOKING FORWARD TO GOING

Write only the missing words **IN CAPITAL LETTERS on the separate answer sheet**.

---

25   The basketball coach will make me train very hard.

MADE

I .... very hard by the basketball coach.

26   'You can watch if you keep quiet,' said the actor.

PROVIDED

The actor said that I could watch .... quiet.

27   I regret not telling you the whole truth.

TOLD

I wish .... the whole truth.

28   After hours of negotiation, they managed to get the new contract.

SUCCEEDED

After hours of negotiation, they .... the new contract.

29   She tried to stay cheerful although she felt sick.

SPITE

She tried to stay cheerful .... sick.

30   Mike probably won't come to the party.

UNLIKELY

Mike .... to the party.

PAPER 1 Reading and ▶
        Use of English

PAPER 2 Writing

PAPER 3 Listening

PAPER 4 Speaking

Part 1
Part 2
Part 3
Part 4
Part 5
Part 6
Part 7

You are going to read an article about noise. For questions **31–36**, choose the answer (**A**, **B**, **C** or **D**) which you think fits best according to the text.

Mark your answers **on the separate answer sheet**.

Noise: traveller's enemy or traveller's friend?

'Passport, boarding pass, phone…' As my taxi zips towards the airport, suddenly a cord of panic pulls tight around my chest. I thrust my hand into one compartment of my handbag, then another. It's not anywhere. My mouth opens, and the words, 'Driver, turn around! Now!' almost spring out. But I swallow them. We're halfway to the airport, and I'm already running late. Surely I can survive one trip without my supply of foam earplugs?

I'm a generally good traveller except for one thing that undoes me every time: noise. Ask me about my absolute worst travel experiences, and I'll tell you the story about that night I spent in a cheap hotel that also happens to be the venue for the most popular Saturday night disco in the area. Elsewhere, there were the chickens that always began crowing at 2 a.m. at a rural retreat (no one, I guess, informed them that they shouldn't get going until dawn). And there was also the deeply discounted hotel room with 'swimming pool view' that I was so pleased with myself for finding. The swimming pool, it turned out, was under renovation. Actively. With power drills. Directly below my window.

In my ideal traveller's world I'd control the volume of everything, like a music producer at a giant mixing board. There would be no blasting television sets hanging above public squares or embedded in taxi seats, no cheesy songs playing in the shops. Loud noise would be completely absent. Everywhere. But no traveller can remain in a perfectly controlled sonic bubble. Not when we're moving through a world in which what constitutes noise has so many different interpretations, including whether noise is ever a bad thing. For sound is relative: one person's noise is another person's music, or expression of happiness.

On one of the first extended trips I ever took, I travelled to an island for Carnival, which is basically like deciding to pitch your tent inside a dance hall for three weeks. At any hour, different kinds of music would float through the air and, without warning, straight into my ear. Neighbours shouted to each other over the din, then turned up the volume on their radios. It was a non-stop celebration, during which I

line 24 got very little sleep. It was fabulous. The thing is, the noise that wraps a city in Carnival happiness is more than just noise: it's the sound of a human community. To block it out is to risk missing something really fundamental about a place – and the reassuring feeling of being part of something larger than yourself. Noise brings people together. I've learnt this over and over in my travels, but it hasn't been an easy lesson to accept.

I struggle against my instinct to isolate myself in a cocoon of silence. I really don't want to cut myself off from the thrill of human noise. But I don't want to go crazy, either. Nowadays, unwanted – and largely non-human – sounds push and shove travellers from all directions. Cars, subways, construction, jet engines: their clamour seems omnipresent. Yet instead of lowering the volume of everyday living, we seem to layer noise upon noise. The hotel bar jacks up its techno music to counteract the babble in the lobby. The traveller walking along traffic-choked streets retreats into her iPod.

On the plane, I press my foam earplug deep into my ear. As it slowly expands to fill my ear canal, I savour the journey into the bliss of noiselessness. Thank goodness the convenience store at the airport stocks one of travel's most essential items. The headache-inducing whine of the jet engines magically fades away, and I'm once again the master of my private sonic world. To appreciate the comfort of noise, you also need the comfort of silence. I'll unplug when I get to where I'm going.

31 What is the writer doing in the first paragraph?

    A demonstrating how well organised she is
    B explaining why she is in a particular situation
    C describing something that often happens to her
    D showing how important something is to her

32 What do the writer's worst travel experiences tell us about her?

    A She is annoyed when the facilities advertised are not available.
    B She is willing to stay in places that are not particularly luxurious.
    C She tries to plan ahead in order to avoid certain situations.
    D She finds unusual locations especially attractive.

33 What does the writer say about her 'ideal traveller's world'?

    A She realises it isn't actually the best way to travel.
    B She wishes she didn't have to share it with others.
    C She travels in the hope of finding it one day.
    D She knows other people wouldn't like it.

34 What does 'It' refer to in line 24?

    A getting very little sleep
    B the volume on people's radios
    C the non-stop celebration
    D the neighbours shouting

35 What does the writer say about noise in the fifth paragraph?

    A People are born with a need to hear it.
    B People deal with it by creating more of it.
    C It affects people in a number of different ways.
    D Modern life offers effective protection from it.

36 How does the writer feel in the final paragraph?

    A relieved she will not have to hear any noise at her destination
    B grateful to know she can find earplugs wherever she goes
    C pleased she can decide for herself whether to hear things or not
    D glad to be able to choose what music she'll listen to on the flight

PAPER 1 Reading and ▶	Part 1
Use of English	Part 2
PAPER 2 Writing	Part 3
	Part 4
PAPER 3 Listening	Part 5
PAPER 4 Speaking	**Part 6**
	Part 7

You are going to read an article about an expedition to look at a mountain under the sea. Six sentences have been removed from the article. Choose from the sentences **A–G** the one which fits each gap (**37–42**). There is one extra sentence, which you do not need to use.

Mark your answers **on the separate answer sheet**.

Mountains in the sea

An ocean scientist visits a mountain, or 'seamount', deep under the ocean.

Sealed in our special deep-sea sphere, we wait until we are untied, drifting, a tiny dot on the immense Pacific Ocean. Then we sink into the water, surrounded by bubbles. A diver pokes through the bubbles to make a final adjustment to the camera mounted on the outside of the submersible sphere (known as a 'sub'). Out there with the camera are hydraulics, thrusters, and hundreds of other essential parts that will keep us safe.

Three of us are crammed inside a sphere 1.5 metres in diameter, surrounded by communication equipment, controls, snacks, cameras. **37** Its peaks, rarely seen up close before, rise from the bottom of the Pacific near Cocos Island. The highest peak here is more than 2,200 metres tall.

Seamounts generally form when volcanic mountains rise up from the sea floor but fail to reach the surface (those that break the surface become islands). Scientists estimate that there are some 100,000 seamounts at least one kilometre high. But if you include others that range from small hills to rolling mountains, there may be as many as a million of them. We've seen little of these oases of life in the deep. Of all earth's seamounts, marine biologists have studied only a few hundred. **38**

Scientists don't often explore their slopes first hand – or even their shallower summits: living mazes of hard coral, sponges and sea fans circled by schools of fish. **39** Among this abundance of sea creatures, might there be new species that could produce new chemical compounds that can cure diseases?

Unfortunately, more and more frequently deep-sea fishing trawlers drag nets weighted with heavy chains across seamounts to catch schools of fish that congregate around them. **40** Once these underwater communities are disrupted, it can take hundreds, even thousands, of years for them to re-establish themselves.

We turn a ghostly greenish blue in the light, kept dim so we can see outside. Clear, pulsing jellies glide gently in the dark, bouncing off the sub in every direction. A black-and-white manta ray flexes its wings and soars past for a look. We are still in what is called the photic zone, where sunlight penetrates and provides energy for countless microscopic, photosynthetic ocean plants that create much of the earth's oxygen. **41**

At about 200 metres the sub's dazzling lights bring the bottom into view. **42** We joke that maybe we've found a new wreck, but instead it is the remains of a volcano, perhaps millions of years old. Within minutes the sub is hovering a few centimetres from the bottom, inside an ancient, circular vent of the now extinct volcano that forms Las Gemelas. Its sculptured walls look like the facade of a deep-sea cathedral.

Our sub surfaces after five hours – all too soon. We begin the long journey back to our land-based lives, where we will analyse our data and add one more piece to the puzzle of our global ocean.

A This process also destroys long-lived and slow-growing corals, sponges, and other invertebrates.

B These under-sea mountains have therefore been well known for a number of years.

C Then we descend further, and the ocean around us is completely black.

D More finely detailed maps of the surface of Mars may exist than of the remotest parts of the ocean floor.

E Suddenly something just beyond them rises from the otherwise featureless sea floor.

F We have everything we need for our journey to reach a seamount named Las Gemelas.

G Some of these animals have even lived to be more than a hundred years old.

PAPER 1 Reading and ▶
         Use of English

PAPER 2 Writing

PAPER 3 Listening

PAPER 4 Speaking

Part 1
Part 2
Part 3
Part 4
Part 5
Part 6
Part 7

You are going to read an article in which four young people talk about the experience of taking their driving test. For questions **43–52**, choose from the people (**A–D**). The people may be chosen more than once.

Mark your answers **on the separate answer sheet**.

Which person

failed the driving test three times?	**43**
thought learning to drive would be easier than it was?	**44**
was discouraged from driving by a relative?	**45**
was very nervous at first?	**46**
is going to drive a vehicle at work?	**47**
practised driving on private land?	**48**
nearly missed the test?	**49**
hasn't driven since taking the test?	**50**
will soon own a car?	**51**
could previously use another type of vehicle?	**52**

First steps at driving

How do young people feel about learning to drive?
We asked four youngsters who have recently passed the test.

A Joe Smedley

I used to make models of cars, and I knew a lot about different makes long before I was old enough to drive one. I'd been riding a motorbike for six months before I started taking lessons for my driving test, and I'm sure that experience helped me. On the other hand, learning to drive proved to be quite hard. I thought because I knew how a car works it would make a difference. That was a big mistake! I remember how embarrassed I was when I couldn't even get the car into second gear. By the time I took my test, I felt fairly confident, so I wasn't surprised when I passed first time. The funny thing about it is that I haven't had the chance to drive a car ever since I got my licence because my parents don't have one!

B Hanna Watson

I'm really glad that I have a driving licence because it's so useful, but I wasn't really sure I wanted to take the test at first. I was shaking and my knees were trembling before the first lesson, though I felt better because the instructor was so friendly. Although he assured me I was ready to take the test after 25 lessons, I decided to wait until I had had a few more. I felt very tense about driving, and the test was a disaster. First, I forgot my glasses when I went for the written test, and then, on the practical test, I got there five minutes' late because the bus I was on broke down! It wasn't my fault, and luckily they let me go ahead with it anyway, but I was quite upset. Anyway, for the last few months I've been practising in my father's car, although he only lets me go on quiet country roads.

C Clarissa Holmes

I wanted to get my driving licence as soon as I could. My childhood ambition was to be the first woman Formula One world champion! Actually, the reality of taking my test was completely different from what I'd expected. I didn't pass the test until my fourth attempt, but that was because of the practical test. I kept on making silly mistakes, you see. In fact, the other part of the test wasn't nearly as hard; all you had to do was learn the regulations about driving.

I was getting pretty upset after failing three times, so my aunt, who owns a farm, let me go into a field and drive around, just to get used to the feeling. I think that helped a lot. I've been saving up like mad, and in a couple of weeks I'm confident I'll have enough to buy a decent second-hand car.

D Eddy Fredricks

I didn't really think about taking my driving test right up until I was 18. I had the idea that driving was basically dangerous, and I think that came from my grandmother. She had never got used to driving in busy traffic, and she used to tell me how awful it was, which put me off a lot. But when a couple of my friends passed their tests, I suddenly realised I really wanted to get my driving licence.

Being optimistic, I just booked ten lessons at first, but in the end I needed over three times that many! Having a driving licence is going to be very useful. When the school term finishes in August, I've got a part-time job delivering books for a big bookshop, and I have to use their delivery van, so I couldn't do it if I hadn't passed my test.

You **must** answer this question. Write your answer in **140–190** words in an appropriate style.

<hr />

1   In your English class you have been talking about sport. Now, your English teacher has asked you to write an essay for homework.

Write an essay using **all** the notes and giving reasons for your point of view.

> Is playing a team sport the best way to get fit?
>
> **Notes**
> Write about:
>
> 1. exercising with other people
> 2. how convenient it is
> 3. .... (your own idea)

PAPER 1   Reading and
          Use of English
PAPER 2   Writing   ▶   Part 1
PAPER 3   Listening   Part 2
PAPER 4   Speaking

Write an answer to **one** of the questions **2–5** in this part. Write your answer in **140–190** words in an appropriate style.

2   You see this announcement on an English-language website.

Articles wanted!
Music

How important is music in your life?

What sort of music do you enjoy? Why?

Who do you listen to it with?

Write us an article answering these questions. The best articles will be posted on the website.

Write your **article**.

3   You recently saw a film about a famous historical event in your country. Write a review of the film for your college magazine. Include information about the story, the characters and costumes, and say whether the film was historically accurate.

Write your **review**.

4   (*for FIRST candidates only*)

Your teacher has asked you to write a report about the eating habits of young people in your area. Describe what most young people eat and suggest how they could be encouraged to eat healthier food.

Write your **report**.

(*for FIRST FOR SCHOOLS candidates only*)

You see this announcement in an international magazine for young people.

Stories wanted

We are looking for stories for our magazine. Your story must begin with this sentence:

Helen and Steve looked at each other and burst out laughing.

Your story must include:
   • a photograph
   • a computer

Write your **story**.

5   (*for FIRST FOR SCHOOLS candidates only*)

Answer the following question based on your reading of one of the set books.

Write an **essay** describing an event in the book or short story you have read which plays a main role in the development of the plot and affects the characters.

PAPER 1 Reading and
          Use of English

PAPER 2 Writing

PAPER 3 Listening ▶ | Part 1
                          | Part 2
                          | Part 3
                          | Part 4

PAPER 4 Speaking

🎧 **Track 13**

You will hear people talking in eight different situations. For questions **1–8**, choose the best answer (**A**, **B** or **C**).

1 You hear a woman bringing an MP3 player back to the shop where she bought it.
   What is the problem with it?
   A It plays tracks at the wrong speed.
   B It jumps from one track to the next.
   C It doesn't switch off properly.

2 You hear a woman talking to a waiter.
   What does she want him to bring her?
   A mineral water
   B coffee
   C orange juice

3 You hear a man describing a journey.
   Where did he want to go?
   A Leeds
   B Manchester
   C Crewe

4 You hear an advertisement for a sale in a furniture store.
   Which items have the biggest reductions?
   A sofas
   B beds
   C armchairs

5 You hear a woman talking to a car mechanic.
   What is the problem with her car?
   A It won't start in wet weather.
   B The brakes don't work properly.
   C The engine keeps on stopping.

6 You hear a graphic designer talking about his work.
   How does he feel about the recent change in his job?
   A He thinks his new work is boring.
   B He regrets giving up his previous job.
   C He thinks he's made the right decision.

7 You hear a radio announcement about traffic on a motorway.
   Where are the longest delays expected?
   A between junctions 10 and 11
   B between junctions 13 and 14
   C between junctions 17 and 18

8 You hear a man phoning his local newsagent's shop.
   Which newspaper did he receive by mistake this morning?
   A *the Telegraph*
   B *the Sun*
   C *the Daily Mirror*

🎧 **Track 14**

You will hear a golfer called John Freeman giving a talk about his career. For questions **9–18**, complete the sentences with a word or short phrase.

Golf

John Freeman has been playing golf for (**9**) .... years.

John's father never progressed as a golfer because he couldn't afford

very good (**10**) ....

When he was younger, John wanted to be a professional

(**11**) .... player.

John's father took up golf again after being (**12**) ....

John wishes he had received some (**13**) .... from his

teachers at school.

John says that golf is often seen as a sport for people with a lot of

(**14**) ....

Young golfers should be able to get help from (**15**) ....

The (**16**) .... of British players is likely to raise the

profile of golf.

John's income from golf is (**17**) ....

John used to dye his hair (**18**) ....

PAPER 1 Reading and
         Use of English

PAPER 2 Writing

PAPER 3 Listening ▶

PAPER 4 Speaking

Part 1
Part 2
Part 3
Part 4

 Track 15

You will hear five short extracts in which people are talking about holidays. For questions **19–23**, choose from the list (**A–H**) what each speaker says. Use the letters only once. There are three extra letters which you do not need to use.

A   It made our friendship stronger.

B   I realised I loved long journeys.

Speaker 1 ☐ **19**

C   It gave me a sense of my origins.

Speaker 2 ☐ **20**

D   It provided an escape.

Speaker 3 ☐ **21**

E   I felt closer to my family.

Speaker 4 ☐ **22**

F   It was my first holiday abroad.

Speaker 5 ☐ **23**

G   I felt I had learnt something.

H   I was relieved to be back home.

PAPER 1 Reading and
          Use of English

PAPER 2 Writing

PAPER 3 Listening ▶

PAPER 4 Speaking

Part 1
Part 2
Part 3
Part 4

Track 16

You will hear part of a radio interview with Laura Bartlett, who works as a florist (someone who sells and arranges flowers). For questions **24–30**, choose the best answer (**A**, **B** or **C**).

24 Laura's parents
    A were professional gardeners.
    B had a successful florist's shop.
    C loved cultivating plants.

25 Laura originally wanted
    A to work as a graphic designer.
    B to become an artist.
    C to write articles for a magazine.

26 She became a florist
    A because she didn't know what else to do.
    B as soon as she resigned from the magazine.
    C as the result of an accident.

27 In the beginning, Laura
    A wasn't skilled at working with flowers.
    B didn't work with flowers at all.
    C only delivered flowers to customers.

28 Laura had to learn
    A the names of different species of flowers.
    B which flowers florists could use in their work.
    C how to prepare flowers for arrangements.

29 Laura suggests that a young person who wants to be a florist must be prepared
    A to send flowers to people who are ill.
    B to work long hours at certain times of the year.
    C to spend a lot of time at the flower market.

30 Laura advises young people who would like to become florists
    A to work at a florist's while they are attending courses in floristry.
    B to study floristry full time at a college before they get a job.
    C to learn how to program a computer.

Part 1 (2 minutes)

The examiner (interlocutor) will ask each of you to speak briefly in turn and to give personal information about yourselves. You can expect a variety of questions, such as:

How did you travel here today?
What sort of public transport is available in this area?
What form of transport do you use most often? (Why?)
What do you like and dislike about it?

Part 2 (4 minutes)

You will each be asked to talk for a minute without interruption. You will each be given two different photographs in turn to talk about. After your partner has finished speaking, you will be asked a brief question connected with your partner's photographs.

1 At work

Look at the two photographs on page 168 which show people working in different environments

Candidate A, compare these photographs, and say how you think the people are feeling in these different situations.

Candidate B, which of these jobs would you prefer to do? (Why?)

2 Leisure

Look at the two photographs on page 169 which show people doing different leisure activities.

Candidate B, compare these photographs, and say what sort of person you think would enjoy each of these activities.

Candidate A, which of these activities would you prefer to do? (Why?)

Part 3 (4 minutes)

You will be asked to discuss something together without interruption by the examiner. You will have a page of ideas with a question to help you.

Inventions

Imagine that you are taking part in a television programme about inventions that have changed the course of history. Turn to page 170 which has the names of different inventions and a question for you to discuss. Talk to each other about how these different inventions have changed people's lives. Then decide which two have been the most important.

Part 4 (4 minutes)

The examiner will encourage you to develop the topic of your discussion in Part 3 by asking questions such as:

What are the advantages and disadvantages of using computers?
Do you think technological advances help to improve everyday life? (Why? / Why not?)
What are the disadvantages of modern technology?
Do you think we rely too much on modern technology? (Why? / Why not?)
What inventions could improve people's lives in the future?
How do you think technology will be different in the future?

PAPER 1 Reading and Use of English

▸▸ PART 5

zip (v) to move quickly

thrust (v) to push hard

spring (v) to jump

run late (v) to be later than planned

foam (n) soft sponge-like material

undo (v) to defeat

retreat (n) a quiet place away from crowds

mixing board (n) electronic device for combining audio signals

embedded (adj) permanently part of

cheesy (adj) in bad style

bubble (n) a place where the outside world cannot disturb

constitute (v) to be or form

pitch (v) to put up

fundamental (adj) important, main

din (n) loud continuous noise

cocoon (n) protected place

thrill (n) great excitement

shove (v) to push hard

clamour (n) noise made by a lot of people

counteract (v) to reduce the effect of

babble (n) noise made by many people talking at once

traffic-choked (adj) completely full of traffic

retreat (v) to escape from

savour (v) to enjoy

bliss (n) great pleasure

sonic (adj) of sound

▸▸ PART 6

sphere (n) a ball shape

drift (v) to move slowly in water, pulled by the sea current

adjustment (n) small change

submersible (adj) designed to go underwater

crammed (adj) pushed together in a small space

maze (n) an area in which you can easily get lost because there are lots of similar paths

abundance (n) large number

drag (v) to pull

school of fish (n) large number of fish of the same species swimming together

disrupt (v) to disturb

re-establish (v) to exist in large numbers again

dim (adj) not bright

glide (v) to move elegantly and smoothly

soar (v) to rise quickly

countless (adj) a very large number

dazzling (adj) very bright

wreck (n) remains of a ship that has sunk

hover (v) to stay above a surface in one place

vent (n) a small opening

façade (n) the front of a building

▸▸ PART 7

gear (n) one of several speeds in a vehicle

tremble (v) to shake with fear

instructor (n) a teacher

ambition (n) a desire to succeed, a goal, an objective

attempt (n) an effort

regulation (n) a rule

save up (phr v) to collect money for a particular purpose

decent (adj) proper, good enough

put off (phr v) to make you dislike something or not want to do something

PAPER 1 Reading and ▶ **Part 1**
         Use of English   Part 2
PAPER 2 Writing   Part 3
                          Part 4
PAPER 3 Listening   Part 5
PAPER 4 Speaking   Part 6
                          Part 7

For questions **1–8**, read the text below and decide which word (**A, B, C** or **D**) best fits each gap. There is an example at the beginning (**0**).

Mark your answers **on the separate answer sheet**.

Example:

| **0** | **A** doubt | **B** reason | **C** purpose | **D** motive |

A powerful influence

There can be no (**0**) .... at all that the internet has made a huge difference to our lives. However, there is some concern over whether people spend too much time browsing the internet or playing computer games, (**1**) .... ever doing anything else in their spare time. Are these activities genuinely (**2**) .... to our well-being? Does spending too much time chatting on social networking sites really (**3**) .... our ability to form meaningful relationships in real life?

Quite the reverse, (**4**) .... to some social media experts, who suggest that using websites to keep in touch with friends may (**5**) .... help to enhance personal relationships and provide people with an increased (**6**) .... of belonging.

There may be room for argument in (**7**) .... of limiting time spent online, especially when it may break into study or work time. Research, however, also indicates that spending a healthy amount of time in front of a computer doesn't necessarily (**8**) .... with academic performance.

1	**A** nearly	**B** literally	**C** almost	**D** hardly
2	**A** harming	**B** harmful	**C** hurting	**D** hurtful
3	**A** affect	**B** bother	**C** effect	**D** concern
4	**A** agreeing	**B** corresponding	**C** owing	**D** according
5	**A** completely	**B** probably	**C** actually	**D** rightly
6	**A** function	**B** sense	**C** attitude	**D** meaning
7	**A** favour	**B** help	**C** choice	**D** opinion
8	**A** trouble	**B** interrupt	**C** oppose	**D** interfere

For questions **9–16**, read the text below and think of the word which best fits each gap. Use only **one** word in each gap. There is an example at the beginning (**0**).

Write your answers **IN CAPITAL LETTERS on the separate answer sheet**.

Example: | 0 | W | H | O | | | | | | | | | | | | | | | | |

Driving blind

The idea that a blind person could drive a car sounds crazy. And the concept of someone (**0**) .... can't see driving a car at almost 150 miles per hour sounds even crazier. Miranda Naylor, (**9**) .... blind accountant from the UK, has done exactly that in an attempt (**10**) .... raise money for charity. Mrs Naylor drove a sports car for two miles along the runway of a disused airfield. She was (**11**) .... radio contact with her husband, who gave her directions and advice. Her achievement (**12**) .... expected to raise about £50,000, which will be donated to a company that trains dogs for (**13**) .... blind.

Mrs Naylor (**14**) .... been blind since she was six, and still has some visual memories of the world around her. She admits that (**15**) .... having sight makes life awkward (**16**) .... times, but she says, 'Achieving something can be a great source of self-confidence.' Miranda is now looking for a new challenge and wants to try motorbiking.

PAPER 1 Reading and ▸
          Use of English

PAPER 2 Writing

PAPER 3 Listening

PAPER 4 Speaking

Part 1	
Part 2	
Part 3	
Part 4	
Part 5	
Part 6	
Part 7	

For questions **17–24**, read the text below. Use the word given in capitals at the end of some of the lines to form a word that fits in the gap **in the same line**. There is an example at the beginning (**0**).

Write your answers **IN CAPITAL LETTERS on the separate answer sheet**.

Example: | 0 | E | X | C | I | T | I | N | G | | | | | | | | |

Following swallows

Bert Cook's job doesn't immediately strike you as (**0**)	**EXCITE**
He sits inside a small construction made of cloth and wire and	
watches birds: swallows, in fact, whose (**17**) .... in Britain after	**ARRIVE**
a dangerous flight marks the (**18**) .... of summer. The severe	**BEGIN**
weather caused by (**19**) .... warming makes their journey	**GLOBE**
tougher each year.	
One of their main (**20**) .... is getting enough to eat. Insect	**DIFFICULT**
numbers have declined (**21**) .... , and if the birds do make	**SHARP**
it to Britain, they may still die of (**22**)	**HUNGRY**
Farm buildings such as barns have been converted into	
houses, and as a result, there are now fewer places for birds	
to nest. Bert finds it (**23**) .... to say with any precision how	**POSSIBLE**
far the numbers of swallows have declined in the area	
under (**24**) .... Bird populations can increase considerably	**OBSERVE**
if swallows have had a good breeding season, and for the	
moment at least, scientists are not overly worried.	

PAPER 1 Reading and ▶
       Use of English
PAPER 2 Writing
PAPER 3 Listening
PAPER 4 Speaking

Part 1
Part 2
Part 3
Part 4
Part 5
Part 6
Part 7

For questions **25–30**, complete the second sentence so that it has a similar meaning to the first sentence, using the word given. **Do not change the word given.** You must use between **two** and **five** words, including the word given. Here is an example (**0**).

Example:

0   I'll be very happy when I go on holiday.

   FORWARD

   I'm .... on holiday.

The gap can be filled by the words 'looking forward to going' so you write:

Example: | 0 | LOOKING FORWARD TO GOING |

Write **only** the missing words **IN CAPITAL LETTERS on the separate answer sheet**.

---

25   Our teacher always makes us do our homework before we leave the class.

   ALLOWS

   Our teacher .... leave the class until we've done our homework.

26   It was almost dark when we got home.

   UNTIL

   We .... it was almost dark.

27   Peter woke up early because he didn't want to miss his flight.

   THAT

   Peter woke up early .... not miss his flight.

28   'You'd better not go for a walk,' said my father.

   ADVISED

   My father .... for a walk.

29   I wish I hadn't left the window open.

   SHOULD

   I .... the window open.

30   All the guests enjoyed themselves at the party apart from George.

   WHO

   George was the .... enjoy himself at the party.

PAPER 1	Reading and ▶	Part 1
	Use of English	Part 2
PAPER 2	Writing	Part 3
		Part 4
PAPER 3	Listening	**Part 5**
PAPER 4	Speaking	Part 6
		Part 7

You are going to read an article about photography. For questions **31–36**, choose the answer (**A**, **B**, **C** or **D**) which you think fits best according to the text.

Mark your answers **on the separate answer sheet**.

Photo research

Photographer Jim Richardson tells us how he aims to get the most from photo shoots.

'If you want to be a better photographer, stand in front of better stuff.' That's a simple mantra and I repeat it over and over to myself. I share it with other photographers and I endeavour to follow my own advice. As a result, I spend a great deal of time doing photo research, looking for great locations to shoot. Put simply, I'm a better photographer when I'm standing in front of something wonderful like the Grand Canyon in Arizona, USA.

Seeing wonderful places is bread-and-butter photography – it's just part of the job. But getting there is only half of any great photograph's story. The other half is how the photographer prepares to capture the subject once in front of it. Example: today my mind is absorbed in the long climb up Skellig Michael, a remote island isolated in the Atlantic Ocean off the coast of Ireland, where Celtic monks found their solace in spiritual isolation 1,400 years ago. I have never been on Skellig Michael, though I have come close four times. Each time I was held back by high seas. In my head I am getting ready to be among the little huts in the monastery at the summit, in the mindset of those who sought their spirituality in the vast Atlantic all those years ago.

In four days I'll be setting sail on a cruise of the British and Irish Isles, and I'll have a chance once again to ascend the slopes of Skellig Michael. I want to be ready to seize the day. For me, groundwork is part of photography, as essential as knowing exposure and lighting or recognising the decisive moment to take the shot. Research sounds like a boring task to many photographers, but for others, digging into a subject in advance is part of the pleasure. I'm one of those photographers.

Philosophically, photographers seem to divide along that line. On one side are those who desire only to be in the moment. On the other side are the planners. These folks would never dream of going out the door without a full list of how they're going to approach the shoot. (Actually, there is a third group nowadays. They just capture the whole scene and do all the creative work in Photoshop after the event.) Fortunately, it doesn't have to be an either/or decision. Most photographers I know do both: research extensively to prepare their schedule (and their minds) and then act in the moment once on site.

I do extensive research in order to get ready for a photographic trip. This includes creating a file for each location I'm due to visit. For my upcoming cruise I already know where we are going day by day. So I start a file for each place and begin to compile information. Knowing what the place looks like in advance is invaluable, so I'll hit several internet photo sites. Besides clueing me in to the photographic possibilities
line 29 of the location, this can also show me what angles have already become overused and which I should therefore avoid. But I'll also find angles I didn't expect from locations I hadn't imagined. Armed with these I'll be better prepared to push the boundaries of what people expect.

Above all, I'll look for places and events that are seasonal and timeless. I open my mind to what might make a great subject for a picture. Most travellers tend to think only of places they're visiting, without looking deeper into culture, history or meaning. I try to get in time with the rhythm of the place and in tune with its melody. But most of all I just want to be ready. If I'm ready, I can just about count on being lucky.

31 What is Jim trying to do in the first paragraph?

    A convince the reader that his method of working is appropriate
    B explain his approach towards taking good photographs
    C remind himself that he should listen to the ideas of others
    D clarify what makes a location good to photograph

32 Why does Jim provide an example in the second paragraph?

    A to explain why he hasn't managed to visit Skellig Michael before
    B to describe what he imagines the next place he will visit to be like
    C to offer details of what he has discovered about Skellig Michael
    D to show how he prepares herself mentally before going to a new place

33 How does Jim feel about the cruise he will go on?

    A excited about an opportunity he didn't think he would get
    B uncertain whether he will know when to take the best photo
    C confident he will produce better work than other photographers
    D uninterested in certain aspects of preparing for travel

34 What point does Jim make about photographers in the fourth paragraph?

    A They are unable to decide on the best plan of action.
    B It is possible for them to adopt flexible ways of working.
    C Some of them refuse to try to understand the way others work.
    D The third group are not as imaginative as some of the others.

35 What does 'this' refer to in line 29?

    A having a daily plan of travel
    B knowing which angles to avoid
    C looking at photo websites
    D compiling location files

36 What does Jim suggest in the final paragraph?

    A He is careful about choosing the right place to visit.
    B Many people who travel don't understand what they see.
    C He likes to go to places that few people bother to visit.
    D Some travellers don't spend enough time in a place.

PAPER 1 Reading and ▶
        Use of English

PAPER 2 Writing

PAPER 3 Listening

PAPER 4 Speaking

Part 1
Part 2
Part 3
Part 4
Part 5
Part 6
Part 7

You are going to read a newspaper article about orangutans. Six sentences have been removed from the article. Choose from the sentences **A–G** the one which fits each gap (**37–42**). There is one extra sentence which you do not need to use.

Mark your answers **on the separate answer sheet**.

Almost human

Orangutans and chimpanzees are capable of performing intellectual feats we once thought to be uniquely human. Using language, being self-aware, learning by imitation and problem-solving are high-level abilities that are not limited to humans. Research has shown that orangutans and other great apes, like chimpanzees and gorillas, share these abilities too.

There are several projects studying the use of language by these creatures. Understanding their mechanisms of developing language will help us evaluate our own linguistic abilities. One of the orangutans involved in a project in Virginia, USA, has learnt how to use over 100 words in sign language, the language used by the deaf to communicate with each other. Another orangutan, Hannah, has learnt 13 symbols that represent different nouns and verbs. Hannah can combine the symbols into simple commands like 'open bag'. **37** [ ]

Not really. One of the fundamental elements of human thought is the ability to recognise numbers and express ideas with them within meaningful strings of words. Hannah can recognise numbers from one to three with reasonable accuracy. **38** [ ]

A fundamental difference between humans and orangutans is their ability to comprehend abstract ideas. Abstract concepts are basic to human thinking, while there's little evidence that orangutans can understand abstract ideas at all.

One of the most interesting experiments in the Virginia project concerns memory. **39** [ ] Orangutans, on the other hand, appear to do so according to where they saw them last. This seems a less efficient way of storing

information, so it may well be that orangutans have a limited capacity for memory in comparison to humans.

40 [ ] They feel extremely frustrated when they make an error and they never rush into a task because they don't want to be wrong. Orangutans have idiosyncracies and differences in character. Some are slow learners, while others are more impulsive.

Unfortunately, most of the research on great ape intelligence has been done with animals in captivity. **41** [ ] Studies of orangutans, however, that suffered captivity but were then freed showed that they are capable of learning by imitation. Imitating someone yawn or scratch his head is not a great intellectual accomplishment, but learning a new behaviour just by watching is a very advanced ability. Orangutans could chop firewood or wash dishes without being taught. The only way they could have done it was by watching humans.

Compared to orangutans, chimpanzees are genetically closer to human beings and they are thought to be more intelligent. There are differences in the way the minds of chimps and orangutans work. **42** [ ] The chimps seem to work fast, almost intuitively, while orangutans are slower and more methodical.

One feature of both chimps and orangutans is the ability to recognise themselves in a mirror. This seems to suggest that they both have a concept of 'self' – they know who they are and think of themselves in a particular way. Chimpanzees are manipulative and capable of deception. They are very good problem-solvers, clearly capable of complex cognitive performance, which makes them almost human.

A Orangutans can become very emotional when they fail a test.

B One obvious disadvantage is that we cannot study their behaviour in their natural environment.

C Does this mean she is starting to think in a human way?

D None of these tasks can be performed well by orangutans.

E Humans generally remember things by putting them into groups or categories.

F However, she hasn't yet learnt to use them in sentences.

G This becomes apparent when they are each given the same task to do.

You are going to read a magazine article in which four people talk about running the London Marathon. For questions **43–52** choose from the people (**A–D**). The people may be chosen more than once.

Mark your answers **on the separate answer sheet**.

Which person

didn't like the reactions of the watching crowd?	**43**
began running to accompany a runner?	**44**
didn't finish last year's marathon?	**45**
had an unpleasant experience in his or her first marathon?	**46**
entered the marathon with colleagues from work?	**47**
is not confident about his or her physical condition?	**48**
belongs to a sports group?	**49**
trains under bad weather conditions?	**50**
saw himself or herself on television?	**51**
doesn't have to go far for his or her runs?	**52**

Running for fun

A Peter Chamberlain

I was always keen on sports. Running a long distance is a bit like life too. You start with a sense of anticipation, you go through some great highs and terrible lows, but in the end it seems to be worth it. There is nothing that I enjoy more than a good workout at the gym or a good one-hour run across the local wildlife reserve. Fortunately, where I live, I can reach the open countryside in just a couple of minutes on foot from my front-door step. In my case, participation in the London Marathon was not about winning, it was about doing the best you possibly can. My first marathon was a disaster. Everything was going fine until the twelfth mile when I started to feel a bit of fatigue kicking in and hit the wall between the fourteenth and fifteenth miles.

B Rosalind Masterson

I surprised myself by doing so well, to tell you the truth. It all started when a friend of mine was training for the marathon and asked me to join her a few mornings a week. I didn't think I was very fit when I started, although years ago I'd go cycling three times a week and jogging at weekends. I found the experience enjoyable but realised I preferred jogging on my own. Success depends a lot on your mood. Last year, for example, I was feeling very stressed for one reason or another, and I got tired much more quickly; I didn't even get to the end of the course! This year's been completely different. London was such a success that I've entered for the Berlin Marathon next month, along with three friends. My husband thinks I'm mad, though when we watched the news that night and he could see my face among the crowds, he was fairly impressed.

C Ruth Watson

Long-distance running is not about how fast you can run, it's about how much pain you can take. Long-distance running is a good discipline for life itself. I run with my head and my heart, because physically I don't think I've got a great deal of talent or ability. I was always a very energetic sports person and I have entered the marathon five times so far. Last year I managed to complete a half marathon in 90 minutes, which was quite an accomplishment for someone who did not train systematically. One thing that annoyed me in my last marathon was the attitude of people watching. They took more interest in the fun-runners and celebrities than in the battle of the elite runners chasing qualification times for the Olympic Games.

D John Saddler

An old friend of mine has been a member of a jogging club for years, and he finally persuaded me to go along with him one Saturday to see if I would enjoy it. Well, I felt fairly good afterwards, so I joined the club and started thinking seriously about running. I thought that entering for the marathon would give me a unique opportunity to raise some cash for the Red Cross. In fact, four of us from the office decided to do the same thing, and between us we raised over £25,000, which was great! Running wasn't as hard as I expected. Training can be difficult, especially when it means I have to drag myself out of bed on cold winter mornings and go jogging in the pouring rain. I never train with friends because I find it impossible to concentrate on what I'm doing.

You **must** answer this question. Write your answer in **140–190** words in an appropriate style.

___

1 You have been discussing families in your English class. Now, your teacher has asked you to write an essay for homework.

Write an essay using **all** the notes and give reasons for your point of view.

Growing up in a large family is better than being brought up in a small one. Do you agree?

Notes
Write about:

1. attention from parents
2. relationships with brothers and sisters
3. .... (your own idea)

PAPER 1   Reading and
          Use of English

PAPER 2   Writing   ▶   Part 1
                             Part 2
PAPER 3   Listening

PAPER 4   Speaking

Write an answer to one of the questions **2–5** in this part. Write your answer in **140–190** words in an appropriate style.

_____

2   You see this announcement in an English-language music magazine.

> **Do you enjoy listening to traditional music?**
>
> Do you think traditional music from your country is old-fashioned, or should it continue to be promoted in the modern world? If so, how is it possible to get more people interested in traditional music?
>
> We'd love to receive your articles. The best one will be published next month!

Write your **article**.

3   This is part of an email you have received from your English-speaking friend, Kim.

> I heard you've moved from the city to a small country village. Can you tell me about it? What are the differences between living in each of the places? How do you feel about the change in lifestyle?
>
> I can't wait to hear from you!
>
> Kim

Write your **email**.

4   You recently saw this notice in an English-language magazine called *TV News*:

> Send us your review of the best or worst TV programme you have seen this year. Include information on what the programme was about and say what made the programme so good/bad. Do you think another programme should be made on the same theme?
>
> We will publish the best reviews in a special summer supplement.

Write your **review**.

5   (*for FIRST FOR SCHOOLS candidates only*)

Answer the following question based on your reading of **one** of the set books.

Your friend has asked you to recommend something to read on holiday. Write a **letter** to your friend about the book you have read, giving reasons why this particular book would be suitable for him/her.

PAPER 1 Reading and
           Use of English

PAPER 2 Writing

PAPER 3 Listening   ▶ Part 1
                              Part 2
PAPER 4 Speaking   Part 3
                              Part 4

Track 17

You will hear people talking in eight different situations. For questions **1–8**, choose the best answer (**A**, **B** or **C**).

1 You hear a tour guide talking about her job.
   What does she like best about being a tour guide?
   A the places she visits
   B the people she works with
   C the different types of food she eats

2 You hear the start of a radio programme about cars.
   Who is the guest on this programme?
   A a car designer
   B an electrical engineer
   C a mechanic

3 You hear a businesswoman talking to her assistant.
   What does she want him to do?
   A write a report
   B make a phone call
   C send an email

4 You hear two friends talking about an evening out.
   Where did they go?
   A to the cinema
   B to the theatre
   C to a party

5 You hear a man talking about his aunt.
   What was her profession?
   A doctor
   B lawyer
   C actress

6 You hear a brother and sister talking about a present for their mother.
   What have they bought?
   A a book
   B a DVD
   C a cooking pot

7 You hear an announcement in a multiplex cinema.
   Which screen is showing the film *Racing Fever*?
   A screen 3
   B screen 5
   C screen 6

8 You hear a ballet dancer talking about an injury.
   What part of his body has he hurt?
   A his back
   B his feet
   C his arm

Track 18

You will hear part of a talk by a man called David Barns, who is the director of a company that will be building a new shopping mall. For questions **9–18**, complete the sentences with a word or short phrase.

Whitesea shopping mall

The mall is expected to open in (**9**) .... next year.

The total cost will be (**10**) .... billion pounds.

A new (**11**) .... will be built next to the shopping mall.

The car park will be situated (**12**) .... and will have
spaces for 3,000 cars.

Three (**13**) .... will be provided to help shoppers
with children.

One section of the mall has a (**14**) ....

There will be (**15**) .... cinemas showing a wide range
of the current films.

(**16**) .... films will be shown twice a day.

There will be walkways with (**17**) .... between different
areas of the mall.

There will be an exhibition focusing on the (**18**) .... of
the area.

PAPER 1 Reading and Use of English

PAPER 2 Writing

PAPER 3 Listening

PAPER 4 Speaking

Part 1
Part 2
Part 3
Part 4

Track 19

You will hear five short extracts in which people are talking about how they got their current jobs. For questions **19–23**, choose from the list (**A–H**) what each speaker says. Use the letters only once. There are three extra letters which you do not need to use.

A I'd done some unpaid work experience at the company.

B I saw an advertisement on a careers website.

Speaker 1 | 19

C I had a contact who worked at the company.

Speaker 2 | 20

D I heard about it from a friend.

Speaker 3 | 21

E I was lucky with a phone call.

Speaker 4 | 22

F I approached the boss face to face.

Speaker 5 | 23

G I was promoted from a previous position.

H I found out about the company through social media.

Track 20

You will hear a radio interview with a doctor called Ann Winters, who is an expert on memory. For questions **24–30**, choose the best answer (**A**, **B** or **C**).

24 Ann compares the human memory to a hard drive because
    A both can be negatively affected by external factors.
    B both can be trained to expand and improve.
    C both can store an unlimited number of images.

25 We are told that people suffering from Alzheimer's disease
    A don't understand the mechanism of life.
    B can't remember who they are.
    C forget how to perform simple tasks.

26 Research has shown that people who have mentally active jobs
    A will never develop Alzheimer's disease.
    B are more likely to develop Alzheimer's disease.
    C are less likely to develop Alzheimer's disease.

27 Apparently, our memories are harmed by
    A doing too many physical exercises.
    B devices designed to help us remember things.
    C forcing ourselves to try to remember too much.

28 Ann says we can remember things if we
    A connect them with a physical object.
    B look at them very carefully first.
    C encourage people to remind us about them.

29 The technique Ann describes works best for people
    A who like pictures.
    B who are used to abstract thought.
    C who can visualise ideas well.

30 Doing crosswords is an example of activities that
    A can prevent ageing.
    B can extend life expectancy.
    C can delay memory decline.

Part 1 (2 minutes)

The examiner (interlocutor) will ask each of you to speak briefly in turn and to give personal information about yourselves. You can expect a variety of questions, such as:

Who do you prefer to spend your free time with? (Why?)
Do you prefer to spend your free time outdoors or indoors? (Why?)
What kinds of things do you like doing with your friends / family?
What's your favourite part of the day? (Why?)

Part 2 (4 minutes)

You will each be asked to talk for a minute without interruption. You will each be given two different photographs in turn to talk about. After your partner has finished speaking, you will be asked a brief question connected with your partner's photographs.

1 Means of transport

Look at the two photographs on page 171 which show different forms of transport.

Candidate A, compare these photographs, and say why you think people use these different means of transport.

Candidate B, which of these means of transport do you prefer to use? (Why?)

2 Fashion

Look at the two photographs on page 172 which show different sorts of clothes.

Candidate A, compare these photographs, and say why you think the people have chosen to wear these sorts of clothes.

Candidate B, which of these sorts of clothes do you prefer to wear? (Why?)

Part 3 (4 minutes)

You will be asked to discuss something together without interruption by the examiner. You will have a page of ideas and a question to help you.

Environmental problems

Imagine you are helping to prepare a poster to raise environmental awareness in your area. Turn to page 173 which has ideas for images that could be included and a question for you to discuss. Talk to each other about which images on a poster would be useful to raise environmental awareness. Then decide which two images should be included.

Part 4 (4 minutes)

The examiner will encourage you to develop the topic of your discussion in Part 3 by asking questions such as:

Are school clubs and societies, such as a photographic club and a computer club, useful for students? (Why? / Why not?)

What kind of after-school activity did you or would you enjoy at school? (Why?)

What do you think people learn from activities which are not connected with schoolwork?

Should schools try to become active parts of the local community? (Why? / Why not?)

How can schools raise people's environmental awareness?

What other useful things can schools teach young people?

PAPER 1 Reading and Use of English

▶▶ **PART 5**

mantra (n) a commonly repeated word or phrase

endeavour (v) to try very hard to do something

capture (v) to record something by camera/on film

be absorbed in (adj) to give all your attention to something that you are doing

remote (adj) far away

solace (n) comfort

summit (n) the highest point of a mountain

mindset (n) mental attitude

ascend (v) to go up

seize the day (phr) to enjoy the moment

groundwork (n) preparation

exposure (n) the length of time light falls on the digital sensor/film (photography)

decisive moment (n) perfect, ideal time

dig into (v) to find out about

approach (v) to deal with

compile (v) to put together

invaluable (adj) extremely useful

clue in (v) to provide someone with a clue

angle (n) the direction from which you look at something

push the boundaries (expr) to experiment

timeless (adj) unaffected by time

be in tune with (expr) understand

▶▶ **PART 6**

intellectual (adj) related to thinking

evaluate (v) to estimate worth, to determine the value of something

accuracy (n) something that is correct and true

fundamental (adj) basic, primary

comprehend (v) to get the meaning of something, to understand

capacity (n) the ability to do something

idiosyncrasy (n) an odd habit or characteristic

impulsive (adj) doing things without considering the possible dangers or problems

captivity (n) a condition of holding someone or something by force against their will, confinement, imprisonment

accomplishment (n) a difficult task done well, success, achievement

genetically (adv) related to genes or genetics

intuitively (adv) related to feelings, not learnt knowledge, instinctive

methodical (adj) systematic, careful, in a step-by-step manner

apparent (adj) obvious, clear

▶▶ **PART 7**

anticipation (n) pleasant expectation

workout (n) a session of physical exercise

fatigue (n) great tiredness

kick in (phr v) to begin to have an effect

hit the wall (phr) to collapse, to be unable to go on

enter for (phr v) to put your name on the list of people taking part in something

impress (v) to cause others to admire

discipline (n) training

persuade (v) to lead a person or group to believe or do something by arguing or reasoning with them

pouring (adj) raining hard

For questions **1–8**, read the text below and decide which word (**A**, **B**, **C** or **D**) best fits each gap. There is an example at the beginning (**0**).

Mark your answers **on the separate answer sheet**.

Example:

0   **A**   life   **B**   living   **C**   alive   **D**   live

0	A	B	C	D

Old and active

It is a well-known fact that Japanese people have a longer (**0**) .... expectancy than the population of most other countries. They also expect to remain healthier for longer.

Scientists are trying to work (**1**) .... what keeps elderly Japanese people so healthy, and whether there is a lesson to be (**2**) .... from their lifestyles. Should we (**3**) .... any changes to our eating habits, for instance? Is there some secret (**4**) .... in the Japanese diet that is particularly (**5**) .... for the human body?

Although the (**6**) .... of a longer, healthier life is a good thing for the individual, it can (**7**) .... create a social problem. The number of people over the age of 65 in the population has doubled in the last 50 years. Japan could soon be (**8**) .... an economic problem: there are more elderly people who need to be looked after, and relatively fewer younger people working and paying taxes to support them.

1	**A** for	**B** out	**C** in	**D** off
2	**A** learnt	**B** gathered	**C** understood	**D** gained
3	**A** do	**B** make	**C** set	**D** give
4	**A** ingredient	**B** component	**C** portion	**D** helping
5	**A** caring	**B** supportive	**C** positive	**D** beneficial
6	**A** view	**B** outlook	**C** prospect	**D** wish
7	**A** therefore	**B** actually	**C** even	**D** as well
8	**A** facing	**B** meeting	**C** adopting	**D** obtaining

PAPER 1 Reading and
Use of English

PAPER 2 Writing

PAPER 3 Listening

PAPER 4 Speaking

Part 1
Part 2
Part 3
Part 4
Part 5
Part 6
Part 7

For questions **9–16,** read the text below and think of the word which best fits each gap. Use only **one** word in each gap. There is an example at the beginning (**0**).

Write your answers **IN CAPITAL LETTERS on the separate answer sheet**.

Example: | 0 | B | Y |

Acoustic archaeology

Acoustic archaeology studies the role played (**0**) .... sound in the ancient world. It examines the connection (**9**) .... acoustics and religious or spiritual sites. The main question is whether the acoustics of a place are relevant to the way (**10**) .... was used.

Archaeologists have noticed that a number of ancient sites have echoes at very low frequencies. When sounds are as low as this, you feel them in your body, rather (**11**) .... just hearing them, and this creates a feeling of happiness and contentment.

If you stand in (**12**) .... of the Maya Temple in Mexico and clap your hands, you can hear an echo that sounds (**13**) .... the chirp of the Maya sacred bird. This echo (**14**) .... produced because the steps of the long temple staircase are at different distances from the listener. Some archaeologists claim that the Maya deliberately constructed this temple (**15**) .... achieve this sound. Similar acoustic phenomena have been observed in sites (**16**) .... over the world.

For questions **17–24**, read the text below. Use the word given in capitals at the end of some of the lines to form a word that fits in the gap **in the same line**. There is an example at the beginning (**0**).

Write your answers **IN CAPITAL LETTERS on the separate answer sheet**.

Example: | 0 | C | O | M | P | E | T | I | T | I | V | E | | | | | | | | | |

The sport of kings

The (**0**) …….. racing of horses is one of humankind's most   **COMPETE**
ancient sports. Horse racing was an organised sport in all major
(**17**) …….. from Central Asia to the Mediterranean and became   **CIVILISE**
an (**18**) …….. with the public in the Roman Empire. The sport   **OBSESS**
has (**19**) …….. been associated with royalty and the nobility. It   **TRADITION**
became a professional sport at the beginning of the eighteenth
century. It is the second most (**20**) …….. attended spectator sport   **WIDE**
in the US, after baseball.

In the UK, the Jockey Club, founded in 1750, has complete
(**21**) …….. for horse racing. It is also responsible for the   **RESPONSIBLE**
(**22**) …….. regarding the breeding of racehorses. Although   **REGULATE**
science has been (**23**) …….. to find a breeding system that   **ABLE**
guarantees the birth of a champion, it is possible to produce
horses that are successful on the racetrack. Commercial
breeding is a very (**24**) …….. business, and racehorses can   **PROFIT**
be worth millions of pounds.

For questions **25–30**, complete the second sentence so that it has a similar meaning to the first sentence, using the word given. **Do not change the word given.** You must use between **two** and **five** words, including the word given. Here is an example (**0**).

Example:

0   I'll be very happy when I go on holiday.

FORWARD

I'm .... on holiday.

The gap can be filled by the words 'looking forward to going' so you write:

Example: | **0** | LOOKING FORWARD TO GOING |

Write **only** the missing words **IN CAPITAL LETTERS on the separate answer sheet**.

---

25   I don't know how wide that river is.

WHAT

I don't know *what the width* .... of that river is.

26   Her parents didn't let her go to the rock concert.

ALLOWED

She *wasn't allowed to* .... go to the rock concert.

27   My father last went abroad in 2010.

BEEN

My father *hasn't been abroad since* .... 2001.

28   'Did you read the book or not?' the teacher asked me.

WHETHER

The teacher asked me *whether I had read* .... the book or not.

29   I find that kind of music really irritating.

GETS

That kind of music really *gets me on my* .... nerves.

30   He cycled across Italy in three weeks.

HIM

It *took him three weeks to* .... cycle across Italy.

PAPER 1	Reading and Use of English	▶	Part 1
			Part 2
PAPER 2	Writing		Part 3
			Part 4
PAPER 3	Listening		**Part 5**
PAPER 4	Speaking		Part 6
			Part 7

You are going to read an article about a park in New York. For questions **31–36**, choose the answer (**A, B, C** or **D**) which you think fits best according to the text.

Mark your answers **on the separate answer sheet**.

Miracle above Manhattan

New Yorkers can relax over busy streets in an innovative park called the High Line.

Parks in large cities are usually thought of as refuges, as islands of green amid seas of concrete and steel. When you approach the High Line in the Chelsea neighbourhood on the lower west side of Manhattan, in New York, what you see first is the kind of thing urban parks were created to get away from – a harsh, heavy, black steel structure supporting an elevated rail line that once brought freight cars right into factories and warehouses and that looks, at least from a distance, more like some abandoned leftover from the past than an urban oasis.

line 7 Until recently that's precisely what the High Line was, and a crumbling one too. Many people couldn't wait to tear it down. Almost a decade later, it has been turned into one of the most innovative and inviting public spaces in New York City. The black steel columns that once supported abandoned train tracks now hold up an elevated park – part promenade, part town square, part botanical garden.

Walking on the High Line is unlike any other experience in New York. You float about eight metres above the ground, at once connected to street life and far away from it. You can sit surrounded by carefully tended plantings and take in the sun and the Hudson River views, or you can walk the line as it slices between old buildings and past striking new ones. I have walked the High Line dozens of times, and its vantage point, different from that of any street, sidewalk, or park, never ceases to surprise and delight. Not the least of the remarkable things about the High Line is the way, without streets to cross or traffic lights to wait for, ten blocks pass as quickly as two.

The High Line is a wonderful idea that was not only realised but turned out better than anyone had imagined. The real heroes of the story are Joshua David, a freelance writer who lived near the midsection of the High Line, and Robert Hammond, an artist who also lived nearby. 'I saw an article saying that the High Line was going to be demolished, and I wondered if anyone was going to try to save it,' Hammond said to me when I interviewed them. 'I was in love with the steel structure, the rivets, the ruin. I assumed that some civic group was going to try and preserve it, and I saw that it was on the agenda for a community meeting. I went to see what was going on, and Josh was sitting next to me. We were the only people at the meeting who were interested in saving it.'

'The railroad sent representatives who showed some plans to reuse it, which enraged the people who were trying to get it torn down,' David explained. 'That's what sparked the conversation between me and Robert – we couldn't believe the degree of rage some of those people had.' David and Hammond asked railroad officials to take them to look at the High Line. 'When we got up there, we saw a mile and a half of wildflowers in the middle of Manhattan. New Yorkers always dream of finding open space – it's a fantasy when you live in a studio apartment,' David said. And that's how the project began.

From the day the first section of the High Line park opened, it has been one of the city's major tourist attractions. Yet it is just as much a neighbourhood park. When I was there on a sunny day last autumn, a section the designers had designated as a kind of sundeck was jammed, and there seemed to be as many locals treating the area as the equivalent of their own beach as visitors out for a promenade. Sometimes dreams really do come true.

31 What does the writer say about the High Line park in the first paragraph?

    A It may initially appear unattractive.
    B It is most easily reached by train.
    C People may wonder where the plants are.
    D People are amazed to find out how old it is.

32 What does 'that' refer to in line 7?

    A an urban oasis
    B a black steel structure
    C a leftover from the past
    D a group of factories and warehouses

33 When walking on the High Line, the writer notices that

    A the weather seems much better there.
    B he seems to walk further in a shorter time.
    C new buildings keep being built around it.
    D he can see everything in the streets below.

34 Why did Robert Hammond go to the community meeting?

    A He was told about it by his friend Josh David.
    B He was responding to an appeal for volunteers.
    C He believed other people there would share his views.
    D He thought he could persuade people to join his campaign.

35 How did Joshua David feel about what happened at the meeting?

    A pleased to realise they might succeed
    B encouraged by everyone's determination
    C worried that their way of life might change
    D surprised by the reaction to the ideas proposed

36 What does the writer say about the park in the final paragraph?

    A It satisfies a range of different needs.
    B Local people wish fewer tourists came to see it.
    C Some of its features are not being used as intended.
    D Its popularity has increased recently.

PAPER 1	Reading and ▶	Part 1
	Use of English	Part 2
PAPER 2	Writing	Part 3
		Part 4
PAPER 3	Listening	Part 5
PAPER 4	Speaking	**Part 6**
		Part 7

You are going to read a newspaper article about people who have difficulty counting. Six sentences have been removed from the article. Choose from the sentences **A–G** the one which fits each gap (**37–42**). There is one extra sentence, which you do not need to use.

Mark your answers **on the separate answer sheet**.

People who can't count

A recent study has discovered that dyscalculia, the mathematical equivalent of dyslexia, affects about 5% of children in Britain. An expert on the subject, Professor Maria Singelton, claims that the government should recognise dyscalculia, inform parents and teachers and provide support for those suffering from it. Unfortunately, there is no simple way of diagnosing dyscalculia and kids with this learning disability are usually labelled unintelligent.

37 [ ] Unlike most people, dyscalculics cannot recognise three or four objects unless they count them one by one. The majority of us, if shown three or four similar things, can immediately recognise them. People with dyscalculia have to go through the routine of counting even a small number of objects. For example, they need to count the three books on the table before they can say how many there are.

Dyscalculics have huge problems using numbers at all. They cannot understand, for instance, why two and three makes five. **38 [ ]** Laboratory experiments have shown that animals such as monkeys and rats have developed a specific region of their brain to deal with numbers and related concepts. It's possible that dyscalculics, though intelligent, have not developed the part of the brain responsible for processing numbers.

Dyscalculics have difficulty with the abstract concept of time. **39 [ ]** If your best friend is always late, he or she might be suffering from dyscalculia. Dyscalculics cannot keep track of time, they never know how much

time they have spent getting ready and how long it will take them to get to work.

You cannot rely on a dyscalculic to give you directions about how to get to the nearest train station. Inability to read maps and orientate themselves is common among dyscalculics. They may take a left turning instead of a right and end up miles away from their intended destination. **40 [ ]**

Research has shown that they behave oddly in social situations like going shopping or having dinner at a restaurant. They never know how much they should tip the waiter or how much money they have got left after a shopping trip. **41 [ ]** This poor ability in arithmetic can explain why they never know how much change they are due or what kind of budget they need for their summer holiday. Discalculia can also affect areas like sports or music. Dyscalculics cannot coordinate the movements of their body or remember the rules of games. They would find it impossible to recall the complicated step sequences of a dance and would rarely choose to do aerobics or play an instrument in their free time.

42 [ ] People suffering from discalculia can become painters, sculptors or poets. Dyscalculia does not seem to prevent or delay language acquisition. Dyscalculic children acquire language at the same time as, if not earlier than, most children and have no problem learning to read or write. Dyscalculia is a learning disability like dyslexia, not a general indication of intelligence.

A Another problem is not being able to tell, just by looking at two groups of objects, which group contains more objects than the other.

B On top of getting lost, they often misplace things and may spend endless hours looking for their car keys or passport.

C These stories are extremely upsetting for parents and children alike.

D What exactly is this learning disability in arithmetic?

E Dealing with cash, taking money from a cashpoint or using travellers' cheques can cause anxiety and fear.

F This can account for their difficulty in reading schedules and remembering the order in which things happened in the past.

G On the other hand, dyscalculics are very good at creative arts.

PAPER 1 Reading and ▶ Part 1
Use of English   Part 2

PAPER 2 Writing   Part 3
              Part 4
PAPER 3 Listening   Part 5

PAPER 4 Speaking   Part 6

Part 7

You are going to read an article in which four writers talk about the first book they wrote. For questions **43–52**, choose from the people (**A–D**). The writers may be chosen more than once.

Mark your answers **on the separate answer sheet**.

Which writer

took six months to write the book?	43
was upset at something their editor said?	44
did not like part of the book design?	45
had written the book years before it was published?	46
has never written that type of book since then?	47
produced a certain amount of writing each day?	48
revised the manuscript because the main character was boring?	49
wrote for a set amount of time each day?	50
wrote short stories before the first book?	51
won something for the first book?	52

The first book

A Harry Holden

I remember my first book very clearly; I suppose every writer does. But I also remember it because I've changed so much since then. It was a biography of the Duke of Wellington, which I'd been asked to write by a friend of mine, a publisher, who knew I was very interested in the subject. I'd had no experience of writing but I have to say the book was actually quite good. In fact, I was awarded the General Haig Memorial Prize for the book the year it was published. By the time it was finally finished, I was completely exhausted. I'd been working on it more or less full time for five years, and I vowed I'd never write a biography again. So since then, I've concentrated on detective stories. They're far easier!

B Marcia Onslow

My first book was quite successful, although to be completely frank, looking back, I think I was very lucky. I attended a creative writing course at university, intending to concentrate on short stories for magazines, which is quite a lucrative market. As a project in my final year, I was asked to write a long work of fiction, and I decided to write a love story set in America during the California gold rush. Anyway, I'd been advised to establish a strict schedule, so I would write ten pages every morning and correct them every evening. Then I left university, started writing stories for publication, and I more or less forgot about the book for about ten years, until my publisher suggested I might try writing a novel. So I just handed it to her, all finished, and she published it right away!

C Maria Delangelo

When I wrote the first draft of my first novel, *Chasing William,* it wasn't much like the version that was eventually published; my editor told me I would have to make some changes to the hero, William, because he wasn't interesting enough. Naturally, I was pretty offended at the time, but I'm glad to say I had the good sense to listen to my editor, who was completely right. The problem was that I had based the whole story on the real adventures of my uncle, William Hargreaves, simply describing my uncle's character. When you write a work of fiction, you have to make the main character intriguing, but describing a real person isn't always the best way to do that. Funnily enough, in the short stories I'd had published previously I never tried to use real people. I'm glad my editor talked me out of doing it in the novel.

D John Hopkins

I learnt a few important lessons from my first book, one of which is that you have to leave certain things to the publisher. For instance, the editor gave me a lot of advice about how to structure my book, a study of the Industrial Revolution. I was a bit hesitant in the beginning, but then I decided to follow his advice and I haven't regretted it. It was the same with the artistic work on the cover, which I really hated at first. But in the end the book was very successful, and I suppose the design must have been right. The other lesson I learnt   was about working methods. I'm quite an impetuous person, and I don't like being tied down to fixed ways of doing things. I discovered I had to be strict about how long I would work for and not write any more than that, even though it meant I spent half a year writing it. Otherwise I'd have been completely exhausted and never actually finished it!

You **must** answer this question. Write your answer in **140–190** words.

1 In your English class you have been talking about fast food. Now, your English teacher has asked you to write an essay.

Write an essay using **all** the notes and give reasons for your point of view.

Is fast food always a bad thing?

Notes
Write about:

1. health
2. cost
3. .... (your own idea)

Exam Essentials

Write an answer to **one** of the questions **2–5** in this part. Write your answer in **140–190** words in an appropriate style.

2   You see this notice in an international magazine:

Can one day change your life?

Have the events on a single day had a major influence on your life?
Write about your experience, and say how it changed your life.

We will publish the best articles in our magazine.

Write your **article**.

3   You recently attended a performance of a play. Write a review for your college English-language magazine giving your own opinion of the play. Include information about the story, the acting, the sets and costumes.

Write your **review**.

4   (*for FIRST candidates only*)

The editor of your college English-language magazine is going to publish a special issue about part-time summer jobs for teenagers. You have been asked to write a report about a summer job you did, describing your job and explaining why it was a positive or negative experience.

Write your **report**.

(*for FIRST FOR SCHOOLS candidates only*)

You see this announcement in your school English-language magazine.

Stories wanted

Write a story for our magazine! Your story must begin with this sentence:

Nola knew that today would be a very special day.

Your story must include:
• a journey
• some friends

Write your **story**.

5   (*for FIRST FOR SCHOOLS candidates only*) Answer the following question based on your reading of one of the set books.

'The theme of a good book, the message we take away after reading it, must help us in our everyday lives.' Do you agree or disagree with this statement? Write an **essay**, giving your opinions with reference to the book or short story you have read.

PAPER 4 Speaking

🎧 **Track 21**

You will hear people talking in eight different situations. For questions **1–8**, choose the best answer (**A**, **B** or **C**).

1   You hear a girl talking about a new film.
    Why does she want to see it?
    A   to have a better understanding of the novel it is based on
    B   because her friends have recommended it
    C   because she likes action films

2   You hear a man talking about a car journey he made recently.
    Where was the biggest traffic jam?
    A   coming out of London
    B   near the airport
    C   getting off the motorway

3   You hear a woman talking about a present.
    What was she given?
    A   a piece of clothing
    B   some jewellery
    C   a drawing

4   You hear a boy talking about his favourite footballer.
    Which team does he play for?
    A   Arsenal
    B   Liverpool
    C   Birmingham

5   You hear a man booking theatre tickets by phone.
    How much will they cost altogether?
    A   £73
    B   £75
    C   £78

6   You hear a woman talking about moving to Scotland.
    How did she feel when she met her neighbours?
    A   pleased they were so friendly
    B   annoyed because she couldn't understand their accent
    C   surprised that they treated her like a foreigner

7   You hear a radio advertisement for a museum.
    What period does the special exhibition deal with?
    A   the 1940s
    B   the 1920s
    C   the 1950s

8   You hear two friends talking about a television programme they have both seen
    What sort of programme was it?
    A   a quiz show
    B   a documentary
    C   a soap opera

🎧 **Track 22**

You will hear a talk by a man called Graham Jones, who designs model railways in Britain. For questions **9–18**, complete the sentences with a word or short phrase.

Model railways

In the 1980s and 1990s, models were considered to be

(**9**) ....

Britain is the (**10**) .... railway model market in Europe.

For parents, model railways are a (**10**) .... alternative
                                                              to computers and videogames.

Most people who buy model railway equipment nowadays are

(**11**) ....

Purchasers of model trains include lawyers, business executives and

(**12**) ....

Children will always be interested in toy models of

(**13**) .... objects.

Model railways will continue to appeal mainly to

(**14**) ....

Companies that make model railways are now investing in countries in

(**15**) ....

Manufacturers will be promoting their products at international

(**16**) ....

Model trains are available that are (**17**) ....
                                                              by computers.

PAPER 1 Reading and
          Use of English

PAPER 2 Writing

PAPER 3 Listening   ▶

PAPER 4 Speaking

Part 1
Part 2
Part 3
Part 4

 Track 23

You will hear five short extracts in which people are talking about their memories of their first day at school. For questions **19–23**, choose from the list (**A–H**) what each speaker remembers about the experience. Use the letters only once. There are three extra letters which you do not need to use.

___

A   I was late for the first class.

B   The building seemed very big.

Speaker 1 | 19 |

C   A relative of mine was already there.

Speaker 2 | 20 |

D   I felt very lonely.

Speaker 3 | 21 |

E   I was glad there wasn't a uniform.

Speaker 4 | 22 |

F   I wasn't wearing the right clothes.

Speaker 5 | 23 |

G   I had to walk to school alone.

H   I had a positive feeling from the very start.

Track 24

You will hear part of a radio interview with a law student called Mark Stone, talking about his life at university. For questions **24–30**, choose the best answer (**A**, **B** or **C**).

24 Why did Mark decide to study at Gramwell University?
   A It offers a very good course in his subject.
   B His parents advised him to go there.
   C It is near where he grew up.

25 When Mark arrived at Gramwell, he was surprised by
   A the weather.
   B the architecture.
   C the atmosphere.

26 What does Mark say about his studies?
   A It is difficult to manage his time well.
   B It is less demanding now than it used to be.
   C It is worth studying hard.

27 Why did Mark get a part-time job?
   A He wanted experience working as a librarian.
   B He had to cover the cost of his accommodation.
   C He was getting bored in his spare time.

28 What does Mark say about his lecturers?
   A They like to communicate with students.
   B They are hard to get to know.
   C They only occasionally want to see students.

29 What does Mark say about his friends at Gramwell?
   A Most people he knows study law.
   B They study a variety of different subjects.
   C The subjects they study are more interesting than law.

30 How does Mark feel about his social life?
   A He wishes he could go to more parties.
   B He worries about wasting time.
   C He believes he studies better after doing sport.

Part 1 (2 minutes)

The examiner (interlocutor) will ask each of you to speak briefly in turn and to give personal information about yourselves. You can expect a variety of questions, such as:

Who are the most important people in your life?
How many brothers and sisters do you have?
Do you have much contact with your aunts and uncles, cousins, etc.?
What do you most enjoy doing with your family?

Part 2 (4 minutes)

You will each be asked to talk for a minute without interruption. You will each be given two different photographs in turn to talk about. After your partner has finished speaking, you will be asked a brief question connected with your partner's photographs.

1 Painters

Look at the two photographs on page 174 which show painters and their work.

Candidate A, compare these photographs, and say which painting you like most and why.

Candidate B, which of these paintings do you prefer? (Why?)

2 Shops

Look at the two photographs on page 175 which show places where people shop.

Candidate A, compare these photographs, and say what the advantages of shopping in each place are.

Candidate B, which of these places would you prefer to shop in? (Why?)

Part 3 (4 minutes)

You will be asked to discuss something together without interruption by the examiner. You will have a page of ideas with a question to help you.

Holiday resorts

Imagine that a travel company is deciding on the best holiday resorts to include on its website. Turn to page 176 which shows different facilities and a question for you to discuss. Talk to each other about how important each facility is for visitors to a holiday resort. Then decide which two are the most important.

Part 4 (4 minutes)

The examiner will encourage you to develop the topic of your discussion in Part 3 by asking questions such as:

Would you prefer to spend a holiday in a small village or in a city? (Why?)
Would you prefer to go on holiday to somewhere cold or somewhere hot? (Why?)
Do you think school holidays are long enough in your country? (Why? / Why not?)
Do you think it's a good idea for teenagers to go away on holiday without their parents? (Why? / Why not?)
Where do people in your country like to go on holiday? (Why?)
What do most people in your country like to do while they're on holiday? (Why?)

PAPER 1 Reading and Use of English

▸▸ **PART 5**

refuge (n) a place where you can get away from unpleasant conditions

amid (prep) among

urban (adj) city

freight car (n) part of a train used for transporting goods

crumbling (adj) breaking into small pieces

tended (adj) looked after

vantage point (n) a place from which there is a clear view

cease (v) to stop

spark (v) to start

designate (v) to choose, appoint

▸▸ **PART 6**

equivalent (n) something that is the same

claim (v) to state that something is true, especially when there is some doubt

region (n) a part, a section

abstract (adj) unclear, vague

orientate (v) to find your position with a map

budget (n) an amount of money set aside for a purpose

recall (v) to remember something

acquisition (n) the act of getting new skills or knowledge

indication (n) a sign, a signal

coordinate (v) to harmonise

schedule (n) a list of timed, planned activities or events

▸▸ **PART 7**

biography (n) the history of a person's life

award (v) to give a prize (honour, praise, etc.) to someone

exhausted (adj) extremely tired

vow (v) to swear, to solemnly promise

frank (adj) open, direct, unafraid to express the truth

lucrative (adj) producing a lot of money, profitable

fiction (n) a type of literature based upon the author's imagination as opposed to true stories

gold rush (n) a rush of people to a place where gold has been discovered

publish (v) to print and distribute something to the public

draft (n) one version of something written

offend (v) to hurt the feelings of people

talk someone out of doing something (phr v) to discourage someone from doing something

intriguing (adj) interesting, fascinating, causing curiosity

hesitant (adj) unsure, reluctant

impetuous (adj) done quickly, often without thinking, impulsive

tie down (phr v) to restrict

For questions **1–8**, read the text below and decide which word (**A, B, C** or **D**) best fits each gap. There is an example at the beginning (**0**).

Mark your answers **on the separate answer sheet**.

Example:

0   **A**   mysterious   **B**   secret   **C**   hidden   **D**   confidential

| 0 | **A** | B | C | D |

The bobcat

Native to North America, the bobcat, sometimes called 'wildcat', is a (**0**) .... and nocturnal animal and is (**1**) .... seen by people. Bobcats are (**2**) .... twice the size of the average domestic cat. Most have a grey to brown coat and a short, black-tipped tail, which seems to be cut off or 'bobbed', hence its name. They have long legs, large paws, and tufted ears (**3**) .... to those of their larger relative, the Canada lynx.

Bobcats roam (**4**) .... much of North America and are able to adapt to such (**5**) .... habitats as deserts, forests, swamps, and have even been seen in suburban areas. On the rare occasion that these solitary animals are spotted, they are usually (**6**) .... Females tend to find quiet, undisturbed dens to (**7**) .... a litter of one to six kittens, which will stay with their mother for between nine months and a year, when they will learn to hunt before finally (**8**) .... out on their own.

1	**A** almost	**B** rarely	**C** little	**D** slightly
2	**A** greatly	**B** considerably	**C** roughly	**D** relatively
3	**A** same	**B** similar	**C** like	**D** as
4	**A** throughout	**B** during	**C** near	**D** among
5	**A** many	**B** mixed	**C** various	**D** diverse
6	**A** individual	**B** lonely	**C** separate	**D** alone
7	**A** rise	**B** grow	**C** raise	**D** provide
8	**A** setting	**B** being	**C** leaving	**D** entering

PAPER 1 Reading and Use of English ▶	Part 1
	Part 2
PAPER 2 Writing	Part 3
	Part 4
PAPER 3 Listening	Part 5
	Part 6
PAPER 4 Speaking	Part 7

For questions **9–16**, read the text below and think of the word which best fits each gap. Use only **one** word in each gap. There is an example at the beginning (**0**).

Write your answers **IN CAPITAL LETTERS on the separate answer sheet.**

Example: | 0 | O | N | E | | | | | | | | | | | | | | | | |

The origin of our language

Sir William Jones, born in 1746, was undoubtedly (**0**) .... of the greatest linguists who ever lived. He had an amazing talent (**9**) .... languages and learnt several at a young age. (**10**) .... the time of his death, he had a thorough knowledge of 13 languages and knowledge of a further 28.

Apart (**11**) .... studying languages, he also studied law and became a judge in India. He was fascinated by this vast subcontinent and wrote about Indian life. He also translated important works of Indian literature.

Jones noticed (**12**) .... Sanskrit, a classical Indian language, was similar to Greek and Latin in a number of ways. The resemblance (**13**) .... not be a coincidence. Several other people (**14**) .... also noted similarities, but Jones was (**15**) .... first to suggest that these three languages had a common origin. He also suggested that they could be grouped together with other European and Asian languages into one family, known (**16**) .... Indo-European languages, which included English.

For questions **17–24**, read the text below. Use the word given in capitals at the end of some of the lines to form a word that fits in the gap **in the same line**. There is an example at the beginning (**0**).

Write your answers **IN CAPITAL LETTERS on the separate answer sheet.**

Example: | 0 | P | O | P | U | L | A | T | I | O | N | | | | | | | |

Left-handedness

Ten per cent of the (**0**) .... is left-handed. Traditionally, there	**POPULATE**
has been a lot of social (**17**) .... against left-handed people.	**DISCRIMINATE**
How hard is it for them to live in a right-handed world?	
A number of (**18**) .... items such as scissors have been	**PRACTICE**
(**19**) .... for right-handed people. It can be very	**DESIGN**
(**20**) .... for 'lefties' to be sitting next to 'righties' during	**CONVENIENT**
dinner. Commonly-used computer keys are on the right	
of the keyboard. Lefties have to use their own sports	
(**21**) .... Less frequently-used car controls such as	**EQUIP**
headlight switches are also on the right.	
Forcing children to use their right hand can cause	
(**22**) .... at school, which may then have an impact on	**DIFFICULT**
left-handed students' academic (**23**) .... It can also result	**DEVELOP**
in learning problems like dyslexia. Trying to make lefties	
use their right hand can explain potentially rebellious	
(**24**) .... at school, as well as causing clumsiness	**BEHAVE**
and frustration.	

For questions **25–30**, complete the second sentence so that it has a similar meaning to the first sentence, using the word given. **Do not change the word given.** You must use between **two** and **five** words, including the word given. Here is an example (**0**).

Example:

0   I'll be very happy when I go on holiday.

FORWARD

I'm .... on holiday.

The gap can be filled by the words 'looking forward to going' so you write:

Example: | **0** | LOOKING FORWARD TO GOING |

Write only the missing words **IN CAPITAL LETTERS on the separate answer sheet**.

---

25   The village is the same as it was in the 1950s.

CHANGED

The village .... the 1950s.

26   Our cat was sleeping on the sofa all afternoon.

SPENT

Our cat .... on the sofa.

27   It was so hot that she fainted.

IF

She .... it hadn't been so hot.

28   I enjoy watching football more than motor racing.

RATHER

I .... motor racing.

29   Please reply immediately on receipt of this notification.

SOON

Please reply .... this notification.

30   The coffee machine in our office hasn't worked for three months.

OUT

The coffee machine in our office .... for three months.

PAPER 1	Reading and Use of English ▶	Part 1
		Part 2
PAPER 2	Writing	Part 3
		Part 4
PAPER 3	Listening	**Part 5**
PAPER 4	Speaking	Part 6
		Part 7

You are going to read part of a story about a mountain climber. For questions **31–36**, choose the answer (**A**, **B**, **C** or **D**) which you think fits best according to the text.

Mark your answers **on the separate answer sheet**.

A steep learning curve

Journalist Dan Greenbaum abandons his laptop and learns how to climb

Living in an area of the country where there's little more than a slight incline to stroll up on the way to the shops, the highest climb I'd ever done was up the stairs to bed. As a writer on an adventure sports magazine, I'd always fought shy of doing the adventurous stuff myself, preferring instead to observe the experts from a safe distance and relay their experiences to readers in the form of prose. So, when I was challenged to take part in a mountain climb in aid of raising money for charity – and to write about it afterwards – I was unwilling to say the least.

Despite their awe-inspiring strength and agility, even experienced climbers fail to make climbing look simple. I knew a mammoth task lay before me if I was to get into even half-decent physical shape before the four thousand-metre climb, which would involve sheer rock faces and steep, snow-covered terrain. I set about consuming not only energy-boosting food to help me get through my intense training regime, but also devouring every climbing magazine I could get my hands on.

I was lucky enough to have a brilliant climbing coach called Keith, who put me through my paces after the daily grind at the keyboard was over. My mentor imparted keen knowledge about everything from the importance of building specific muscle groups to how to combat fatigue through nutrition. I listened, speechless, while he went into great detail about everything to do with the sport. It quickly became apparent that the mechanics of climbing were more complex than I could have imagined. And there wasn't only the strength and endurance-building to contend with, but the gear, too. I had to get to grips with an array of equipment and techniques I'd never even heard of: 'crampons', 'glissade' and 'self-arrest', all of which I learned would come in handy on the snow-capped peak I'd be ascending in a few months' time.

line 21 Aware of the challenge that lay ahead, Keith made a detailed action plan and I forced myself to stick to it diligently, doing a daily workout at the gym, eating carbohydrates, and going on long hikes with a heavy backpack. I perfected my technique on the climbing wall and even squeezed in a weekend away to the Scottish mountains to get in some vital experience of trekking through snow and ice. My self-belief increased alongside my muscle power and I became not only confident about finishing the climb, but determined to do it with flying colours.

All too soon I was on a plane to my destination – Switzerland. Early one clear spring morning I peered out of a hostel window and up at the mountain I would attempt to ascend that day. My hard-won confidence took a nose dive as the enormity of what I'd let myself in for struck me as suddenly as an avalanche: I sank down on my bed and for a brief moment considered fleeing. And then I remembered all the hard work I'd done to get here and how disappointed Keith would be if I ducked out at the last minute – not to mention letting down the charity and the sense of failure I'd experience myself. With a deep breath I tied my boot laces, gathered my gear and headed out to into the sunshine to meet the rest of the group.

And as I sit here now, tapping away on my laptop, with the ordeal safely behind me, I'm amazed at the detail in which I can recall every second of the climb; the burning muscles, the sheer exhaustion, the minor setbacks along the way. Could I have been better prepared? Possibly. Would I be back for another go? Thankfully not. The exhilaration of standing on top of the world is a never-to-be-repeated experience, but one I will cherish forever nonetheless.

31 In the first paragraph, the writer reveals his

    A difficulty in accurately recounting the stories of expert sportspeople.
    B disappointment in the exercise opportunities available in his town.
    C lack of interest in listening to professional climbers' personal tales.
    D lack of enthusiasm for the challenge he'd been offered.

32 In the second paragraph, we know that the writer is

    A keen to learn as much about mountain climbing as he is able to.
    B worried that he won't have time to prepare well enough for the climb.
    C amazed by how easy professional climbers make the activity seem.
    D concerned about the difficulty of climbing in certain conditions.

33 What do we learn in the third paragraph?

    A The coach makes the writer realise how complicated climbing is.
    B The writer doesn't think he'll be able to cope with the equipment he needs to use.
    C The writer is confused by the information about food that the coach gives him.
    D The coach doesn't believe the writer is doing enough work towards his climb.

34 What does 'it' refer to in line 21?

    A a daily workout at the gym
    B the challenge
    C a detailed action plan
    D the writer's coach

35 How does the writer use the example of an avalanche in the fifth paragraph?

    A to highlight a strong and unexpected feeling
    B to explain the way he sat down on his bed
    C to describe what he could see from his window
    D to emphasize how quickly he wanted to run away

36 How does the writer feel looking back on his climb?

    A satisfied that he had done his best
    B relieved that he wouldn't have to do it again
    C surprised that he had managed to complete it
    D regretful that it hadn't gone as smoothly as it could have

PAPER 1 Reading and ▸
        Use of English
PAPER 2 Writing
PAPER 3 Listening
PAPER 4 Speaking

Part 1
Part 2
Part 3
Part 4
Part 5
Part 6
Part 7

You are going to read a newspaper article about a pirate radio station. Six sentences have been removed from the article. Choose from the sentences **A–G** the one which fits each gap (**37–42**). There is one extra sentence, which you do not need to use.

Mark your answers **on the separate answer sheet**.

Pirate radio stations

In 1964, a radio station on a boat off the coast of Britain began broadcasting pop music. Radio Caroline's style was young and fresh – and the station itself was outside British law.

The British government now grants licences for people to operate radio and TV stations, but in the 1960s the only radio stations that existed legally in Britain were run by the BBC, the state-owned broadcasting company, and the government would not allow anyone to operate a private radio station. **37** The Irishman who founded Radio Caroline simply put the radio equipment on a boat and anchored it just outside the three-mile limit.

Why would anyone go to so much trouble to start up a radio station? One reason was the BBC's policy on the kind of music it broadcast. During a period when pop music was extremely popular, the BBC played very little of it on its radio stations. It was felt that the BBC should cater for more conservative tastes in music. **38** It was only a matter of time before an enterprising businessman who managed some pop music bands realised that here was a huge potential market.

There was, in fact, a radio station operating outside Britain at the time transmitting programmes that could be received in the country: Radio Luxembourg. **39** It was only after Radio Caroline went on the air that people were able to listen to pop music broadcast in English all day.

As well as playing the sort of music that young people liked, Radio Caroline was popular with listeners for other reasons. The disc jockeys didn't have the typical BBC pronunciation, which was considered by many to be formal and old-fashioned. Instead they spoke with regional accents, they used colloquial English, they were cheeky and informal. Audiences loved it and soon large numbers of listeners were tuning in.

Then other pirate radio stations began to spring up and the British government decided that some action had to be taken. **40** However, it soon became clear that the authorities were being forced to face the new situation created by the pirate radio stations. These had shown that pop music was here to stay, and that young people desperately wanted to listen to radio stations that played it.

Was there a lesson to be learnt from all this? Indeed there was! The BBC decided to start up its own pop music radio station, Radio 1, and before long Radio Caroline disc jockeys were working there. **41**

In a further development, the British government decided to allow commercial radio stations to operate in the country. This meant stations could now do legally what Radio Caroline had been doing illegally – and in far more comfortable conditions. **42** Its situation became even worse when the ship from which it was operating sank. The crew and disc jockeys had to be rescued.

Today Radio Caroline still exists although it is no longer as popular as it was in the 1960s. But it made history by forcing the BBC to change its policy on pop music and the nature of its relationship with its listeners.

A The radio station went on to become a legend, and its disc jockeys won fame and fortune.

E But this station used to play only a short section of each song – and this was clearly not satisfactory.

B Not surprisingly, Radio Caroline found itself in serious financial difficulties.

F However, the government's power only extended to the country itself and the seas around it up to around five kilometres from the shore.

C As a result, there were large numbers of young people who wanted to listen to a particular type of music, but couldn't.

G In 1967, a new law was passed making it illegal to advertise or supply an offshore radio station from the UK.

D What is more, increasing numbers of listeners were switching from the pirate stations to the eminent broadcaster.

PAPER 1 Reading and ▶ Part 1
Use of English Part 2

PAPER 2 Writing Part 3
Part 4
PAPER 3 Listening Part 5
PAPER 4 Speaking Part 6
Part 7

You are going to read an article in which four people talk about their experiences of playing a musical instrument. For questions **43–52**, choose from the people (**A–D**). The people may be chosen more than once.

Mark your answers **on the separate answer sheet**.

Which person

mentions other people's reluctance to do what's required?	**43**
mentions an initial confidence in their ability?	**44**
experienced indirect musical input from others?	**45**
says that a certain belief is relevant to other activities?	**46**
recognises a particular advantage of studying music?	**47**
proved another person right?	**48**
had an unexpected understanding of what they were trying to do?	**49**
prefers to keep their skills to themselves?	**50**
is keen to disprove a particular opinion?	**51**
wanted to fulfil someone else's wish?	**52**

Musical magic

A Andrea Beecham

I play the bass guitar in a band. Everyone assumes that it's just one of those teenage things – something I'll get bored with or grow out of. They reckon I'm just in it because I want to be famous but nothing could be further from the truth. Sure, the money would be fantastic, but I'd rather not experience being recognised everywhere you go. The reality is that I just love performing, and striving to produce something that other people want to listen to. You've got to be patient and persevere and practise, practise, practise if you want to get any better at an instrument – which I think a lot of people tend to overlook. That's why they tend to give up before they've even started. I guess you could apply that same principle to lots of things – you only get out what you put in.

B Mike Tindale

I wouldn't say I had any particular desire to learn an instrument, but when I was about eight my parents insisted I give it a go. They'd both turned down the chance to learn the piano when they were younger because they thought it looked like hard work, and they both regretted their decision. So I went along to my first lesson just to keep them happy. To my surprise, I took to it really quickly and was keen to get ahead. I still play now and, although I'll let my own kids decide for themselves whether they want to take up an instrument or not, I've noticed there are some benefits to keeping your mind active in this way. I like to think I have pretty good coordination skills, which I put down to learning an instrument that requires you to use both hands, both feet and engage your brain simultaneously!

C Dave Warwick

I remember hearing someone play the violin on the radio when I was little and that was it! I pestered my dad to let me have some lessons, and he was happy to indulge me in what he thought was just another phase. We hired an instrument from a local music shop and I went along brimming with enthusiasm and excitement to my first lesson, convinced I was about to become a famous musician. More fool me! I was shocked by the awful scraping sound which I produced and suddenly realised what I'd let myself in for. This was going to be no easy task and it would be a very long time before I'd come close to the beautiful singing violin I'd heard on the radio. I never went back. Do I regret not sticking it out? Maybe. But I think I'd rather listen to the professional musicians. I know they do it so much better than I ever could.

D Maria Perez

I'm pretty shy when it comes to getting up on stage and showing people what I can do on my drum kit, even though my friends are always really encouraging. I've been messing about on drums as far back as I can remember – my mum plays them, so there was always a kit in the house. I never had any formal training, I'd just pick up the rhythms I heard Mum play and then imitate them. I'm glad I grew up in such a creative environment – there were always loads of other musicians hanging around the house when I was a kid and some of them were pretty inspirational. It's just that performing isn't really my thing – I've only ever played the drums for my own amusement, rather than intending to make a career out of it.

You **must** answer this question. Write your answer in **140–190** words in an appropriate style.

1 In your English class you have been talking about fashion. Now, your English teacher has asked you to write an essay.

Write an essay using **all** the notes and give reasons for your point of view.

It's important to wear the latest fashions. Do you agree?

Notes
Write about:

1. cost
2. your image
3. .... (your own idea)

PAPER 1 Reading and
          Use of English
PAPER 2 Writing   ▶   Part 1
PAPER 3 Listening   Part 2
PAPER 4 Speaking

Write an answer to **one** of the questions **2–5** in this part. Write your answer in **140–190** words in an appropriate style.

2   This is part of an email from your English-speaking friend.

> Thanks very much for inviting me to stay with you and your family last weekend. It was fun! Would you like to stay with me and my family for a weekend next month? What would you like to do? Is there anything you can't eat?
>
> Write soon!
>
> Li

Write your **email**.

3   You recently saw this notice in an English-language magazine called *Young Film Critic*:

> **WANTED: GREAT FILMS WITH GREAT STORIES**
>
> Films can rely too much on special effects instead of a good story or good acting. Write a review of a film that used many special effects. How good or bad was the film? Did it rely too heavily on special effects?
>
> We'll publish the best reviews next month!

Write your **review**.

4   (*for FIRST candidates only*)

Your teacher has asked you to write a report about what facilities there are for young people in your local area. Describe what facilities are available and explain whether they are suitable for young people's needs. Suggest what other facilities young people might like to have.

Write your **report**.

(*for FIRST FOR SCHOOLS candidates only*) You see this announcement in an English-language magazine for teenagers.

> **Stories wanted**
>
> We are looking for stories for our magazine. Your story must begin with this sentence:
>
> *If I had known what was going to happen, I would never have made that phone call.*
>
> Your story must include:
> * a bus journey
> * a stranger you meet

Write your **story**.

5   (*for FIRST FOR SCHOOLS candidates only*) Answer the following question based on your reading of **one** of the set books.

'If a story is good, it doesn't matter where and when it is set. Good stories have universal appeal.' Do you agree or disagree with this statement? Write an **essay**, giving your opinions with reference to the book or short story you have read.

🎧 **Track 25**

You will hear people talking in eight different situations. For questions **1–8**, choose the best answer (**A**, **B** or **C**).

1   You hear two school friends talking about a drumming workshop they will take part in.
    How does the boy feel about it?
    A   worried that he won't understand what to do
    B   excited by the prospect of learning something new
    C   nervous about a particular part of it

2   You hear a woman talking about a shopping trip.
    What does she say about it?
    A   She fulfilled the original aim of the trip.
    B   She spent more than she had intended to.
    C   She had planned what to buy herself in advance.

3   You hear a man talking about a car he used to own.
    Why did he decide to sell it?
    A   because he wanted to economise
    B   because he no longer needed it
    C   because he needed a more comfortable car

4   You hear a woman phoning the reception desk of her hotel.
    What is the problem with her room?
    A   The heating doesn't work.
    B   The television is out of order.
    C   The door doesn't close properly.

5   You hear a girl talking to her father about a school trip.
    What is her father concerned about?
    A   The activities may not be interesting for the students.
    B   The students might spend too much time alone.
    C   The trip will cost more than he can afford.

6   You hear a man describing a trip in a hot-air balloon.
    How did he feel when the balloon started to rise?
    A   astonished at the silence around him
    B   nervous because the basket was not steady
    C   worried that they would drift out of control

7   You hear two friends talking about an exercise routine.
    What do they agree about?
    A   how unlikely it is to work
    B   how easy it must be to maintain
    C   how tiring it sounds

8   You hear a woman talking about a magazine she used to read as a teenager.
    What did she like most about it?
    A   the fashion tips
    B   the interviews with pop stars
    C   the stories

Track 26

You will hear part of a presentation by a woman called Linda Brown, who is the director of a new college. For questions **9–18**, complete the sentences with a word or short phrase.

Woodley community college

Summer school classes start on (**9**) ....

People expressed interest in the college after several
(**10**) .... were broadcast on the radio.

The (**11**) .... will declare the college open.

Other figures at the opening ceremony, include a famous
(**12**) .... , who will make a speech.

Local (**13**) .... will teach courses at the college.

The emphasis will be on (**14**) .... subjects.

The college will be (**15**) .... about who it allows to enrol for courses.

Students may not have the (**16**) .... required by
traditional colleges.

It is hoped that an (**17**) .... office in the city centre will
generate interest in the college.

People interested in courses should first refer to its
(**18**) .... for more information.

PAPER 1 Reading and
         Use of English

PAPER 2 Writing

PAPER 3 Listening ▶

PAPER 4 Speaking

Part 1
Part 2
Part 3
Part 4

 Track 27

You will hear five short extracts in which people are describing what they like most about the city of New York in the USA. For questions **19–23**, choose from the list (**A–H**) the reason each speaker gives for why the city appeals to them. Use the letters only once. There are three extra letters which you do not need to use.

A There are plenty of sightseeing opportunities.

B It has a mixture of ethnicities.

Speaker 1	19

C It is a fantastic place for shopping.

Speaker 2	20

D The local people have a great sense of humour.

Speaker 3	21

E It's a very energetic and lively place.

Speaker 4	22

F The architecture is very impressive.

Speaker 5	23

G There's a wide choice of places to eat.

H The museums and galleries are fascinating.

PAPER 1 Reading and
Use of English

PAPER 2 Writing

PAPER 3 Listening ▶

PAPER 4 Speaking

Part 1
Part 2
Part 3
Part 4

🎧 **Track 28**

You will hear an interview with a man called Ray Garrett, who is a professional deep-sea diver. For questions **24–30**, choose the best answer (**A**, **B** or **C**).

24 Ray became a deep-sea diver because he
   A lost his job as an office manager.
   B didn't enjoy working in an office.
   C had worked as a diving instructor.

25 What did Ray's parents think of his new career?
   A They knew he didn't have enough experience to do the course.
   B They thought that he wouldn't be able to complete the course.
   C They believed that he didn't have the strength to do the course.

26 Most of the work that Ray does
   A is boring but completely safe.
   B keeps him underwater for over two hours.
   C is not in very deep water.

27 According to Ray, accidents happen when divers
   A dive down to the sea bed.
   B work on shipwrecks at the bottom of the sea.
   C forget to think about possible dangers.

28 At the moment, Ray
   A is repairing a ship in America.
   B is working on a ship that sank off the coast of America.
   C is looking for a ship that sank 150 ago.

29 What does Ray say about the ship, the SS Union?
   A It was travelling to the northern states when it sank.
   B It might have been carrying a valuable cargo.
   C It sank towards the beginning of the twentieth century.

30 According to Ray, if a shipwreck breaks up, a diver
   A might be unable to return to the surface.
   B might suffer from air embolism.
   C might have to dive too deep.

Part 1 (2 minutes)

The examiner (interlocutor) will ask each of you to speak briefly in turn and to give personal information about yourselves. You can expect a variety of questions, such as:

Are you a student or do you work?
What do you enjoy about what you do? (Why?)
What are your plans for the future?
What do you think is the ideal job? (Why?)

Part 2 (4 minutes)

You will each be asked to talk for a minute without interruption. You will each be given two different photographs in turn to talk about. After your partner has finished speaking, you will be asked a brief question connected with your partner's photographs.

1 Special moments

Look at the two photographs on page 177 which show people enjoying special moments in their lives.

Candidate A, compare these photographs, and say what makes these moments special for these people.

Candidate B, which of these do you think is more memorable? (Why?)

2 Climates

Look at the two photographs on page 178 which show different types of climate.

Candidate B, compare these photographs, and say what you think it would be like to live in each of these climates.

Candidate A, which climate would you prefer to live in? (Why?)

Part 3 (4 minutes)

You will be asked to discuss something together without interruption by the examiner. You will have a page of ideas and a question to help you.

Evening and weekend classes

Imagine your local college intends to run some evening and weekend classes. Turn to page 179 which shows some classes that could be offered and a question for you to discuss. Talk to each other about how each class might attract different people. Then decide which two of the classes you think should be offered by the college.

Part 4 (4 minutes)

The examiner will encourage you to develop the topic of your discussion in Part 3 by asking questions such as:

What other classes do you think people might enjoy taking? (Why?)
Why do you think people attend classes outside of school or work?
Why do you think some people don't like to learn new things?
Do you think schools and colleges should offer classes in the evenings or weekends? (Why? / Why not?)
What sort of subjects would you like to learn about? (Why?)
What benefits are there of doing activities which are different from work or schoolwork?

PAPER 1 Reading and Use of English

▶▶ **PART 5**

hut (n) a small dwelling of simple construction, especially one made of natural materials

livid (adj) dark bluish grey

loosen (v) to make or become less tight or firm

grip (v) to grasp or seize firmly, to hold fast

tumble (v) to fall

face (n) a steep, high side of a mountain

awkward (adj) difficult

despise (v) to hate, to detest

haul (v) to pull slowly and with difficulty

bound (v) to jump

cannon (v) to knock into someone or something

hum (v) to make a continuous sound

gaze (v) to look at something for a long time

skip (v) to run in a hopping way

overhanging (adj) sticking out over

canopy (n) a cover

thump (n) the sound of a heavy object when it hits the ground

tug (v) to pull hard

clamp (v) to hold something tightly

arch (v) to form a curved shape

crush (v) to press something so hard that it breaks

hoop (n) a circular tube

snatch (v) to take something quickly, to grab, to seize

sideways (adv) to one side

mountaineer (n) a mountain guide or person who climbs mountains for fun

▶▶ **PART 6**

grant (v) to allow someone to have something that they have asked for

found (v) to start something such as an organisation or school

anchor (v) to lower a piece of heavy metal to the bottom of the sea to prevent a ship from moving

policy (n) a way of doing something that has been officially agreed by an organisation

cater for (phr v) to provide a particular group of people with the things they need or want

conservative (adj) traditional

enterprising (adj) having the ability to think of new ideas and make them work

transmit (v) to send out electronic signals, etc. using radio, television or other equipment

regional accent (phr) a way of pronouncing words, which shows that you do not come from the capital city, but from a particular part of the country

colloquial (adj) of language, used mainly in informal conversations

cheeky (adj) rude or disrespectful in a way that is amusing

tune in (phr v) to listen to a broadcast on radio

spring up (phr v) to appear suddenly, to start to exist suddenly

switch (v) to change from doing one thing to doing another

eminent (adj) famous, important and respected

extend (v) to affect

▶▶ **PART 7**

assume (v) to think that something is true, without question or proof

strive (v) to try very hard to do or achieve something

persevere (v) to keep trying

principle (n) basic idea

desire (n) a strong feeling you want to do something

turn down (phr v) to refuse an offer or request

take to something (phr v) to like and learn a new skill

benefit (n) an advantage

simultaneously (adv) at the same time

pester (v) to ask repeatedly in an annoying way

indulge (v) to let someone do what they want

phase (n) a stage or period

brimming (adj) full

stick something out (v) to continue to do something to the end

imitate (v) to copy

PAPER 1	Reading and Use of English ▶	**Part 1**
		Part 2
PAPER 2	Writing	Part 3
		Part 4
PAPER 3	Listening	Part 5
		Part 6
PAPER 4	Speaking	Part 7

For questions **1–8**, read the text below and decide which word (**A, B, C** or **D**) best fits each gap. There is an example at the beginning (**0**).

Mark your answers **on the separate answer sheet**.

Example:

| 0 | **A** huge | **B** vast | **C** large | **D** immense |

The old gate

In the Middle Ages the (**0**) .... majority of European cities had walls around them. They (**1**) .... to defend the city, but they also kept out undesirable people, like those with contagious (**2**) ....

Most of London's gates had been (**3**) .... by the end of the eighteenth century. However, by a (**4**) .... of luck, the last of them was preserved. This gate is, in (**5**) .... fact, not called a gate at all; its name is Temple Bar, and it marked the (**6**) .... between the old City of London and Westminster. However, as the (**7**) .... of traffic through London increased, Temple Bar became an obstacle to its free flow. In 1878 it was decided to take it down, so its stones were numbered, dismantled and put in (**8**) ....

In the 1970s the Temple Bar Trust was set up with the intention of returning the gate to the City of London. Today, Temple Bar stands next to St Paul's Cathedral.

1	**A** supposed	**B** served	**C** expected	**D** meant
2	**A** injuries	**B** symptoms	**C** wounds	**D** diseases
3	**A** devoted	**B** demolished	**C** deleted	**D** decreased
4	**A** stroke	**B** wave	**C** hit	**D** blow
5	**A** real	**B** current	**C** actual	**D** definite
6	**A** division	**B** part	**C** line	**D** boundary
7	**A** bulk	**B** quantity	**C** amount	**D** number
8	**A** storage	**B** store	**C** storeroom	**D** stock

For questions **9–16,** read the text below and think of the word which best fits each gap. Use only **one** word in each gap. There is an example at the beginning (**0**).

Write your answers **IN CAPITAL LETTERS on the separate answer sheet**.

Example: 0 | O | F | | | | | | | | | | | | | | | | | |

Learning the language

Illiteracy is the condition (**0**) .... being unable to read and write. Illiteracy is also used (**9**) .... describe the condition of being ignorant in a particular subject or field. Computer illiteracy is (**10**) .... we call the inability to use a computer programming language.

Most of us (**11**) .... use computers can send emails, or know (**12**) .... to create a new folder. But we know almost (**13**) .... about programming languages, the artificial languages used to write instructions that can be executed by a computer. Only a very small percentage of computer users are able to read or write (**14**) .... kind of computer language. Should we make the effort to learn computer languages, especially when (**15**) .... are so complicated?

The answer is yes. Because of computer illiteracy, users are (**16**) .... the mercy of software manufacturers. Our society has become dependent on information technology, and this will no doubt be a problem for us for years to come.

For questions **17–24**, read the text below. Use the word given in capitals at the end of some of the lines to form a word that fits in the gap **in the same line**. There is an example at the beginning (**0**).

Write your answers **IN CAPITAL LETTERS on the separate answer sheet**.

Example: | 0 | A | S | S | O | C | I | A | T | I | O | N | S | | | | |

Film festivals

Film festivals are events staged by private organisations, local
governments, arts (**0**) .... or film societies. They provide an   **ASSOCIATE**
opportunity for both famous and (**17**) .... film makers to   **KNOW**
present their movies to a real live audience and to have them
reviewed by (**18**) .... critics.   **PROFESSION**

Some festivals welcome a wide range of films, but other
festivals are more specialised. They may accept only comedies,
or only films made by female (**19**) .... Most festivals accept   **DIRECT**
submissions from any film maker, regardless of his or her
past experience.

Each festival has its own set of rules. (**20**) .... , film-makers   **GENERAL**
are given a deadline by which they have to submit their films.
Submitting a film to the wrong festival is likely to end in
(**21**) .... However, if a movie is accepted, the organisers   **REJECT**
(**22**) .... the film-maker. Film festivals are (**23**) ....   **NOTE**
divided into categories like drama, documentary   **TYPICAL**
or animation. Films are judged for their production value,
(**24**) .... and overall impression.   **CREATE**

For questions **25–30**, complete the second sentence so that it has a similar meaning to the first sentence, using the word given. **Do not change the word given.** You must use between **two** and **five** words, including the word given. Here is an example (**0**).

Example:

0   I'll be very happy when I go on holiday.

   FORWARD

   I'm .... on holiday.

The gap can be filled by the words 'looking forward to going' so you write:

Example: | 0 | LOOKING FORWARD TO GOING |

Write **only** the missing words **IN CAPITAL LETTERS on the separate answer sheet.**

---

25   You've got to decide what you really want to do with your life.

   TIME

   It's .... what you really want to do with your life.

26   Each month he goes to the local hairdresser's for a haircut.

   HAIR

   Each month he .... at the local hairdresser's.

27   It was a mistake for you to insult Sarah.

   SHOULD

   You .... Sarah.

28   I'm sure Chris hasn't forgotten about the meeting.

   HAVE

   Chris .... about the meeting.

29   It's a pity we don't have a bigger apartment!

   ONLY

   If .... a bigger apartment!

30   The doctor told me to reduce the amount of sugar in my diet.

   CUT

   The doctor told me .... the amount of sugar in my diet.

PAPER 1 Reading and ▶   Part 1
          Use of English   Part 2
                                 Part 3
PAPER 2 Writing   Part 4
                             Part 5
PAPER 3 Listening   Part 6
                                 Part 7
PAPER 4 Speaking

You are going to read part of an article about a pilot. For questions **31–36**, choose the answer (**A**, **B**, **C** or **D**) which you think fits best according to the text.

Mark your answers **on the separate answer sheet**.

Flying high

Barrington Irving is very good at rising above obstacles. Literally. Raised in Miami's inner city, surrounded by crime, poverty and failing schools, he beat the odds to become the youngest person ever to fly solo around the world. He built a plane himself, made his historic flight, graduated with excellent marks from an aeronautical science programme, and founded a dynamic educational non-profit-making organisation.
line 5 Then he turned 28.

His message for kids: 'The only thing that separates you from chief executives in corner offices or scientists in labs is determination, hard work, and a passion for what you want to achieve. The only person who can stop you from doing something great is you. Even if no one believes in your dream, you have to pursue it.' The secret, he believes, is having a dream in the first place, and that starts with powerful learning experiences that inspire kids to pursue careers – particularly in science, technology, engineering, and mathematics.

The moment of inspiration for Irving came at the age of 15 while he was working in his parents' bookstore. One of their customers, a Jamaican-born professional pilot, asked Irving if he'd ever thought about becoming a pilot. 'I told him I didn't think I was smart enough; but the next day he gave me the chance to sit in the cockpit of the commercial airplane he flew, and just like that I was hooked. There are probably millions of kids out there like me who find science and exploration amazing, but lack the confidence or opportunity to take the next step.'

To follow his dream, Irving turned down a full football scholarship to the University of Florida. He washed airplanes to earn money for flight school and increased his flying skills by practising at home on a $40 flight simulator video game. Then another dream took hold: flying solo around the world. He faced more than 50 rejections for sponsorship before convincing several manufacturers to donate individual aircraft components. He took off with no weather radar, no de-icing system, and just $30 in his pocket. 'I like to do things people say I can't do.'

After 97 days, 26 stops and dozens of thunderstorms, monsoons, snowstorms and sandstorms, he touched down to a roaring crowd in Miami. 'Stepping from the plane, it wasn't all the fanfare that changed my life. It was seeing so many young people watching and listening. I had no money, but I was determined to give back with my time, knowledge and experience.' He's been doing it ever since. Irving's non-profit-making organisation, Experience Aviation, aims to boost the numbers of youth in aviation and other science- and maths-related careers. Kids attend summer- and after-school programmes tackling hands-on robotics projects, flight simulator challenges and field trips to major industries and corporations. In his Build and Soar programme, 60 students from failing schools built an airplane from scratch in just ten weeks and then watched Irving pilot it into the clouds.

'We want to create a one-of-a-kind opportunity for students to take ownership and accomplish something amazing,' he notes. 'Meaningful, real-world learning experiences fire up the neurons in kids' minds. If you don't do that, you've lost them. Purposeful, inspiring activities increase the chance they'll stay on that learning and career path. We've had one young lady receive a full scholarship to Duke University to study mathematics, and several young men are now pilots, engineers, and aircraft mechanics.' Perhaps Irving's
line 39 most compelling educational tool is the example his own life provides. After landing his record-breaking flight at age 23, he smiled out at the airfield crowd and said, 'Everyone told me what I couldn't do. They said I was too young, that I didn't have enough money, experience, strength, or knowledge. They told me it would take forever and I'd never come home. Well ... guess what?'

31 Why does the writer say 'Then he turned 28' in line 5?

    A   to explain why Irving was ready for a change in his lifestyle
    B   to emphasise how much Irving had achieved in his life so far
    C   to show why Irving's organisation had become so successful
    D   to justify the enthusiasm Irving demonstrated through his actions

32 According to Irving, what is the most important requirement for success?

    A   having friends who believe you will eventually succeed
    B   having something specific that you want to accomplish
    C   having plenty of opportunities to study different subjects
    D   having contacts in organisations who can share their knowledge

33 What does Irving say about what happened in his parents' bookshop?

    A   He realised immediately how lucky he was.
    B   He felt too embarrassed to refuse the offer.
    C   He was initially doubtful about his own abilities.
    D   He understood that his efforts would be rewarded.

34 What do we learn about Irving in the fourth paragraph?

    A   Once he knew how to fly he took on a further challenge.
    B   He chose to get by on as low a budget as possible.
    C   He was eventually given just enough money to keep going.
    D   The most useful flying tips he picked up were from a game he bought.

35 Why did Irving set up his non-profit-making organisation?

    A   He wanted to help improve the schools in his area.
    B   He hoped to avoid becoming a celebrity pilot.
    C   He thought he could teach people more than the flight schools could.
    D   He saw there was widespread interest in what he was doing.

36 What does 'compelling' mean in line 39?

    A   exciting and demanding
    B   interesting and amusing
    C   powerful and effective
    D   clear and simple

PAPER 1 Reading and ▶
        Use of English
PAPER 2 Writing
PAPER 3 Listening
PAPER 4 Speaking

Part 1
Part 2
Part 3
Part 4
Part 5
Part 6
Part 7

You are going to read an article about robot shops. Six sentences have been removed from the article. Choose from the sentences **A–G** the one which fits each gap (**37–42**). There is one extra sentence which you do not need to use.

Mark your answers **on the separate answer sheet**.

The robot shop

Like most ideas that seem absolutely revolutionary, the concept behind the robot shop is actually very simple. In fact, it has already been around for many years in the form of vending machines selling bars of chocolate or drinks. This idea has been further developed to create the first robot shop, which may eventually change the future of shopping.

The prototype robot shop in a suburb of London looks like a giant vending machine. **37** ☐ The display on the right is refrigerated and holds items such as milk, yoghurt and cheese, while the display on the left has an impressive selection of biscuits, coffee, cakes and crisps. It does not have the variety of conventional shops, but it can cope with a late-night request for bread or painkillers.

A central console is what allows you to actually do your shopping. You key in the code numbers of the goods you want, which are displayed just underneath each item in the window, and a huge robot arm reaches out and picks up each item, bringing it over to the console inside the shop.

An electronic display shows you the total you have to pay. **38** ☐ Unlike supermarkets, in robot shops you can only collect the goods after you've paid. When the robot arm finds the things you want, it drops them into a hatch and you reach inside to take them out. If this happened before you paid, you could easily walk off with the goods without having paid for them.

The system couldn't yet be described as entirely efficient. There's a lot of room for improvement. The robot arm represents one of the biggest problems. **39** ☐ The arm has to be very accurate in order to pick up the item it has reached for, carry it to the hatch and safely drop it into it.

The difficulty of judging customer attitudes is another reason why the robot shop has to be tested. Customers are still cautious about doing most of their shopping in a robot shop, but this is only to be expected; every new invention has been regarded with some suspicion at first. **40** ☐

The manufacturers of robot shops suggest that the small shopkeeper in inner-city areas represents their biggest potential client. **41** ☐ People in the area value the convenience of being able to pop out virtually all hours of the day and night for some item they have forgotten or suddenly feel like buying. Small shopkeepers are likely to invest in robot shop equipment, rather than employ part-time staff to work twenty-four hours a day.

The question is whether customers will prefer the impersonal service of a robot shop to the conventional type of shopping where there's human contact. **42** ☐ Machines do not take lunch breaks, they hardly ever make mistakes and they are never rude to customers. Isn't this the sort of efficiency people want from a shop these days?

A Not least of which are concerns about mechanical failure, especially when they occur in the middle of the night.

B The first thing you notice are the two large display windows which are absolutely packed with goods.

C The real question is whether, over the three-month testing period, enough people will overcome their doubts and start shopping here in significant numbers.

D For security reasons, you have to do this before the robot arm starts gathering your goods.

E Many shops like these only survive because they stay open late, or even around the clock in some cases.

F Experience with similar mechanised service equipment, such as cash dispensers, suggest that there are considerable advantages for both customers and shop owners.

G The challenge is to create a piece of machinery which will be delicate enough to pick up eggs but at the same time strong enough to pick up bottles of mineral water and baked-bean cans.

You are going to read part of an article in which four people talk about the sports lessons they had at school. For questions **43–52** choose from the people (**A–D**). The people may be chosen more than once.

Mark your answers **on the separate answer sheet**.

Which person

thinks sports encourage cooperation?   **43** ☐

believes that experience of losing is important?   **44** ☐

thinks one benefit of sports is learning to concentrate?   **45** ☐

compares academic subjects to sports?   **46** ☐

believes the Olympic spirit is essential today?   **47** ☐

thinks sports help non-academic pupils?   **48** ☐

thinks sports can teach objectivity and justice?   **49** ☐

thinks schools should teach unusual sports?   **50** ☐

thinks diet and health should be taught with sports?   **51** ☐

thinks sports can make some children feel uncomfortable?   **52** ☐

Sports at school

A Diane Townson

Looking back, I did enjoy sports lessons at school, even though I think most schools in those days assumed sports were basically for boys, and girls weren't encouraged to do well at sports. That attitude really annoys me, because the whole point of sports at school is to help kids develop the right attitudes, and it doesn't matter really how good you are. If you can't run as fast as an Olympic athlete, that doesn't matter – what matters is that you run as fast as you can. Schools are highly competitive environments and sports can teach children the importance of teamwork. To do well in almost everything else at school, like maths or history, you are rewarded for individual effort, but sports are about working together towards a common goal. Sports at school give children who are not high achievers a chance to excel at something.

B Colin Campbell

My own memories of sports lessons at school aren't particularly good, but that's mainly because of the type of school I went to. It was very unusual by British standards, with old-fashioned ways of teaching, and the headteacher didn't really think sports mattered at all. The school rarely organised sports events and never invested in sports equipment. There was very little emphasis on the importance of eating sensibly and the benefits of keeping fit and exercising properly. I believe that issues like obesity, anorexia, nutritional value of food, etc. should be included in sports lessons at school. Children should be encouraged to take part in competitive sports. Being competitive is part of human nature, and doing sports can provide an excellent outlet for this aggressiveness. Winning at sports can build up your self-esteem and confidence. On the other hand, since you can't expect to win every time, sports can also teach you how to be humble and realistic.

C Roger Dias

There are obvious benefits in having good sports classes at school. Children stay fit and learn the importance of fair play. Schools can introduce children to sports they would never otherwise have the opportunity of doing. For instance, I grew up in a big city, and we hardly ever travelled to the countryside as a family. At school we had a climbing wall in the gym, and we learnt rock climbing in sports class. When I moved to Europe, I took up rock climbing and was surprised by how good I was at it. Schools should offer a wide range of sports from the most popular ones, like football and basketball, to the less popular ones, like table tennis and climbing. Unfortunately, sports are often regarded as a sort of optional extra by certain schools and this is also reflected in the children's attitude to them.

D Helen Smith

The main point about sports is that they encourage peaceful competition. I think that's the basis of the Olympic spirit of Classical Greece, which nowadays is more important than ever before. Sports can teach you how to discipline yourself, how to remain focused on what you're doing and how to apply yourself to achieving a goal. I don't think sports are really about the sort of aggression and rage that you see sometimes in football matches, for instance. I certainly think teachers should discourage any form of aggression during sports classes. On top of that, we need to be more sensitive towards the feelings of children who are not fit or good at sports. Taking part in a sports lesson can be a major source of embarrassment and a traumatic experience for less athletic children.

You **must** answer this question. Write your answer in **140–190** words in an appropriate style.

1   In your English class you have been talking about free time. Now, your English teacher has asked you to write an essay.

Write an essay using **all** the notes and give reasons for your point of view.

Some people say we all have too much free time and should spend more time studying or working. Do you agree?

Notes
Write about:

1. work or study hours
2. seeing family and friends
3. .... (your own idea)

Write an answer to **one** of the questions **2–5** in this part. Write your answer in **140–190** words in an appropriate style.

2 A new shop has recently opened in your area and your English teacher has asked you to write a review of it for the college English-language magazine. Describe the shop, what it sells and give your opinion of the staff in the shop. Would you recommend this shop to other people your age?

Write your **review**.

3 You see this announcement in an international magazine.

> **Do local traditions really matter?**
>
> As the world becomes smaller and globalisation has a greater effect on us all, is there any place for local traditions? Tell us about any traditions that you feel should be preserved.

Write your **article**.

4 (*for FIRST candidates only*)

You see this announcement on an English-language website.

> **Free photography course in New York!**
>
> Ten lucky people can attend a four-week photography course in New York for free, including accommodation and food!
>
> We are looking for people with an interest in photography, but beginners are welcome.
>
> Write to Mr Harvey Green, explaining why you should be offered a place.

Write your **letter of application**.

(*for FIRST FOR SCHOOLS candidates only*) You see this announcement on an English-language website.

> We are looking for stories from all over the world! Your story must begin with this sentence:
>
> *Dan knew he might regret answering the text message, but he did it anyway.*
>
> Your story must include:
> * a car
> * a present

Write your **story**.

5 (*for FIRST FOR SCHOOLS candidates only*) Answer the following question based on your reading of one of the set books.

Characters in books have to make important decisions. Write an **essay** about a decision that one of the characters had to make in the book or one of the short stories you have read. You should also say whether you would have made the same decision as the character.

Track 29

You will hear people talking in eight different situations. For questions **1–8**, choose the best answer (**A**, **B** or **C**).

1   You hear a man talking to his friend about his choice of career.
    What does he say?
    A   He wishes his current job was more exciting.
    B   He has plans to change his profession.
    C   He regrets not following his dream.

2   You hear a woman talking about being a student at university.
    Why did she study French?
    A   because her parents wanted her to
    B   because she had enjoyed her visit to the country
    C   because she wanted to become a translator

3   You hear a man talking about acupressure.
    Which of the following does he say acupressure can do?
    A   relieve headaches
    B   change people's mood
    C   prevent colds

4   You hear an actress talking about her new role.
    What character is she playing?
    A   a bank manager
    B   a mother
    C   a taxi driver

5   You hear two students talking about remembering new vocabulary.
    What do they agree about?
    A   The memorisation technique is boring.
    B   The association technique is time-consuming.
    C   The picture technique is effective.

6   You hear the captain of a plane talking to his passengers.
    Which city are they closest to at the moment?
    A   Brussels
    B   Rotterdam
    C   Amsterdam

7   You hear a woman talking about taking up dancing as a hobby.
    How does she feel about it now?
    A   surprised by the progress she's already made
    B   very upset by her obvious lack of skill
    C   motivated to improve her ability

8   You hear a man and a woman talking about an author's latest work.
    What does the woman think is a masterpiece?
    A   the author's collection of short stories
    B   the author's latest novel
    C   the author's latest film script

Track 30

You will hear part of a careers talk by a nurse called Anne England. For questions **9–18**, complete the sentences with a word or short phrase.

Being a nurse

Anne was inspired to become a nurse when she heard her

(**9**) .... talking about the job.

Anne's teachers told her she would need to improve her

(**10**) .... a bit if she wanted to be a good nurse.

Anne hadn't expected to go to so many (**11**) .... when
she was a student.

Anne's (**12**) .... helped her with some of her student
projects.

Anne found learning how to (**13**) .... people safely was
particularly useful.

When Anne got her first job, she had to go to work by

(**14**) .... every day.

Anne didn't enjoy having to do a lot of (**15**) ....

People say Anne is much more (**16**) .... than she used
to be.

One of Anne's patients gave her a (**17**) .... which she
always wears.

If Anne wasn't a nurse, she would like to be an (**18**) ....

PAPER 1 Reading and
Use of English

PAPER 2 Writing

PAPER 3 Listening ▶

PAPER 4 Speaking

Part 1
Part 2
Part 3
Part 4

 Track 31

You will hear five short extracts in which people are talking about a journal or magazine they read regularly. For questions **19–23**, choose from the list (**A–H**) what each speaker says. Use the letters only once. There are three extra letters which you do not need to use.

A	The fashion photography is excellent.		
B	It provides an excellent news round-up.	Speaker 1	19
C	It presents a variety of different views.	Speaker 2	20
D	It features the best photographs.	Speaker 3	21
E	It has good travel information.	Speaker 4	22
F	It has information on things I buy.	Speaker 5	23
G	It is both entertaining and informative.		
H	It has the most up-to-date information about fashion.		

🎧 **Track 32**

You will hear a radio interview with a woman called Kay Stanley who is talking about a condition called dyslexia. For questions **24–30**, choose the best answer (**A**, **B** or **C**).

24   The Stanley Trust
   A   helped Kay a lot when she was a child.
   B   was started by Kay to help other people with dyslexia.
   C   was founded by Kay's father.

25   How did Kay's parents first realise she had dyslexia?
   A   She didn't know stories that other children could read.
   B   Her mother found her memorising audio books.
   C   She couldn't spell words that other children knew.

26   What was Kay told by an expert on dyslexia?
   A   She has a milder form of the condition.
   B   She will be able to overcome her problems by reading.
   C   Spelling will always be a particular problem for her.

27   How does dyslexia affect the way people think?
   A   It can make people think more creatively.
   B   It prevents them from solving problems effectively.
   C   It makes it harder for them to follow logic.

28   What made Kay work hard to improve her reading?
   A   It was the only way she could study acting.
   B   She didn't want people to think she was stupid.
   C   Her father encouraged her.

29   Kay feels that children with dyslexia should
   A   attend special schools.
   B   have special training to help them read.
   C   be treated like all other children at school.

30   How does Kay want to publicise the problem of dyslexia?
   A   by acting in a film about the subject
   B   by giving talks to parents of dyslexic children
   C   by setting a positive example

Part 1 (2 minutes)

The examiner (interlocutor) will ask each of you to speak briefly in turn and to give personal information about yourselves. You can expect a variety of questions, such as:

Do you enjoy going to the cinema or the theatre? (Why?)
Is the cinema in your town or district popular?
Was the last film you saw at the cinema or on television? What was it about?
What's your favourite TV programme? (Why?)

Part 2 (4 minutes)

You will each be asked to talk for a minute without interruption. You will each be given two different photographs in turn to talk about. After your partner has finished speaking, you will be asked a brief question connected with your partner's photographs.

1 Learning environments

Look at the two photographs on page 180 which show different learning environments.

Candidate A, compare these photographs, and say what you think about these two learning environments.

Candidate B, which of these learning environments would you prefer? (Why?)

2 Holidays

Look at the two photographs on page 181 which show different types of holiday.

Candidate B, compare these photographs, and say why you think the people have chosen these different types of holiday.

Candidate A, which of these two holidays would you prefer? (Why?)

Part 3 (4 minutes)

You will be asked to discuss something together without interruption by the examiner. You will have a page of ideas with a question to help you.

The shopping centre

Imagine your town is going to have a new shopping centre. Turn to page 182 which shows some ideas for how a new shopping centre could attract customers and a question for you to discuss. Talk to each other about how useful these ideas would be for attracting customers. Then decide which two ideas the shopping centre should have.

Part 4 (4 minutes)

The examiner will encourage you to develop the topic of your discussion in Part 3 by asking questions such as:

Do you prefer to shop alone or with friends?
Where do you like to go shopping? (Why?)
Do people in your country like shopping in small local shops? (Why? / Why not?)
What are the disadvantages of shopping in large shopping centres?
Are there any products that you can only find in large shopping centres?
Are there any special products sold in your town/city that would be impossible to buy in another country?

PAPER 1 Reading and Use of English

▸▸ PART 5

obstacle (n) something that makes it difficult to succeed

beat the odds (expr) to succeed even though there is little chance of doing so

dynamic (adj) active and energetic

non-profit-making organisation (n) an organisation whose aim is to help people, not to make money

smart (adj) clever

cockpit (n) the part of an aeroplane where the pilot sits

hooked (adj) wanting to do something all the time

scholarship (n) money given to a student to help pay for their studies

flight simulator (n) something that imitates the conditions inside an aircraft

take hold (expr) to begin to be important

donate (v) to give for no charge

component (n) a part

touch down (phr v) to land

fanfare (n) excitement and attention

boost (v) to increase

tackle (v) to deal with

from scratch (phr) without any previous knowledge

neuron (n) a type of brain cell

▸▸ PART 6

revolutionary (adj) completely different from what was done before

concept (n) an idea

prototype (n) an early example

conventional (adj) traditional and ordinary

console (n) central control panel

key in (v) to enter (numbers or information)

hatch (n) an opening

cautious (adj) taking care to avoid risks or danger

regard (v) to consider

suspicion (n) a doubt

potential (adj) possible

virtually (adv) almost

impersonal (adj) unemotional, lacking human contact

overcome (v) to deal with and control a problem

gather (v) to collect together

delicate (adj) gentle

▸▸ PART 7

attitude (n) a feeling about or toward someone or something

competitive (adj) involving or demanding competition, aggressive

individual (adj) working on your own

achiever (n) a person with a record of successes

excel (v) to do very well

equipment (n) useful items needed for a purpose (work, sports, etc.)

obesity (n) the condition of being too fat

anorexia (n) prolonged loss of appetite, resulting in low body weight

outlet (n) a release for emotions or energy

aggressive (adj) unfriendly, hostile, competitive

self-esteem (n) a sense of self-worth

fair play (expr) playing fairly and according to rules; not cheating

optional extra (phr) something additional that you can choose

reflect (v) to show or be a sign of a particular situation or feeling

discipline (v) to train to control the mind and body

sensitive (adj) understanding, aware

embarrassment (n) a feeling of shame, discomfort or self-consciousness

traumatic (adj) shocking, harmful

athletic (adj) having ability in sports

CAMBRIDGE ENGLISH
Language Assessment
Part of the University of Cambridge

Do not write in this box

Candidate Name
If not already printed, write name
in CAPITALS and complete the
Candidate No. grid (in pencil).

Candidate Signature

Examination Title

Centre

Supervisor:
If the candidate is ABSENT or has WITHDRAWN shade here ▭

Centre No.

Candidate No.

Examination Details

Candidate Answer Sheet

Instructions
Use a PENCIL (B or HB). Rub out any answer you wish to change using an eraser.

Part 1: Mark ONE letter for each question.

For example, if you think **B** is the right answer to the question, mark your answer sheet like this:

| 0 | A | B | C | D |

Parts 2, 3 and **4:** Write your answer clearly in CAPITAL LETTERS.

For Parts 2 and 3 write one letter in each box. For example:

| 0 | EXAMPLE |

Part 1

1	A	B	C	D
2	A	B	C	D
3	A	B	C	D
4	A	B	C	D
5	A	B	C	D
6	A	B	C	D
7	A	B	C	D
8	A	B	C	D

Part 2

Do not write below here

9		9 1 0 u
10		10 1 0 u
11		11 1 0 u
12		12 1 0 u
13		13 1 0 u
14		14 1 0 u
15		15 1 0 u
16		16 1 0 u

Continues over ➡

Part 6

	A	B	C	D	E	F	G
37	A	B	C	D	E	F	G
38	A	B	C	D	E	F	G
39	A	B	C	D	E	F	G
40	A	B	C	D	E	F	G
41	A	B	C	D	E	F	G
42	A	B	C	D	E	F	G

Part 7

	A	B	C	D
43	A	B	C	D
44	A	B	C	D
45	A	B	C	D
46	A	B	C	D
47	A	B	C	D
48	A	B	C	D
49	A	B	C	D
50	A	B	C	D
51	A	B	C	D
52	A	B	C	D

SAMPLE

Part 3 (Remember to write in CAPITAL LETTERS or numbers)

Do not write below here

17
18
19
20
21
22
23
24

	1	0	u
17	1	0	u
18	1	0	u
19	1	0	u
20	1	0	u
21	1	0	u
22	1	0	u
23	1	0	u
24	1	0	u

Part 4 (Remember to write in CAPITAL LETTERS or numbers)

Do not write below here

25
26
27
28
29
30

	2	1	0	u
25	2	1	0	u
26	2	1	0	u
27	2	1	0	u
28	2	1	0	u
29	2	1	0	u
30	2	1	0	u

SAMPLE

Part 5

	A	B	C	D
31	A	B	C	D
32	A	B	C	D
33	A	B	C	D
34	A	B	C	D
35	A	B	C	D
36	A	B	C	D

Continues over

TEST 1

▶▶ **PART 2**

Candidate A

Language bank

The first photograph might be a village in Asia, because of the style of the boats. People seem to be living in these boats.

On the other hand, the second photograph shows skyscrapers, probably with very expensive apartments for wealthy people. This could be a photo of any big, modern city.

Perhaps the people who live on the houseboats in the first photograph also work on the water. They might catch fish for a living, or use their boats to transport goods. This could be the reason why they have chosen to live on these boats.

I suppose the people who live in the skyscrapers want to be in the centre of the city. Maybe they work in the city and have chosen to live near their workplaces or they just prefer city life.

Why have people chosen to live in these places?

▶ 1

▶ 2

▶▶ **PART 2**

Candidate B

Language bank

The first photograph shows people in a very big theatre or opera house, and everyone is wearing formal clothes. It could be a classical music concert or opera.

In contrast, the people in the second photograph are younger, and it looks as if a concert is taking place outdoors. Unlike the people in the first photo, these people are casually dressed. This could be a pop or rock concert.

The people in the first photograph look quite serious, but they could be thinking about what they're going to see or hear when the performance starts. The second photograph shows people who are excited and seem to be enjoying themselves.

Both photos show people who like music, and are probably glad to be attending these performances.

> **How are the people feeling?**

1

2

▸▸ **PART 3**
Candidates A and B

Language bank

A mobile phone would be useful for contacting friends or family, and if we had any problems, we would be able to phone for help. I agree, although we might not be able to use a mobile phone if we were in a remote place.

I think we would have to take a first-aid kit because someone could be hurt in an accident. But this might not be the most important thing to take.

If we had a torch, it would make it much easier to do lots of things, like putting up the tent in the dark, for example. I would agree with you about that.

Let's try to reach a decision. Are we agreed that we should take a torch? Unfortunately, I can't agree with you on that.

▶▶ **PART 2**

Candidate A

Language bank

Both these photos show people who seem to be working hard.

The young woman in the first photo is in a library, reading a book at a table; the young man behind her looks as if he's working hard too. The library is modern and light, and there are a lot of books on the shelves behind her.

Perhaps the woman has chosen to study in the library because she likes to work in a quiet place where other people are studying too. I imagine she can get any book she needs for her studies very easily in the library, so maybe she likes it for that reason as well.

The young man is in a busy café, working on his laptop. He looks as if he is concentrating hard, even though the people around him are talking. Maybe he's going to meet a friend there later, or maybe he prefers to work in a more relaxed atmosphere.

Personally, I prefer to study in quiet places, like at home or in a library. I find I work more efficiently if I'm not disturbed by other people making a noise.

Why are the people working in these places?

1

2

▶▶ PART 2

Candidate B

Language bank

The first photograph shows a small family consisting of a man and woman and a little girl who is probably their daughter. The parents are about thirty, and the girl is about ten years old. They seem happy and relaxed, and they're sitting on the grass, perhaps in a park.

The second photograph is more formal, as if a photographer asked the people to sit like this. There are three children sitting on the floor at the front, a girl aged about eight and two boys, probably her brothers, aged about five and twelve. There are four adults on the sofa behind them. Two of the adults are probably the parents of the children. And there is an older couple, probably the grandparents.

I suppose in a small family the child might get more attention from the parents, but the child could also be lonely. In a big family, with grandparents and several children, it could be harder to have some time to yourself, but you'd never be lonely, and you might grow up to be more sociable.

> What would it feel like to grow up in these families?

▶ 1

▶ 2

Language bank

Who do you think would like that type of film? What sort of person would that type of film appeal to? Do you think the people in our class would prefer this type of film or that one?

I suggest we talk about each kind of film first. Let's decide who would like each of the films. Why don't we decide which kind of film we think would be most suitable? What about choosing the kind of film we like best?

I agree with you about a love story. I disagree that a thriller would be a good choice, because not everyone likes that sort of film. I don't think you're right about that. Do you agree that an action film would be popular? Don't you think we should choose a western?

▶▶ **PART 2**

Candidate A

Language bank

The first photograph shows a man in a shirt and tie sitting in what looks like a hotel restaurant or terrace. The hotel might be quite expensive. He looks as if he's drinking coffee, and there's fruit juice on the table, so he must be having breakfast. He's looking at something on his computer. Perhaps he's reading a work email.

In the second photograph some people are having a picnic. They're sitting on a rug or blanket on the grass. I think it's a mother and father and their two children, a boy and a girl. My impression is that they're having lunch.

I think the man in the first photo looks relaxed, while the people in the second photo look really happy and they're probably having fun.

Personally, I wouldn't like to stay in a posh hotel because I wouldn't feel relaxed. I enjoy being in the countryside, so I'd rather have a meal outdoors like the people in the second photograph.

How do the people feel in these situations?

▶ 1

▶ 2

▶▶ **PART 2**

Candidate B

Language bank

In the first photograph a man is driving a sports car down a mountain road. The car seems to be coming towards the camera at high speed. It looks like a very expensive car.

The car in the second photograph is red and could be a vintage car. As in the first photo, a man is driving and looks as if he's enjoying himself. The car appears to be in excellent condition.

I think it would be exciting to drive both of these cars. I get the feeling that the car in the first photo is a lot faster than the one in the second photo. I often feel nervous if someone drives fast, but I like travelling by car. Being able to drive is important, and having a driving licence gives you a feeling of freedom and independence.

How would it feel to travel in these cars?

▶ 1

▶ 2

▶▶ PART 3
Candidates A and B

cycling

hiking

What are the advantages and disadvantages of these outdoor activities?

sailing

horse-riding

rock-climbing

Language bank

What do you think are the advantages of this activity? Do you think this activity would be suitable for young teenagers? Does this activity have any disadvantages in this situation?

I'd say rock-climbing is exciting, but it might take a long time to learn to do properly. On the one hand, hiking can be very satisfying, but some of the teenagers might find it terribly boring. I think teenagers would love sailing, which is very good fun and less dangerous than climbing.

If we have to choose two of these activities, I'd suggest sailing and cycling. Would you agree with me on that? Don't you think young people would learn a lot from these activities? I think they would, too.

It seems that we don't agree on this, because you believe climbing would be a suitable choice here, and I don't share that view.

▶▶ **PART 2**

Candidate A

Language bank

Both photos show different working environments.

There is a woman working at a desk with a pile of papers and files next to the computer. She's concentrating hard. She could be an accountant or a lawyer.

The woman might be thinking about all the work she has to do. I would imagine that she must be feeling overworked and stressed.

The man in the second photo is standing in a building or wooden structure, hammering a nail into some wood. I would guess that the man is helping to build this. He is wearing casual working clothes and a hat to protect his head.

This man must be quite fit, and perhaps he enjoys working with his hands. He is concentrating on his work and seems to be making sure he is doing everything properly.

> How are the people feeling in these different situations?

▶ **1**

▶ **2**

▶▶ **PART 2**

Candidate B

Language bank

Both photos show leisure activities.

The boy in the first photo is balancing on a skateboard with one arm up in the air, and it looks as though he might have just jumped off a wall on his skateboard. You would have to be fit and active to enjoy this, and I think the sort of person who would go skateboarding would love adventure and taking risks in life.

The woman in the second photo looks relaxed. She is sitting on a sofa, reading a book. It looks as though she is concentrating on what she is reading, so I'd say the book is probably very interesting. Someone who likes reading would enjoy this activity, or perhaps someone who has been working hard and deserves a rest.

Reading is a more passive activity compared to skateboarding.

> **What sort of person would enjoy each of these activities?**

▶ **1**

▶ **2**

▶▶ **PART 3**
   Candidates A and B

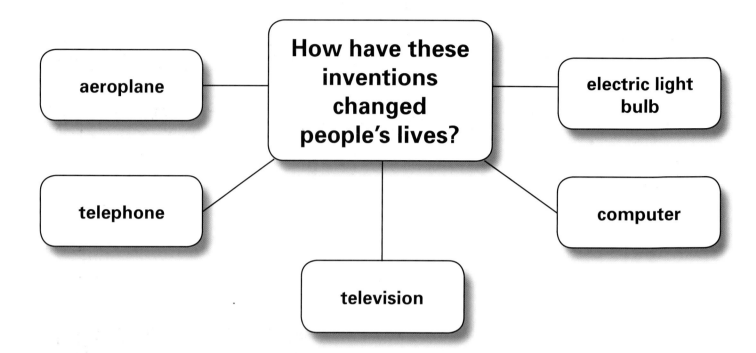

Language bank

Let's think about how important these inventions have been to us. Which ones have changed people's lives, would you say?

If the electric light bulb hadn't been invented, our lives today would be very different. Do you agree with me on that?

It's hard to imagine life without some of these inventions, like the telephone. On the other hand, air travel has made the world smaller and changed many people's lives.

If we think of inventions we could not do without today, I'd say the computer is the most important.

You're right about that. However, in terms of changing people's lives, I'd say the electric light bulb is the most important.

I agree to a certain extent. But I also think that television has improved the quality of our life.

Shall we make a decision?

▸▸ **PART 2**

Candidate A

Language bank

I get the impression that this type of train is very modern and fast, so perhaps it's designed for public transport in a big city or between cities. It would seem to me that people who are in a hurry and have no time to waste would choose to travel by train.

The bus looks very crowded and the people look quite bored or fed up. Perhaps the people who are standing up would prefer to have a seat. I imagine this is a local city bus, because it doesn't look very luxurious. The passengers are probably travelling a short distance.

They might have chosen to travel by bus because it's cheaper or because they really had no other choice.

> **Why do people use these different means of transport?**

▸ **1**

▸ **2**

▶▶ **PART 2**

Candidate B

Language bank

The man and woman in the first photograph look very happy and are both laughing. They are wearing very formal clothes and look very smart.

I assume these people have dressed formally to go to a wedding reception, celebrate an anniversary or have dinner in a posh restaurant.

The man and woman in the second photo are younger and are wearing casual clothes that would not be suitable for a formal celebration.

The people look relaxed and happy, and their clothes look comfortable and suitable for the weather. It looks as though they are out riding their bikes, and they would need to wear this type of clothing for the activity.

Why have the people chosen to wear these sorts of clothes?

▶ 1

▶ 2

▶▶ **PART 3**
   Candidates A and B

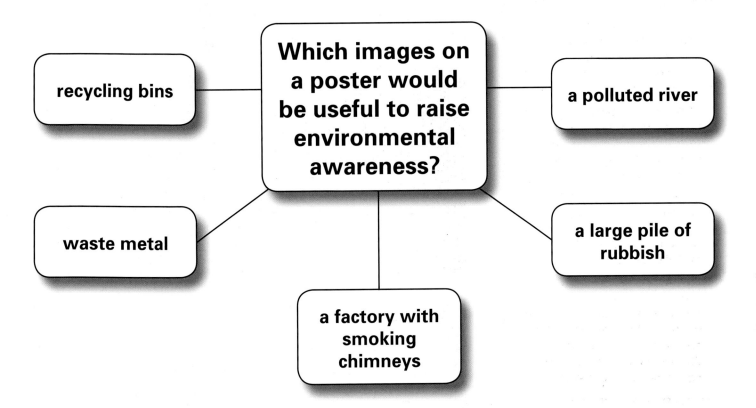

Language bank

Would you like to start?

The poster should illustrate ways of dealing with pollution. Don't you agree?

I would prefer a photo that illustrates the problems that pollution can cause to the environment. Do you see my point?

If I had to choose between a photo of a factory with smoking chimneys and one of waste metal, I would definitely go for the first one.

I'm afraid I disagree. Don't you think a photo of recycling bins would be more effective?

We haven't talked about this one. What do you think of it?

Perhaps you're right. I think we should make a decision now, so shall we choose the factory and the recycling bins?

▸▸ **PART 2**

Candidate A

Language bank

In the first photograph the artist appears to be painting the scene around him. I think an artist should paint a picture that is true to life. In my view, a picture should reflect the real world around us.

I would like to have this painting because it shows a peaceful landscape. I like the relaxed and tranquil mood of the first painting.

The artist in the second photograph is also facing slightly away from us, working on her painting. The photograph may have been taken inside the artist's studio, or she could be painting a wall in a school, for example, or even outdoors.

The painting in the second photo has a lot of faces, which look quite childish. People who appreciate modern, more abstract ways of expression would probably prefer this painting to the first one.

Which painting do you like most and why?

▶▶ **PART 2**

Candidate B

Language bank

The two women in the first photo seem to be choosing fruit or vegetables from a stall. One of them has a basket in her hand. It isn't clear whether this is a market stall or a stall outside a greengrocer's shop.

If you shop like this, you can select the things you want and check them carefully, which is an advantage. I imagine things are often cheaper in a market, too. Some customers might enjoy the friendly, personal atmosphere of shopping in a market or at a local greengrocer's.

The second photograph shows part of a supermarket, with a lot of vegetables on display. Some of the vegetables are loose, and others are in plastic packaging.

Supermarkets have a very wide variety of goods of different brands. Some things, such as clothes, may be cheaper in supermarkets. It is more convenient to go to a supermarket and do all your shopping in one place, especially for families who perhaps go shopping once a week. On the other hand, supermarkets can be very impersonal.

What are the advantages of shopping in each place?

▸▸ **PART 3**

Candidates A and B

How important is each facility for visitors to a holiday resort?

- a tourist information centre
- a water-sports centre
- an airport nearby
- a local hospital
- a car rental agency

Language bank

The point I'd like to make is that the majority of visitors would appreciate an airport nearby more than any other facility.

I don't completely agree with you. A lot of people these days want to visit places while on holiday, so a car rental agency would be a good idea.

That may be true, but I'd say most holidaymakers like to know medical care is available if necessary, so having a small hospital in the resort would be essential.

I think that the hospital should be the number one priority. Now, let's discuss what other facility the resort should have. What about a tourist information centre?

That's a very good point; a tourist information centre can help you organise your holiday, plan visits and sightseeing tours, but is this more important than a water sports centre, for example?

I consider the tourist information centre essential, so perhaps we have different views on this.

Well, we'll just have to agree to disagree!

▶▶ **PART 2**

Candidate A

Language bank

The young man in the first photo is holding a sports trophy, so he must have won a competition or have been in the winning team. Judging by his clothes, I'd say he is probably a basketball player.

In the background I imagine that there are a lot of spectators; this is probably an important sporting event, so the man must feel very proud of himself and pleased with his achievement. He must be feeling both exhausted after training and practising hard and relieved that the game or competition is over.

The young man and woman in the second photo are holding a small baby; it looks as though the baby is only a few weeks old, and they may still be learning how to look after him or her.

I'm sure the parents will never forget the day their baby was born. Both parents are smiling at the baby, and there can be no doubt that they are absolutely delighted to have a son or daughter.

What makes these moments special for these people?

▶▶ **PART 2**

Candidate B

Language bank

The first photo shows people in a desert. There are some large tents in the desert. We can see the desert stretching out into the distance. There are quite a few people here, wearing long robes and with their heads covered. There are also several camels walking along.

It must be very hot here, although I suppose people who are born here become accustomed to the heat. I don't think I could get used to living in such a hot climate. I expect it would be very dry and dusty as well as hot.

The house in the second photograph has a thatched roof. It looks old-fashioned and picturesque. Behind the house there are some trees, and there are more hills in the background. The sky is blue with some clouds, but I think the sun is shining.

The green grass and trees suggest the climate is quite wet, which might make life a bit uncomfortable. I think I would prefer this climate to the desert climate in the first photo.

What would it be like to live in each of these climates?

▶ 1

▶ 2

▶▶ **PART 3**

Candidates A and B

Language bank

I suppose sport and fitness classes would appeal to a lot of different people, of all ages. Perhaps the college should make these classes a priority.

I disagree; I think cookery classes would be more popular with people in a small town.

I see your point, but on the other hand, people learn to cook in their families; photography classes would be more entertaining and enjoyable.

What's your view on acting classes? Don't you agree that they would mainly attract younger people?

Since we have to choose two classes, can we agree that one of them should be a hobby and the other should be something useful, like the cookery class?

That sounds reasonable. In that case let's say one class should be cookery. We've got four options left. Which one should be our second choice?

▶▶ PART 2

Candidate A

Language bank

The teenagers in the first photo are sitting in a classroom writing something. They seem to be concentrating hard. They are all sitting in a row, and there are probably other students doing the same thing in front of them. There is a board behind them with some writing on it, and there's probably a teacher in the classroom with them. People can learn a lot in a classroom environment, especially if all the students are focusing quietly on their work.

The second photograph shows a group of younger children standing in front of a pile of plastic bottles. The man could be their teacher, and he must be talking to them about the benefits of recycling.

This is a more relaxed learning environment, and the children look motivated and interested in the subject. It seems to be quite a small group of children, so I suppose a pupil would get more attention from the teachers at this school.

| What do you think about these two learning environments? |

▶ 1

▶ 2

▸▸ **PART 2**

Candidate B

Language bank

The first photograph shows a group of people in the desert, with the Sphinx in the background, so this must be Egypt. It looks as though the people are tourists and one of the people at the front might be a guide explaining the history of the pyramids.

A tour like this might be a cheaper and easier way to see some interesting historical sights, because you would have an expert guide to explain everything.

It could be that these people have chosen to have a holiday in a group because they are members of a club or society, perhaps people with a common interest, or they may just be on a guided tour organised at the site.

The second photograph shows a man relaxing by a lake, with a pile of books next to him. He is looking at a laptop computer. This type of holiday would be more relaxing than the type of holiday shown in the first photo.

It would probably appeal to people who want to stay in a beautiful place and have a quiet time and who may not be particularly interested in going sightseeing or visiting tourist attractions.

Why have the people chosen these different types of holiday?

▸ **1**

▸ **2**

▸▸ **PART 3**
   Candidates A and B

Language bank

Why don't we start by looking at the ideas?

My first choice would be the children's play area. I think that most families go shopping with their children, and having a place to leave them would be a good way to attract customers.

I couldn't agree more, but perhaps we're overlooking a very simple point: customers want to save money when they go shopping, so shops that have sales and reduced prices would be very popular.

Obviously, that is an important point, but what about the idea of having different kinds of restaurants? Don't you feel that would attract customers?

As we have to choose two of these ideas, I suggest choosing the car park and the reduced prices.

Preparing, planning and checking

▶▶ Preparing for the Writing Paper

One of the best ways to improve your writing skills is to read as widely as possible. This will help you to expand your range of vocabulary and grammatical structures. You also need to study the basic text types which you may be asked to produce in the exam, and have a good understanding of their basic features: layout, organisation, style and register (level of formality). You should also practise completing writing tasks in the time allowed in the exam. Remember the criteria the examiners will use in awarding marks:

- Has the candidate achieved the purpose stated in the instructions?
- Does the text have a positive general effect on the target reader?
- Does the text cover all the content points?
- Is the text well organised and are ideas linked appropriately?
- Has language been used accurately?
- Does the text show a good range of vocabulary and grammatical structures?
- Is the register appropriate for the task?
- Is the layout appropriate?

If possible, ask an experienced teacher to provide feedback on pieces of writing you produce when you are practising for the exam. This will help you to learn what kind of mistakes you frequently make so that you can avoid them. For example, if you often make mistakes with a certain tense, you can ask your teacher to explain it to you again, or you can use a good grammar guide to help you. It's also a good idea to make a list of expressions that you can include in your exam text, such as the useful phrases you find with the model answers in this section.

▶▶ Planning your answer

The most useful lesson to learn about writing is the importance of planning what to write before you actually start writing. In the exam you will only have time to write your text once, so you should make time to write a plan before you begin writing. This will help you to write your exam text more easily.

Always read the question carefully and make sure you understand the following:

- Who are you writing for (a friend, a teacher, other students)?
- What are the points you must include in your answer?

- Does the text type (an email, an article, a report, a review) have any particular layout requirements?
- Do you have the necessary vocabulary to answer the question on the topic?

When you are sure you understand what you have to do to answer the exam task, prepare a plan of what you are going to write. It doesn't matter if you change your plan or cross things out – nobody will read it. But it has to show clearly the different sections of your writing and which points you must include in which section (i.e. in the introduction, main body, and conclusion). When you look at the plan carefully, you might want to change it; for example, one point might be better in a different paragraph, or you might realise you will be repeating yourself. When you are satisfied with your plan, you will find it much quicker to write your text. Give yourself five minutes to make your plan before you start writing.

▶▶ Question 5, the set text task (*FIRST FOR SCHOOLS* only)

If you choose to write about one of the set texts, remember that the question may ask for an essay, article, email or letter. You may be asked to write about the characters, relationships or themes in the book. Make sure you know the story well, as you will need to support your views with examples from the book. When answering the question, think carefully about the target reader, and plan your answer accordingly.

Remember: Do **NOT** answer the set text question if you have not read the book.

▶▶ Checking

Most people make more mistakes than usual when they are writing under exam conditions. Always give yourself at least five minutes at the end to read through your work. First, check that you have answered the question correctly and that you have included all the information that was required. Second, check for mistakes in grammar, spelling, punctuation, etc. You should have enough writing experience by now to know where you often make mistakes – spelling certain words, for example, or using a particular type of punctuation.

If you need to change something in your text, make the correction carefully and make sure it is still easy for the examiner to read your work. If you need to cross out something you have written, just put one line through the word or words.

1 Essay

▶▶ **Exam task – Part 1**

You **must** answer this question. Write your answer in **140–190** words in an appropriate style.

In your English class you have been talking about the internet. Now, your English teacher has asked you to write an essay.

Write an essay using **all** the notes and give reasons for your point of view.

Do you think the internet has a negative effect on people's lives?

Notes

Write about:

1. communicating with friends
2. news and current affairs
3. .... (your own idea)

Useful phrases

Introducing the topic

To begin with ...
The first point I would like to make is ...
As some of us know, / As we all know, ...
Most people believe ...

Expressing opinions

It seems / appears to me that ...
I agree / disagree with ...
I am in favour of / I am against ...
For me, the most important ... is ...

Discussing pros and cons

On the one hand, ... / On the other hand, ...
However, ...
Nevertheless, ...
There are many arguments against / in favour of ...

Giving examples

For example / instance, ...
One example of ... is ...
... such as ...

Conclusion

To sum up, I believe there are advantages ...
In conclusion, ...
On balance, ...

▶▶ **Approach**

▶ Make sure your writing is well organised and clearly paragraphed, starting with an introduction and ending with a conclusion summarising your opinion.

▶ You need to write about the two elements in the notes, as well as adding an idea of your own. This third idea must be different from the other two, and cannot simply be your conclusion at the end of the essay. Think about what your own idea will be before you start writing. Read the question carefully and write a brief plan so you know what to include in each paragraph.

▶ The register should be neutral or semi-formal, and even if you have strong opinions on the topic, you should try to express them in an objective way and look at both sides of the argument.

▶▶ Model answer

State the general topic in the first paragraph.

The use of the internet is now widespread. It is part of most people's lives, and some believe that its overall effects are harmful to society.

As we all know, the internet makes it easy to keep in touch with friends or family, for example by using social networking sites. You can also find out about events in the wider world almost as soon as they have happened. Moreover, students use the internet to find useful information for homework and college projects.

One way of writing this kind of essay is to present the advantages of the statement or situation in one paragraph. Use the two points in the notes and add one of your own (here, the third point is about using the internet to help with homework).

You can present the disadvantages of the statement or situation in a separate paragraph.

On the other hand, there are disadvantages too. For example, people can spend so much time chatting to friends on their computers that they rarely meet them face-to-face. Furthermore, the news that people see on the internet is not always accurate. Accuracy can also be a problem for students using the internet for their homework: unless it is from a reliable website, it may be incorrect.

Use linking words or expressions to list the main points (advantages or disadvantages) in your paragraph.

Sum up the main points and say whether there are more advantages than disadvantages. Show clearly whether you agree, disagree or partly agree with the statement.

On balance, I think there are more advantages than disadvantages to using the internet. As long as people are careful and do not automatically believe everything they see on it, then the internet can be a positive part of their lives.

2 Email

▶▶ Exam task – Part 2

You have received this email from your English-speaking friend, Adam.

> **From:** Adam
>
> **Subject:** Exchange programme
>
> I've been offered the opportunity to come to your town on an exchange student programme. How easy is it to find accommodation? What is the transport like? And what is life like in your area? Do you think I should take up the offer?
>
> Write soon!
>
> Adam

Write your **email**.

▶▶ Model answer

Useful phrases

Introduction
Thanks for your message / email.
Sorry I haven't written before.
I'm really glad / sorry / pleased
  to hear …

Body of email
In my view / opinion, …
It would be a good idea to …
You should / shouldn't …
Don't forget to …
If I were you, I would / I'd …

Conclusion
Well, that's all for now.
I hope this is helpful.
Do keep in touch.
Write soon.
Look after yourself.
Give my love / regards to …

Dear Adam,

In the introduction greet your friend.

I was really pleased to get your email last week and to hear that you might be coming on an exchange programme. Sorry I haven't written back before now, but I've been very busy working in my parents' shop.

In your email you asked me about accommodation. There is a student residence not far from our apartment; I can find out if you could get a room there, and how much it will cost.

Divide your email into short paragraphs. Make sure each paragraph is on a different topic.

The bus service here is very efficient and reliable. The college is within walking distance from the town centre, and it would take you about 20 minutes to walk there.

The exam question requires you to give information about your area and advice about the exchange programme.

I think the exchange programme is a wonderful opportunity for you to spend time away from New York. Life here is very relaxing, the pace of life is slow, and the people are friendly. If I were you, I wouldn't think twice!

I'm really looking forward to seeing you here and showing you around my favourite places. Do write and tell me what you decide.

Finish your email in an informal way. Send greetings and ask the reader to write back.

Look after yourself,

Mike

3 Review

▶▶ **Exam task – Part 2**

You see this announcement in your college English-language magazine.

> ### Everyone has a favourite film.
>
> What makes a certain film mean so much to us?
>
> Write a review of your favourite film, and tell us why you like it so much.
> If we publish your review, you will win free film tickets for two people.

Write your **review.**

Useful phrases

Adjectives
exciting, amusing, gripping, absorbing, excellent, outstanding, hilarious, fascinating

Adverbs
extremely, incredibly, awfully, terribly, amazingly, surprisingly, particularly

Film-related vocabulary
The story is set ...
The main characters ...
It is produced / directed by ...
The performance is ...
The pace is slow / fast ...
The message conveyed is ...
The special effects are ...
low-budget film, script, audiences, blockbuster

▶▶ **Model answer**

A review is a piece of writing where you are asked to give your opinion about a TV programme, a film or play you have watched.

Decide how formal the language should be; if you are writing for a magazine, the language can be quite informal.

Provide a brief summary of the plot and comment on the main characters.

List the things that you liked most about the film.

Film review: **Titanic**

My favourite film is Titanic, a wonderful story with incredible special effects. Titanic is not only a commercial success but also a good film.

In this film a rich young woman on the luxurious Titanic meets a struggling artist and they fall helplessly in love. When the ship sinks, he saves her life but drowns. The young woman never forgets him or stops loving his memory. The two main characters are fascinating and they have a wonderful on-screen chemistry.

The film is very realistic and the scenes when the ship is sinking are extremely dramatic. You can feel the panic of the people trying to get away, and this part of the film is particularly gripping! Although the film's success is partly based on its amazing special effects and action sequences, the director also focuses on how characters act in the crisis, which makes it an emotional film to watch.

The sinking of the Titanic may be one of the most important lessons for humanity. The great ship was thought to be unsinkable. People thought they had conquered nature. Its maiden voyage proved how wrong they were.

Make the introduction interesting without giving details about the film.

Try to make the review interesting by using dramatic and sophisticated language. Avoid repeating simple adjectives like *good*, or *bad*. Use adjectives like *fascinating, gripping* or *dramatic* to describe people or things.

The conclusion should summarise what you have said in the review or focus on the main message of the film.

4 Article

▶▶ **Exam task – Part 2**

You have seen this announcement in an English-language magazine.

We want your articles!

Giving gifts

What's the most thoughtful gift you've ever received? Why do you think giving gifts is important? Do you think the best gifts are the most expensive ones?

We'll publish the best articles in our magazine next month.

Write your **article**.

Useful phrases

Ordering language
First of all, ...
Secondly, / Next, ...
Another point is ...
Finally ...

Involving the reader
Have you ever ...?
Can you imagine ...?
I think you will agree that ...
What would you do if ...?

Giving your opinion
It seems to me that ...
In my opinion ...
To my mind ...
As far as I'm concerned ...
(Personally), I think / believe that ...

▶▶ **Model answer**

An article is a piece of writing on a particular topic for a newspaper, magazine, newsletter, website or other publication.

Use neutral language for your article (not too formal or informal). You can address the reader personally by using 'you'.

Make your article lively and entertaining. Use descriptive language.

Conclude your article with a summary of what you have said, and give your opinion if appropriate.

Have you ever received a really thoughtful gift? The best gift I've ever been given was a picture from my ten-year-old niece, which she had drawn for my birthday. It wasn't an expensive gift, but it was one of the most thoughtful I've ever received. The picture was decorated with hand-drawn images of the things I love best: flowers, ice cream and birds.

Personally, I think it's important to give gifts to show you care about the people in your life. The picture my niece made was so nice because it demonstrated that she understands the things that make me happy. As far as I'm concerned, you don't have to spend a fortune on a gift: something home-made and personal is just as lovely to receive as a diamond ring or a fast car. And you don't need to wait for a special occasion such as a birthday; you can give gifts any day of the year to show someone you love them.

Remember, it isn't how much you spend on a gift that matters, but the thought you put into giving something you think the other person will enjoy.

Gain the reader's interest in the title and introduction, for example, ask a question to attract the reader's attention.

An article expresses your personal point of view and it does not need to be objective.

5 Report (for FIRST candidates only)

▶▶ **Exam task – Part 2**

Your local tourist office is preparing a brochure for tourists. Write a report suggesting a local tradition that you think should be included in the brochure. Include details about the tradition, such as what it means to local people, and what people do to celebrate the tradition.

Write your **report**.

Useful phrases

Introduction
This report is intended / designed to …
The purpose of this report is to …
The aim of this report is to …

Making suggestions / recommendations
I would recommend …
I suggest that …

Conclusion
In conclusion, …
In my view, / opinion, …

▶▶ **Model answer**

You can use paragraph headings, numbering or bullet points to organise the information in a clear way.

The purpose of this report is to suggest a tradition which could be included in the brochure which might be of interest to visitors to our region. I would recommend including the tradition of Bonfire Night in the UK.

State the aim of the report in the introduction.

What is Bonfire Night?

Bonfire Night is a British celebration which takes place on 5th November each year. Originally, the tradition celebrated a historical event, although nowadays it is a social occasion.

What happens on Bonfire Night?

Bonfire Night is celebrated in the autumn, when it goes dark early in the evening. Fireworks are lit and big fires are made. In many towns, public firework displays are organised, and bonfire parties are held in people's gardens. Special food is eaten, too, such as toffee apples or jacket potatoes.

The language should be formal and impersonal (e.g. passive forms).

What does Bonfire Night mean to people?

Bonfire Night celebrations bring friends and families together in order to share a night of fun and a sense of community.

In the conclusion you should give your opinion and/or make a recommendation, depending on the wording of the exam question.

Conclusion

In conclusion, I suggest that the brochure for tourists should also include photographs relating to Bonfire Night. In my view, the local tradition mentioned in this report would appeal to visitors.

Don't write your name at the end of the report.

6 Letter of application (*for FIRST candidates only*)

▶▶ **Exam task – Part 2**

You see this advertisement in your college English-language magazine.

Summer jobs!

Could you be a guide for visitors to your area?

Excellent pay for part-time job guiding English-speaking visitors.

You must be available to work evenings and weekends.

Write your letter of application to the manager of *Visitors Unlimited*, Mr Sadler.

Write your **letter of application**.

Useful phrases

Introduction

I have seen your advertisement in our local newspaper …

I am writing in connection with the job vacancy you have advertised …

I am writing about …

I am writing to apply for …

Body of letter

I am … years old and I …

I have a good command of …

I have a good knowledge of …

I have worked …

I would be suitable for the job …

Conclusion

I would welcome the opportunity to …

I look forward to hearing from you / to your reply.

▶▶ **Model answer**

In a formal letter start with Dear *Mr / Mrs* …

> Dear Mr Sadler,

In the introduction say briefly why you are writing.

> I am writing in connection with the job vacancy you have advertised for a guide for visitors to this region.

Give information about yourself if you are writing to apply for a job.

> I am 19 years old and have just finished my first year at university, studying Economics. I would be available to work from the beginning of June until the end of August, including evenings and weekends. I lived in London for a year when I was younger, and I am fluent in English. I am an outgoing person with a good sense of humour, and I am confident I would get on with visitors to this region.

Express the information in the exam question in your own words. Don't copy directly from the question.

Make sure you include all the necessary information given in the exam question.

> I have travelled extensively in this part of the country, and I am familiar with several places that would be of interest to visitors. For example, the Folk Museum in the centre of town has fascinating exhibitions, the cathedral is popular with sightseers, and the old town has some interesting traditional restaurants.

> I would welcome the opportunity of meeting you in person to discuss this. I look forward to your reply.

Finish by saying that you look forward to hearing from the other person.

If you know the person's name, end with *Yours sincerely*. If not, end with *Yours faithfully*.

> Yours sincerely,
> Maria Barone

7 Story (for FIRST FOR SCHOOLS candidates only)

▶▶ **Exam task – Part 2**

You have seen this announcement in an international English-language magazine for teenagers.

Stories wanted

We are looking for stories for our magazine for teenagers. Your story must begin with this sentence:

There was no moon that night, and we were not expecting a storm.

Your story must include:
- a boat
- a mobile phone.

Write your **story**.

Useful phrases

Setting the scene
There were three of us …
My family had rented a cottage …
It was a cold winter night …
I had never been to …

Sequencing events
At the beginning …
As soon as …
First …
Then …
Afterwards …
Finally …
In the end …

Reaction to events
I was petrified …
I was numb with fear …
I was shocked …
I stood there speechless …
I was so embarrassed …

▶▶ **Model answer**

The exam question asks you to use the sentence at the beginning of the story. Don't change what the sentence says or change its position.

There was no moon that night, and we were not expecting a storm. There were three of us in the boat: my uncle, my aunt and myself. I felt nervous and excited. I had never been sailing before.

Begin the story in an interesting way. Set the scene: explain who the narrator is, say when and where the story takes place.

Try to use vocabulary imaginatively (similes, metaphors, vivid descriptions of people and things).

When we left the harbour, the wind began to get stronger. The boat was jumping up and down like a dog pulling at a lead. Then the rain started, and I could hardly see the lights of the houses in the harbour. The boat struggled against the howling wind, and I was absolutely petrified!

Describe the events and people's feelings and reactions to them.

Suddenly, there was a terrible crash! We had hit some rocks, and for a minute I thought the boat was going to sink. The storm was getting worse and the rain was coming down in torrents. Then I realised that the boat had got stuck between the rocks.

Present the main events of the story in chronological order. Use narrative tenses (past simple, past continuous, past perfect, etc.) and linking words (*when, by the time, within seconds,* etc.) to sequence events.

Bring the story to a conclusion.

Luckily, Uncle John had his mobile phone, and he called for help. But in the end it was nearly an hour before the coastguards could rescue us. I was so glad to be on dry land again!

TEST 1

▶▶ **PART 1**

1

I've been learning about child development on my college course and it's interesting to see how my young cousin matches up to the different stages. Every day he's up to something new and he's developing in leaps and bounds. Yesterday I turned round and there he was on his own two feet. I can't wait to hear him utter his first words, as we've gone into that in detail – it's fascinating. I'm looking forward to putting what I've studied into action – that's if I'm lucky enough to find a job in the childcare field after my degree, and of course, if I'm still into the whole thing by that point!

2

A: Can I help you?
B: Yes, I'd like to buy some flowers for my mother's birthday.
A: Did you have anything particular in mind? We've got some tropical bouquets which are rather distinctive.
B: They're beautiful! And a little over my budget, I'm afraid. I think she'd prefer something a bit more traditional. I've been looking into roses, which she likes growing. Perhaps she'd like a variety she's less familiar with.
A: Let me think ... I'm expecting a delivery this afternoon of a new hybrid rose. It's been a winner with our customers so far. Why don't you pop back in about an hour's time and I'll show you?
B: Sounds perfect.

3

A: How did you get on in maths today? I struggled with that new formula. I just couldn't get my head round it.
B: I'm with you there. Have you seen that new maths app? It's pretty cool – you just download whatever you want to do more practice on, on your mobile.
A: Doesn't help you grasp the concept though, does it? I mean if it's just practice activities?
B: You've got a point – but don't you think that if you keep doing it, you'll eventually get it?
A: I could give it a try. I'd rather ask the teacher to go over it again, though.
B: Well, yes – if it makes you feel more confident.

4

As the day proceeds, we'll see storm clouds building up here on the west coast, moving gradually across the country and bringing temperatures down to well below the seasonal average. Scattered showers over on the west coast will die down during late afternoon. The east coast can expect to get the worst of the bad weather, with very heavy storms hitting during the late evening and in the early part of the night, though the south coast won't escape this entirely; we're forecasting gale-force winds in some areas ...

5

This is a message for John, the plumber. I've got a bit of a leak coming through the kitchen ceiling but I can't seem to track it down. I'm not sure whether it's coming from the bathroom or somewhere else. You've already sorted out that problem with the taps, so I wondered if you might be able to call in at your convenience and check this for me as well. I'm working late this evening but the weekend's fine. In the meantime, I'll have another look into it and see if I can work out where the water's coming from. Can you call me back on this number? Thanks.

6

The sales training session was supposed to be taking place on Thursday afternoon, in which case I could have caught the 10 a.m. train into London. But plans have changed, so I'm thinking of travelling down the day before – it's going to be a nine o'clock start now and there's no way I can get there for that time from where I live. So, I was wondering whether you might be able to put me up for the night since you don't live far from the conference centre. If it isn't convenient, don't worry about it – I can easily make alternative arrangements. Either way, I hope to see you soon.

7

A: Good match, despite the result.
B: Do you think so? We've played better. Good job our goalkeeper was on the mark.
A: He's been doing an impressive job this season. As have the rest of the team.
B: Pity we can't say the same for the referee. He's supposed to be impartial, but I'm sure he was favouring our opponents.
A: Oh, I don't think so! You're just fed up 'cause it was a draw. We'll make it up next time, wait and see.
B: I wish I shared your enthusiasm. We've got a long way to go if we want to win the championship. Though it's not beyond us, I guess.

8

A: So, you want to become a student buddy – helping new students settle in to university life?
B: Yes. When I started at this university as a first-year student myself, I remember feeling a bit disorientated during the first few weeks – I wasn't sure where to find things or who to approach about general student life. I remember feeling really grateful that I could go to the buddies about these things. I guess I feel it's my turn to give something back. I like to think I'm a pretty approachable person and I know the university like the back of my hand – why not help others feel at home?

TEST 1

▶▶ **PART 2**

Thank you for coming to hear my talk about Museums for All. My name's James Edwards and I'm director of the association. Let me start by telling you what the association is. As the name suggests, it's a sort of club with all the museums in the country as members. Although museums themselves have been around for hundreds of years, our part in this is relatively new – two years ago a group of major museums came together and started the association – but we're already making big changes.

So, what's our task? Since the association was formed, we've been putting in a great deal of effort to alter the experience people have of visiting museums. For decades, museums have been seen as stuffy, boring places, but in the next few years we aim to have transformed this belief – and we've got plenty of ideas about how to do this!

My own background isn't actually in this field. As a university graduate, I worked for a marketing firm and made the switch to advertising a few years later. It was while I was working for a large agency in this area that I was approached and asked to think about becoming director of Museums for All. I hope my experience will enable me to apply a fresh point of view.

At Museums for All, we believe we have to publicise museums more effectively as far as attracting visitors is concerned. The age-old way of running a museum has been too passive in this respect, which is why we're committed to being more active in that sense.

I can quite understand why traditional museums are the way they are – it's all to do with the history of museums, and the whole way of thinking about museums in the past, when they were mainly for people with high levels of education. All that has changed, but people in general still don't feel very much at home in museums. We're working on ways to change that.

The best way to encourage interest in museums, I think, is to get children into the idea from an early age. Ideally, I'd like to see close links between museums and schools in the area, so the children can feel that the museum belongs to them. It's important that we reach out to the community and connect with them in this way.

Many people find museums a little threatening – they're often silent places in dark old buildings. We want museums to be much more friendly places, much like shopping malls are – with things like cafés and gift shops. We envisage museums with a central area and wings or corridors leading off that area towards the exhibitions and other facilities. That would allow people to return to the central area after wandering around for as long as they want.

A trip to a large museum can leave people feeling overwhelmed. There's so much to see that visitors don't know where to begin. At Museums for All, we think that we can make a museum visit a far less exhausting experience, which for some people, is the case. By changing their appearance and improving visitor flow, we think people will come to enjoy the experience much more than they ever have.

Rebuilding museums, however, is rather expensive, but they are really important: investing in museums is investing in the future of the country, just like investing in other services for the community – and the government has to realise that.

We certainly have a huge challenge ahead of us in the next few months, but I feel very optimistic about what we have to do. I'm sure we'll see more and more people visiting museums in the near future through our programme of planned cultural events. Next year in June, we're organising a Museum Festival, which is intended to attract people who wouldn't normally go to museums. I'm convinced it will be a huge success. I think that's really all we've got time for right now, but are there any questions?

TEST 1

▶▶ PART 3

1

Our History Society organised a trip to Kent, where we spent a fortnight digging up some Roman remains. I didn't know a thing about archaeology before, but that summer I really got interested in the subject, and the dig was fantastic. I got to know two girls and we've become really close since then. I also fell in love with Kent – that's what I call a great trip. I'm now pretty busy making preparations for another trip – this time to Egypt! It'll be my first solo trip to join a professional team out there and I can't wait to go. I've even learned some Arabic phrases!

2

One year our geography teacher organised a ski trip to the French Alps. It was great! None of us had been skiing before, and I don't think any of us had seen such wonderful scenery before, either. I thought later that if we'd learnt some of the basics about skiing before we went, it would have helped a lot, because the first week we were basically stuck in the ski school and couldn't go out on the slopes by ourselves. But in spite of all that, it was still a really good trip.

3

Our school had a cottage in the Lake District, where some of us went for weekends during the summer. I was about 14 when I went for the first time. It was quite nice, really, but we were a bit disappointed because we didn't realise we'd have to go walking round the mountains all day. We wanted to have more time to ourselves, just to go and look round the lakes, but of course looking back, I can see why the teachers had to supervise us closely and make sure we kept safe.

4

One summer our Spanish teacher organised a trip to Spain, which was fascinating! She knew all about the history of the country, and she'd prepared a very good programme of sightseeing tours. She'd taught us some good communicative language – though we didn't use it much. The area we stayed in was great – there was tons of stuff to do. The teacher gave us lots of time to explore on our own as well – the only downside was that the trip didn't go on long enough! My friends and I were really sad to come home. Hopefully I can convince my parents to take me back on holiday there this year!

5

Our English teacher also taught drama, and he was really keen on us seeing as much live theatre as we could. One of my most memorable experiences was going to London to see *Hamlet* at the National Theatre. We stayed overnight in a youth hostel. I was about 15, and I'd never been to London before, so it was really exciting for me. We must have had a big discount at the theatre and the youth hostel, because I remember the whole thing only cost £35, which was pretty cheap.

TEST 1

▶▶ PART 4

Interviewer: This evening on *Young and Gifted* I am joined in the studio by Julia Emerson, the young Scottish writer who's recently had a screenplay accepted by a major Hollywood studio. Julia, I'm glad you could be with us today. Could I start by asking you to explain exactly why what you've done is so unusual?

Julia Emerson: Well, Hollywood films these days don't start off with a screenplay. The screenplay only gets written after the producers have come up with an idea for a film. Then they contact agents to find at least one major star who will act in it. The next step is to get a team of anything up to 20 writers working on the screenplay. Now, I was inexperienced enough to think that I could simply write a screenplay and send it to a number of studios. Which is what I did. When I didn't get an answer, I wrote another one. And this time, by some amazing chance, they accepted it!

Interviewer: I think everyone has been stunned by the fact that you've been successful with a screenplay at such an early age. But in fact, this isn't the first piece of writing you've had published, is it?

Julia Emerson: No, it isn't. I won a short-story competition in a magazine when I was 15, and ever since then I've been writing in my spare time. I've had a number of articles published in teen magazines. I've always been fascinated by television and the cinema, and I even tried to develop an idea for a TV series, but somehow it didn't feel right. Then I tried putting down an idea for a film, and the writing just flowed.

Interviewer: Do you think you're influenced very strongly by films you've seen?

Julia Emerson: Yes, but I have to watch out, or I might end up writing a slightly different version of a classic! I suppose everyone who does anything creative has to think about that, though.

Interviewer: Can you tell us something about this screenplay that's been bought by Planet Studios. What's it about?

Julia Emerson: It's about two sisters, who are stranded in the jungles of South America after becoming separated from the rest of their tour group. They have all sorts of adventures as they try to get back to civilisation. It's an adventure story, but it's also about the relationship between the two girls. You see, they've never been very close – in fact, at the start of the story they really hate each other. Or at least, they think they do.

Interviewer: How much of the story is based on your own experience?

Julia Emerson: Since I don't have any brothers or sisters, in one way it's clearly not based on my experience! But on the other hand, I have experienced how the feelings we have for our family can go through different stages and transformations, which is the real theme of the story.

Interviewer: And when am I going to be able to see this film in the local cinema?

Julia Emerson: I've got no idea! The studio has paid for the right to use the screenplay, and they have that right – it's called an option – for another six months. They might make the film in that time, or they might buy the option again for another couple of years. It's all out of my hands, in fact. So I try not to get too excited about seeing the story on the big screen one day, because I have no way of knowing when that might be.

Interviewer: I hope it's soon, anyway. Julia Emerson, thanks for talking to us. It's been a pleasure.

Julia Emerson: Thank you.

TEST 2

▶▶ **PART 1**

1
Well, Mr Saunders, we have to take this lower back pain of yours seriously. You'll need to get an orthopaedic mattress, and a chair for your desk that supports your back – and I'll be showing you how to stand properly. Now, for the first exercise, get down on the floor, look straight up at the ceiling, arms by your sides, and lift each foot as high as you can. That's great. I'd like you to repeat that four times, three times a day. Now I'll show you the second exercise.

2
A: Hello?
B: Good evening, Taj Mahal restaurant.
A: Oh, good evening, I'd like to order a takeaway.
B: Certainly. What would you like?

A: I'd like a Madras curry with beef, a hot lamb curry and a mild chicken curry, your special. Oh, and three portions of rice.
B: Did you know the chicken curry is with rice?
A: Oh, I see. Better make that just two portions of rice. Thanks.
B: And would you like anything else with it?
A: No. that's all, thank you.
B: And where would you like it delivered to?
A: 11 Grant Street, Hitchworth Common, Dryswold ...

3
It's incredible how he makes the whole scene come to life. I think this is a perfect example of Impressionism at its best. The colours are so lively, so exciting, and you really have the sense that you know how he felt when he painted it. This is one of his later works, right at the end of the real Impressionists. In fact, art historians generally say the end of the Impressionist movement was 1886, and this was actually painted two years later. But it clearly belongs with the Impressionists ...

4
The football ground? Now let me see – probably the quickest way to get there is to go along this road until you come to a big supermarket on the left, and you turn right just opposite it. That brings you into Oldham Street, and you go straight on. You come to some traffic lights just after a park on the right – you keep on going, and then you take the third turning on your left – at a cinema called the Majestic, you can't miss it – and the football ground's on the right.

5
A: All right, Bill, so you've come up with a new cartoon character. What's his name?
B: Crazy Conrad. Do you think it sounds good?
A: Well, not bad. And Conrad's a horse, right?
B: No, you're holding it upside down. He's a baby elephant.
A: Oh, sorry. Yes, now that I look more closely I can see what you mean. It's got bigger ears than a horse and it's got a trunk. Yes, of course it's not a horse.
B: He was originally going to be a bear, but then I changed my mind.
A: Why was that?
B: I'm not sure, really, I just thought it wouldn't be as funny, somehow.

6
Oh officer, I do hope you can help me. I never thought this would happen to me! Well, I suppose you never do expect these things, do you? Anyway, I didn't notice anything, though someone must have put their hand in my bag. They didn't take the camera, just my purse. The camera's quite expensive, in fact, so I suppose I'm lucky they ignored that! And I thought I was being so careful about the bag, you know, always keeping it closed and where I can see it. So it must have happened in a flash, maybe when I was getting off the bus.

7
And now for our traffic bulletin. The police have issued a warning about long delays on the M63 heading south, between junctions 15 and 16, caused by an accident involving three cars on the A36, just before junction 15, where the A36 and the B636 intersect. The incident on the A36 has produced a long tailback. Delays are expected for the next three or four hours while rescue services clear the road, and police are advising motorists to avoid the area if at all possible. And on the railways ...

8

My mother's been doing this fruit diet, you know where you're supposed to eat only fruit for ten days as a way of losing weight. What she doesn't seem to understand is that if she eventually manages to lose a few pounds, it'll be because she's eating less, rather than because of eating nothing but fruit. It won't do her any harm, of course, but it's quite funny, really. I mean there's no scientific basis for it, in my opinion. At least it's only for ten days, and then she'll be back to her usual diet, which I think is quite healthy and varied.

TEST 2

▶▶ PART 2

Hello, my name's Jane Robertson, and I'm here to talk to you about a language you may not have heard much about before: Gaelic. I work at a Gaelic school in Scotland – I'm the headteacher, in fact. There aren't very many of these schools at the moment, so I'm lucky to have such an interesting job.

Maybe I should start by explaining exactly what Gaelic is. It's a very old language that was spoken in most of Scotland, outside the cities, up to a couple of hundred years ago.

Today, unfortunately, very few people speak or even understand the language – only about 60,000 in the whole of Scotland. Now you may think that sounds like rather a large number of people, but the total population of Scotland is over 5 million. So you can see that the number of Gaelic speakers form a relatively small proportion of the population as a whole.

And according to experts, a language is dead if fewer than 50,000 people speak it. You see, you have to have a large number of people using the language in everyday situations, not just linguists or people who learn it as a hobby. It needs to be a normal part of a lot of ordinary people's lives, or it simply doesn't qualify.

So our aim is to get as many people as possible interested in learning it. And young people – those under 25 – are particularly important. I would like to see a third of them speaking and writing the language – then we could begin to say it was in a healthy state.

At my school all the teaching is in Gaelic, whatever subject the children are learning. This is very important, because it has been discovered that very young children learn a language best if they are completely exposed to it – hearing and speaking the language all day. Of course, it's a bit of a shock for them at first, but we have some wonderful teachers, and they're trained to cope with that!

Quite a lot of parents send their children to our school because they want their children to know about the history of the country – cultural reasons like that. But of course it's also well known that it's good for a child to grow up speaking two languages perfectly. And in fact, these children grow up to be bilingual. This gives them many advantages. It's been scientifically proven that bilingual children do better at tests, and there's reliable evidence that they're also more tolerant and imaginative. In this case, an added advantage is that children of Scottish origin are rediscovering Scotland's mother tongue.

Many people feel pessimistic about the future of Gaelic, and I can see why, when you look at the figures, it could appear that there's little hope. But I myself am extremely optimistic.

In fact, when it comes to situations like this, there's an example which is encouraging, and it's quite close to home. Not that long ago, the Welsh language was in real danger of dying out. Some children may have grandparents who speak it as a first language, but in many parts of Wales it's rare for kids to grow up speaking Welsh instead of English at home. However, with a lot of effort it's been possible to save the Welsh language. The important thing is to have government support and enough money available. In Wales, virtually 80% of children now learn Welsh as a second language at school. It's been a real success story and I hope that we'll eventually be able to do the same in Scotland ...

TEST 2

▶▶ PART 3

1

My event is the 100-metres sprint. Athletes never stay in the sport for very long in this kind of event; you just burn up too quickly. It may seem a bit cynical, but I think you have to see it as a way to get your name famous, get some good income from sponsors and advertising, and then put that money into a business – a shop selling sports equipment or a luxury sports club, for example – so it'll take care of you in ten or 15 years' time, when you can't compete any more.

2

Archery isn't a very well-known sport, but it is an Olympic event. I actually started by complete accident, when a friend of mine wanted to go to an archery club, and I said I'd go along just out of curiosity. But now I'm really hooked. Last month I won a regional contest here in Cornwall, and I have my eye on the national championships later this year. Winning it would just be amazing, even if I never become famous; just the feeling that nobody can beat me is exciting enough.

3

Like most athletes, I started at school. We had a really good gym teacher who encouraged everyone to try all the track and field events to find which we were good at. Well, it turned out that I was good at the high jump, and now I'm going to compete in my first international event in the summer. To be honest, I haven't thought beyond that; it's always been my biggest dream to compete at international level for Australia. I know I'm going to be terribly nervous, but it's definitely worth it.

4

Ever since I was about ten years old, I knew I wanted to be a professional footballer. I suppose it was partly because both my elder brothers were really good at school – they were always among the best in their class at maths and things – and I wasn't. My little sister was also getting loads of praise from her teachers, even though she was only little. So I wanted my mum and dad to see I was good at something, at least. Of course, as I got older that part of it became less important, and I found myself loving the game itself.

5

Show jumping is as much a social activity as a sport, you know, and in this part of the country lots of people have horses. It's something people spend a lot of money on and it takes up most of their free time. In fact, most of my friends are interested in things like show jumping or pony clubs. We meet almost every weekend, except in the middle of winter. That's how I started, although there's an awful lot of hard work involved if you get more serious about competing at higher levels. But it's still loads of fun!

▶▶ **PART 4**

Interviewer: This is Kate Green with another edition of *Wild Ones*, the programme about extreme sports. My guest on today's programme is Sam Hall, a mountain climber. Sam, thanks for being with us today. Now, I'd like to start by asking you how you became interested in such a dangerous sport.

Sam Hall: <u>Well, first I'd like to point out that climbing isn't a dangerous sport, as long as you take it seriously and don't get too excited.</u> Almost all the people who have accidents are badly prepared, you see, and this gives the sport a bad name, which isn't really fair.

Interviewer: Is the excitement part of the reason why you are so keen on climbing?

Sam Hall: Only a small part of the reason, if I try to analyse it. The sense of achievement is more important, I suppose. <u>But the main thing is the sensation of being so close to nature, though perhaps that's not the right way to put it</u> ...

Interviewer: I suppose you get a view of mountains that nobody else really sees?

Sam Hall: Yes, that's very true. But at the same time, if I was dropped on the top of a mountain by helicopter, it wouldn't be the same. Less tiring, maybe, but not the same! It's knowing that you've covered the distance to the top yourself, fighting every inch of the way. <u>That's what makes you feel so pleased with yourself when you get to the summit.</u>

Interviewer: Have you always been keen on climbing?

Sam Hall: Ever since I was about 12, when my parents took me on a holiday to the Lake District, and we went walking almost every day. Suddenly, <u>it hit me that I was completely myself when I was in the hills and mountains, and I knew for certain that's what I wanted to do.</u> <u>I think perhaps everyone has a moment like that in childhood,</u> though whether you can do anything about it later in life is a different matter.

Interviewer: How did your parents feel when it became clear that you were hooked on the sport?

Sam Hall: Oh! Very anxious that I should get the proper training and experience, <u>but they've never tried to put me off.</u> They were able to support me financially, which was useful. I'm not sure that it's exactly what they would have chosen for my occupation in life, but they've never said anything.

Interviewer: I'd like to ask you about your last climb, in Peru. It was quite an adventure, wasn't it?

Sam Hall: Definitely. You see, there's a mountain there called Siula Grande, and nobody had ever climbed the west face. So there I was, with an old friend called Tony Gold. We'd done lots of climbs before, so I suppose we felt fairly sure of ourselves. <u>Which, as any experienced climber will tell you, is naturally when it can get dangerous; you make mistakes when you feel confident that you can do it.</u>

Interviewer: And what exactly happened to you?

Sam Hall: We got lost in a storm and had to spend 14 hours longer than we had planned on the mountain. Actually, in the circumstances <u>we were fortunate</u>: it could have been a great deal worse. We were told later that storms in that region can last for as much as a week at that time of the year. <u>But while we were there in sub-zero temperatures, wondering if anyone would ever find us, that's certainly not how it felt!</u>

Interviewer: Well, I'm sure we're all delighted that your adventure turned out happily in the end. Thanks for joining us, and carry on climbing!

Sam Hall: Thank you – I will!

▶▶ **PART 1**

1

I'm a keen gardener and there's nothing I enjoy more than seeing everything I've planted coming up in spring. I think it's nice to put in some early-flowering seeds as soon as winter's properly over – maybe in April so there's less chance of a late frost that you sometimes get in the earlier months of the year. You wouldn't want to leave it as late as May to do any planting if you want to see the results by <u>June, though. You should have a lovely splash of colour in the flower beds by then.</u> You may find they're a little later, depending on whether we get any warmer weather ...

2

A: George! It's so lovely to see you again! It must be ages since we last met.

B: Oh, I suppose it is. But weren't you at Michael's twenty-first party last August?

A: No, I wasn't. I got the flu at the last minute. I think the last time I saw you was three years ago in December, when we all had dinner together in that Indian restaurant ...

B: No, surely we've met since then ... Wait a minute ... <u>it was at Peter's place. When he and Jenny got married.</u>

A: Yes, of course it was! Wasn't it a fantastic reception?

B: One of the best I've ever been to.

3

I suppose the books I've tended to pick up most often are somehow romantic – not in the traditional sense but like *Time to Go* which I've read recently. It's about the lonely individual against the world, about a man's relationship with nature – it's a moving story. I used to be into mysteries in a big way – I just loved the thrill of trying to work out who'd done the crime before the detective did. I started to find the themes repetitive after a while, though. <u>I've actually gone back to my childhood favourite recently. Simple fairy tales may not seem very grown-up, but some of them are real classics.</u>

4

A: <u>I haven't played tennis for ages.</u> I'm sure you'll beat me easily.

B: We can practise for a while first, if you prefer. We shouldn't leave it so long until we play next time, since <u>it's our strongest sport.</u>

A: Sure. I'm not as fit as I should be either ... as you no doubt picked up when we played volleyball at college yesterday.

B: Well, <u>I guess no one puts their best efforts into sports they aren't so keen on.</u> By the way, are you playing in the basketball match on Saturday?

A: No. To be honest I'm thinking of giving it up. It's something I'd much rather watch than play.

B: That's a pity.

5

A: How did that sweater fit?

B: Not bad, actually, though I'm not sure about the colour. Anyway, I think I may abandon my search until another day and concentrate on what I really came in for! <u>I'm going to an important business event next week and need a shirt</u> to go with my suit as nothing I have really seems suitable. Do you have formalwear in stock?

A: Indeed we do. In fact, we have a very wide selection of formal garments, in addition to our casual range. If you follow me over to the formalwear section, I'm sure we'll be able to sort you out with just the right thing.

6

A: How's your new job, Michael? You're part of the theatre lighting team, aren't you?

B: Yeah. Tonight's the first performance I'll be involved with. I expected to be nervous about it, in case I get something wrong. Fortunately, though, the whole responsibility doesn't lie with me to get everything right, and once everything's up and running, I'll be able to enjoy it. Even if I do make one or two errors – the audience probably won't realise. I'm sure I'll be pretty tired by the end of it with all the concentration and so on. It'll be a real buzz, though – I've wanted to work in theatre for so long.

7

I'm pretty good at maths, and I've had some good results in homework projects lately. I just find it ... I don't know ... fairly easy really, which means there isn't much challenge in it for me. My teacher says I'm talented – unlike history, where I struggle to remember all the dates and stuff. I know I should take more interest in it – it just doesn't do it for me. I guess the highlight of the school day is art. That's where I really seem able to let my imagination take over – it takes my attention away from all the serious stuff we have to study for a while.

8

Now, Mr Birch, the good news is that I've been able to arrange a flight for you, getting you to Houston by Wednesday morning for the price you wanted to pay, but the bad news is that it does involve a few stopovers. You see, you first fly to Amsterdam, arriving late Tuesday morning, and then take the transatlantic flight to JFK Airport in New York, where you have to wait for about three hours for your connecting flight to your final destination, which will be coming from Los Angeles ...

TEST 3

▶▶ PART 2

Hello, my name's Tom Botham. Thanks for coming to this talk about newspaper journalism. I'll tell you a bit about how I got into it and there'll be some time at the end to ask any questions. As you know, newspaper journalists report on local and national events – everything from news and business, to culture and sport.

The usual way to become a journalist is by first gaining a qualification in journalism or writing, though these days many newspaper editors welcome people with degrees in other subjects such as economics – which is the route I took – or science. So, if you're already studying another subject like music, all is not lost. Specialising in an unrelated subject can put you in a strong position should you want to work for a specialist publication, for example.

It's difficult to get ahead in the field without having a recognised journalism certificate in addition to your university studies. In preparation for this qualification you can do a course where you'll learn the basics of news reporting and – my personal favourite – how to conduct interviews. You also need editing skills – you know, preparing copy for print.

When you're applying for a journalism role, you have to prove you can actually put pen to paper – or fingers to keyboard – and create a compelling piece that grabs the reader's attention. Potential employers will want to see your portfolio – a collection of articles you've had published. This doesn't have to be in national publications – anything you've had printed in a local magazine or paper will prove your writing ability.

There are lots of ways to get writing experience. Like me, lots of budding journalists contribute to their student magazine doing things like music reviews. My own involvement was as a film critic and my best friend wrote features on student issues. It's great fun and you make loads of good friends – and if you're lucky – some useful contacts in the industry.

Employers aren't only interested in how well you can write, though. Journalists have to be able to demonstrate evidence of other key skills such as organisation, oral communication, and an ability to work under pressure to meet deadlines. On a more personal level, you'll need to have a flexible approach, as well as persistence and motivation.

You also need to think about what else you can offer employers, especially as newspapers are now available in many formats, including online. My brother runs his own web design company and I'd been involved in that as a weekend job while I was studying. Other things, like video skills and understanding social media definitely come in useful for online publishing. My own background certainly helped me progress in my career.

I got my first job as a junior reporter on a local newspaper, which is the usual route. I won't pretend it was the most glamorous job, but it did provide me with invaluable experience and it had its perks – I regularly got to go and watch football matches, which was a real bonus. I also had to go to things like school talent shows and amateur theatre performances, which weren't quite as fascinating!

I currently work on a regional paper, which is a step up from the local one. Working on a smaller paper suits me because I have more responsibility than I would on a national paper. I get involved in all aspects of the job, from deciding what will go where, to what content to include in our daily e-newsletter. I specialise in research – my preferred aspect of the role – and also make sure our advertising copy is consistent.

There are great opportunities for career progression as a journalist. I'm definitely planning on staying in the field, though I wouldn't mind investigating other avenues. Many journalists will tell you that they want to progress to a sub-editor role and eventually land the top job as editor, something I used to want myself. In fact, I fancy trying something totally different and I'm looking into the possibilities of becoming a photographer here. But enough about me. Are there any questions?

TEST 3

▶▶ PART 3

1

I think my favourite film must be *Some Like it Hot*. It's a crazy story about two men – musicians – who pretend to be women to get away from some gangsters and join a women's orchestra. The plot may sound silly, and it's hardly what you'd call realistic, but the film is just hilarious. I've seen it four or five times and every time I see it, I just can't stop laughing. The ending fitted perfectly with the rest of the story, too. I think the director was wonderful. His name was Billy Wilder and he made some great films.

2

I thought *The Hobbit* was brilliant. Fantasy films don't usually do it for me – I prefer more realistic stuff, but I watched *The Lord of the Rings* trilogy with my brother and fell in love with the characters, so I was disappointed when it ended. This prequel's on a similar theme, so when I heard about it, there was never any doubt I'd be first in line for a ticket! <u>The actors' performances were awe-inspiring</u>, which is a good enough reason to see the film, even if it isn't really your thing. The special effects were a bit of a let-down, but the story makes up for that.

3

My favourite film? I would say *Solaris,* by the Russian director, Tarkovsky. It was never a blockbuster or a great financial success, but it's so absolutely gripping, a fascinating psychological study. I don't normally like science-fiction films, but unusually in this case I did. I put it down to the fact that <u>the effects are not used just to impress the audience; there's a reason for them</u>. I liked the actors who played the main characters as well, of course. In a way, Tarkovsky uses a futuristic setting so that we can concentrate on the story he's telling.

4

My favourite film has to be *Skyfall*. It's an action film about a spy called James Bond and follows a long series of films about the character. The theme doesn't vary that much between them but you're on the edge of your seat the whole way through as he's involved in chasing and escaping from the baddies. It all works out OK in the end, of course – <u>you know it will but you still have to watch, just to make sure</u>! That's what makes me love the films so much. I like the main actor – he makes a good James Bond I think. It's completely unrealistic, but I love it.

5

Actually, the film I like best is set in England 300 years ago. It's called *Barry Lyndon,* and it's the story of a man's life in those times. The photography is great, so it's what we call, easy on the eye,: it's lovely to watch. I suppose it really captures the way people feel and talk at any time through the history of mankind! <u>This is what makes it</u> <u>absolutely realistic</u>. I mean, you get the feeling the film is sort of universal in that sense.

 TEST 3

▶▶ PART 4

Interviewer: My guest today is Alice Barker, who has a very unusual ability. Alice, thank you for coming into the studio. What kind of unusual ability are we talking about here?

Alice Barker: Well, it's quite easy to describe. Basically, <u>when I read a word or even think of a particular word, such as Tuesday, I see a colour connected with it</u>. It's not that I imagine a colour – I really see it floating in front of my eyes. People think it sounds really weird, but it feels perfectly normal to me!

Interviewer: How interesting! Is it a sort of medical condition?

Alice Barker: Yes, and just recently doctors have begun to understand it more. They call it synaesthesia, and it means that somewhere in my brain there are links between sections that should really be separate. Synaesthesia affects different people in different ways. Some people experience tastes or smells when they hear a word, for example. <u>Apparently, it's generally passed on from parents to their children, which is the case with me. That means if I have kids, I could pass it on to them</u>.

Interviewer: And do you have brothers or sisters with the same ability?

Alice Barker: Yes, my brother is the same as me. If we start talking about it, people think we're completely crazy – in a funny way, of course! <u>When we were younger, we used to have arguments about things like what colour the word Friday was</u>. It turns out that everyone with this condition sees different colours for different things. I haven't met anyone else with synaesthesia yet, but I think we'll have some fascinating conversations if I ever do!

Interviewer: It sounds as though it could make life quite exhausting.

Alice Barker: I suppose it does, but you see, if you've never known anything different, you don't think of it like that. It does make you aware of your moods, though. I <u>know if I'm starting to feel depressed because things begin to look grey. That's pretty useful actually, as it means I can do something to cheer myself up before I feel too bad</u>!

Interviewer: Are there any other advantages to having synaesthesia, do you find?

Alice Barker: Well, it seems that quite a lot of artists and musicians have this condition, so I guess it can be beneficial if it's combined with some sort of gift or natural talent. Which is not the case with me, unfortunately! But I do find it makes reading very interesting, because <u>sometimes a sentence has a very nice range of colours, so you want to read it again just to experience that</u>. Of course, this makes me quite a slow reader.

Interviewer: When you're listening to someone, do you also see colours connected to that person's words?

Alice Barker: Yes, and that can be pretty distracting! Sometimes I hardly listen to what the other person is saying, because I'm concentrating on the colours I can see. <u>But on the whole, having this condition is not at all unpleasant</u>. At least, now I understand it. I think other people have more difficulty trying to get their heads round it than I do experiencing it.

Interviewer: Did you use to think it could be a dangerous condition?

Alice Barker: When I was a child, yes, but that was because <u>doctors used to think it was a sign of approaching mental illness</u>, so the first doctor I saw, when I was about ten, told my parents I would probably grow up to be insane! At the time there was no name for what we experienced. Now research has shown that synaesthesia is not that uncommon and it may affect one in 25,000 people. It's interesting that for some people smells, tastes or even sounds can have colours!

 TEST 4

▶▶ PART 1

1

Well, I bought this MP3 player a few months ago, and it seems to have developed a fault. <u>When I'm playing a track, suddenly, for no reason, it just stops. And before I can do anything about it, it goes on to the next song.</u> I've tried pressing stop, but that doesn't seem to help. When I start it up again, it goes back to the first track it was playing. I find it very frustrating. I hope you'll be able to fix it, or if that can't be done, then perhaps you could replace it? I'm very surprised this has happened, especially as it was so expensive!

2

A: I'm afraid this isn't what we ordered. You must have got it mixed up with another table. We wanted a mineral water and a grapefruit juice for the children, and a white coffee, no sugar for me!

B: I'm very sorry. I'll be back with your order in a minute.

A: Don't worry about the mineral water and the juice – the kids are quite happy with what they've got. But I really would like my coffee!

B: Yes of course, I'll bring it to you straight away.

A: Thank you! Oh, and could we have a couple more napkins, too? I think the children might need them ...

3

It was awful! First of all, there was some delay on the line from London, so we were late starting, and I was afraid I wouldn't get to Leeds in time. Well, I did miss the connection, but luckily, there was a train to Manchester, so I took that. And then there was a bus for the last part of the journey. I was really exhausted when I finally got there! It was even worse than my last train journey – you know the one where I was stuck in Crewe for an hour when my connection was cancelled?

4

Don't you think it's time to replace some of that old furniture you've had in your home for far too long? Well, this is your opportunity to do so without having to spend a fortune! Don't miss the sensational GFI furniture sale this Monday! Incredible reductions on all items in stock. Armchairs at an amazing half price! Sofas with up to 40 per cent reductions and double beds with 35 per cent reductions! Hurry while stocks last! GFI furniture sale starts Monday at eight o'clock sharp! Don't be late for these amazing bargains!

5

A: Could you please have a look at my car? Do you think you might be able to repair it by the end of the day today?

B: It depends what's wrong with it, doesn't it? What seems to be the trouble?

A: It starts OK, but then the motor just cuts out every time I stop, like at traffic lights. I mean, when I put the brakes on, it slows down OK, but then I have to start the engine again when I want to drive off.

B: Let's have a look at it ...

6

I've been in this business for almost 20 years now, and I have to say it's still very exciting for me. I don't regret for a moment working freelance, although in the beginning I was afraid I might get bored working from home. You hear stories, don't you, about how it just doesn't suit some people? Of course, things are totally different now I've got a lovely little office in the attic, with a new computer and my favourite software. I wouldn't dream of going back to working in a multinational company.

7

Good morning, this is Radio Kent with the latest traffic news for the M2 heading into London. Traffic is pretty heavy, especially between junctions 17 and 18, due to roadworks on the A229 which is causing a bottleneck here. Last week road widening was causing long delays between junctions 13 and 14, though I'm glad to say it has now been completed, and we're getting reports of a steady flow right up to junction 11. And this is where you should expect the longest delays. Delays up to two hours are expected between junctions 10 and 11, lasting right through until evening ...

8

Good morning, this is George MacPherson, at number 50 Regent Avenue. It's about my morning newspaper. I've been getting my *Telegraph* delivered from your shop for the last 25 years, and I really think that entitles me to a bit of service! I came downstairs first thing this morning, looking forward to having my first cup of tea and reading the paper – and what do I find on the doormat? *The Sun*! And a few days ago it was the *Daily Mirror*! This is unacceptable! I expect you to send someone round with my newspaper now!

TEST 4

▶▶ **PART 2**

Hello, my name's John Freeman, and I'm a golfer. I'm delighted to be here today in this magnificent venue to tell you all a little bit about myself and my career in what I consider to be the best sport anyone could possibly play – yes, golf!

I've been playing golf for a long time now, in fact I started about 18 years ago, even though I didn't really think about entering competitions and taking it more seriously until I was 16 or 17.

It was my dad who got me interested first of all. He used to be quite a good player himself – strictly amateur, of course, but still pretty good. Unfortunately he never really progressed any further – the really good equipment was too expensive for him, but he was always very keen on the game. He'd always watch all the international competitions on TV, but he didn't play himself for years.

You might think that with a dad like that, I'd have been very interested myself right from the start, but to tell you the truth, I wasn't much. When I was at school, I was obsessed with soccer, and my ambition was to be a professional one day. But in my mid-teens I realised I wasn't really much good at it. It was hard to give up my dream, but I knew I had to be realistic about my chances of making it.

At about the same time my dad decided to take up his old hobby again, because he was made redundant and suddenly had a lot of time on his hands. So he'd take me along with him, and I started to take more of an interest in it than I had ever done when I was younger.

Looking back, one thing that really annoys me is how teachers at my school reacted. I didn't expect advice on becoming a golfer, of course, but when I told them I wanted to practise golf and become a professional golfer one day, they all tried to put me off. I wish they'd given me a bit of encouragement, but to be honest, I don't think they knew much about the game.

That wasn't particularly surprising, I suppose, especially a few years ago – I mean, I grew up in a fairly poor part of London, and went to the local school, and everyone there thought golf was just a game for people with a great deal of money. Because that's the image golf's got, isn't it?

I think it's a little different today, but not much. I'd like to see a lot more things change. For example, I think the government should do something for young people who play golf, like allowing them to hire good quality equipment at a reasonable price. I go round schools and talk to young people about how wonderful golf is, but I do think some extra support is needed.

Having said that, one thing that really seems to be making a difference and raising the sport's profile among younger people is the huge success of some young British players these days. It doesn't take many, just a few very talented players who are an inspiration to kids all over the country.

I'm in this sport because I like it and I can make a reasonable income from it. It hasn't made me enormously wealthy, but it's given me a great deal of enjoyment over the years. I'd be delighted if I could make kids feel the sport is a possibility for them.

I'll be very happy to answer any questions you'd like to ask – but before that, I'll tell you something I'm asked about wherever I go: why did I dye my hair when I was younger? There were in fact two reasons: I thought it would show up nicely against the green on television – <u>it was blue</u>, as some of you may remember – and it was also just to show that you didn't need to look conventional to take the game seriously.

And now, if you have any questions ...

▶▶ PART 3

1

A few years ago I went cycling in Holland with my mum, dad and Alice, my sister. I hadn't really been looking forward to it; I was a teenager, and I didn't get on with my parents. As I'd expected, the things my family chose to see weren't all that interesting, and for the first couple of days I was in a really bad mood. <u>However, by the end of the first week I found myself having a good time with my parents. I wasn't a kid any more, and I felt that we were forming a friendship.</u>

2

The most unusual holiday I've ever had was before going to university, when a friend dragged me along on an archaeological dig. We were uncovering the remains of a Roman villa in Kent, and I'd somehow imagined we'd just be pottering around in the sun all day. Well, it was very hard work, but I started to feel fascinated by the whole subject of the Romans in Britain and the effect they had on our modern society. <u>The main thing I got from the holiday was the feeling that I had a better understanding of where I'd come from and who I was.</u>

3

I was just 17 when my parents agreed to let me go away with two friends on a holiday in Wales. We were staying in a youth hostel that was next to a farm with horses. I'd always wanted to try horse riding, and on the second day, we visited the farm and got talking to the farmer, and the next thing we knew <u>he'd agreed to show us how to ride. I got a great sense of achievement from that, and I'll always remember the feeling of developing a new skill.</u>

4

Well, one summer this friend from work suggested we should go camping in Scotland. I didn't know what camping was all about because my parents had never done anything like that when I was a child, but it sounded like fun. I couldn't have been more wrong! The holiday was a disaster! The weather was awful, our tent started leaking, and we got soaking wet by the rain. But somehow we kept each other's spirits up, and at the end of the camping trip <u>we felt confident that our friendship could survive anything after that.</u>

5

The year I finished school, three friends and I got those student railcards for Europe. We were looking for something different to do, and most of our classmates had decided to go camping on the coast, which we thought might be a bit boring. Anyway, it was a big mistake! We spent endless hours travelling from

one capital to the next and then went sightseeing to make the best of our holiday. After seven days we were exhausted and decided to get back. <u>I can't describe the feeling of absolute joy when I finally got home</u>!

▶▶ PART 4

Interviewer: Welcome to this week's edition of *Careers for You*. My guest on today's programme is Laura Bartlett, a successful florist. I'm sure there are many young people out there who've never considered floristry as a career. Who knows, they might be inspired by Laura's example! Laura, how did you become interested in floristry?

Laura Bartlett: <u>My parents were keen gardeners. My father used to grow rare varieties of vegetables and my mother grew orchids very successfully.</u> But it was my mother's sister who was the professional. She had a florist's shop, and when I was a kid, I'd help out at weekends. I grew up knowing quite a lot about the business.

Interviewer: So being a florist was something you'd always wanted?

Laura Bartlett: Not exactly! <u>When I was at school, I wanted to be an artist</u> but my art teacher persuaded me to train as a graphic designer instead. After college I got a job working for a magazine, but I hated being in an office all day, so I resigned. I didn't know what I was going to do. I had a number of temporary jobs. <u>And then one day, my aunt fell and broke her arm. She asked me to help out in the shop until she got better. But I liked it so much that I stayed on, and eventually took over from her when she retired.</u>

Interviewer: What exactly did you do?

Laura Bartlett: <u>At first, I did the jobs I'd done as a kid: cleaning, delivering flowers to customers, things like that.</u>

Interviewer: <u>Didn't you work with flowers at all?</u>

Laura Bartlett: <u>Well, that's a skilled job. My aunt's assistant would do the creative stuff and I'd put together simple bouquets – following her instructions.</u>

Interviewer: What kinds of skills did you need to learn?

Laura Bartlett: Lots! Fortunately, I already knew a lot about the different species and varieties of flowers available, but <u>I now had to learn how to look after them, prepare them so they lasted, wire them if necessary.</u>

Interviewer: Wire them?

Laura Bartlett: Yes. In some arrangements, flowers have to keep a certain position, and one of the ways you can make sure they do this is by twisting fine wire round their stems.

Interviewer: Oh, I see. Would you say that being a florist is a good career for a young person?

Laura Bartlett: That depends. You have to love flowers, but you must also be good with people. You see, people come into a florist's for many reasons – often they want some flowers as a gift for a birthday, perhaps they want to apologise to someone, a family member could be ill. They depend on you to help them make the right choice, so you have to take an interest. And it's not all pretty flowers. You have to get up before dawn to buy good quality flowers from the market; it's not much fun when you have to put your hands into freezing water in winter; you stand most of the day; you have to lift heavy containers; and <u>before special occasions like Mother's Day, you need to work through the night to prepare orders.</u>

Interviewer: So if any of our listeners would like to become florists, how should they go about it?

Laura Bartlett: Well, they could try getting a job at a florist's and learn the business on the job. Or they could take a course at a college. My advice would be to look for a part-time job and attend courses in floristry at the same time. That way you get a good knowledge of all aspects of the business. Because it *is a* business. If you want to run your own shop one day, you must learn how to manage a budget, run a website and keep accounts. No matter how talented you are, you will fail unless you can do all the other boring things!

TEST 5

▶▶ **PART 1**

1

Yes, I really love my job as a tour guide! Of course there are drawbacks, and though I get to see some amazing places, I also know some rather too well – sometimes you do end up wishing you could go somewhere new. My colleagues are great, though, they're the best thing really, I wouldn't still be doing this if they weren't such fun to be with. I've had some memorable meals too, not always because I liked them, though! I suppose you do learn to enjoy different things, but I'm still quite a fussy eater so I probably don't take full advantage of all the good things on offer.

2

Good evening, and welcome to a special edition of *Driving Force*, devoted this week to the issue of car security. Engineers are constantly working on the problem, but why is there an increase in the number of vehicles being stolen, despite technological advances in security systems? Can a stolen vehicle be tracked electronically? Do steering wheel locks really work? Can mechanics fit and update new security gadgets easily? With me to discuss these issues is Betty Crawford, designer of the new Vortex GT6, the car which was recently declared Car of the Year.

3

Terry, you know that report from head office we were talking about? The cost-cutting exercise? Well I have to make a few phone calls now and I wonder if you could write a few notes summarising what we discussed? You could email it to HR so they'll know what our position is on the proposed changes before Brenda talks to head office. It needs doing straight away because I know she's in meetings from ten today, and I'd like to make sure our views are taken into account. If you could get on with that now, that would be great.

4

A: Wasn't that great? I really enjoyed it!

B: Yes, what an evening! I really hadn't expected to enjoy myself so much.

A: Oh good, I hoped you'd like it. I read some very good reviews of it on the internet, and those people I met at the party – you know, the ones I was telling you about this afternoon – well, they'd been and they said they'd loved it.

B: Well, I'm very glad you insisted on going. I expected it to be really boring, but it was one of the most exciting plays I've ever seen!

5

My Aunt Maud was rather a rebel for her time. She grew up in the early part of the twentieth century, when women weren't really expected to have any profession. At the time, the common belief in upper middle-class families was that girls couldn't have a career in show business, so her parents were absolutely furious when she told them she had enrolled at drama school and was leaving home! I think they were relieved when her younger brother became a lawyer. And her older brother was a doctor, so that was fine too!

6

A: Amanda, I got Mum's birthday present, but are you sure she's going to like it? A guide to Italy?

B: But it's a guide to the cooking in different parts of the country. You know how Mum likes to experiment with dishes, and she's been getting really keen on Italian cooking.

A: Ah – so she can read about the cooking and then try out the dishes on us.

B: That's right; there's a recipe section in the back. She'll love it! And we can watch that film you have about Italy when we all have time to sit down together!

7

Good evening, ladies and gentlemen, and welcome to Gallery Multiplex. Please check your tickets for the start times of the films, and make sure you go to the right section of the cinema. This evening we have *Crow's Nest* just starting in Screen 1, and at 18.45 *Hurricane* starts in Screen 7. In just over 20 minutes, at 18.55, *Racing Fever* begins in Screen 6, and at the same time *Details of the Fall* starts in Screen 5. Don't forget you can buy soft drinks and snacks in the foyer. We hope you have a very enjoyable evening.

8

I'm a professional ballet dancer, so I'm usually pretty careful about the kind of physical work I do away from rehearsals. I know it was a very stupid thing to do, but one day I needed to change the light bulb, and the ladder I used looked quite stable ... I was just reaching my arm up to the bulb when it collapsed. All of a sudden, there I was on the ground! I'd never realised back pain could be so awful! Eventually, I painfully pulled myself to my feet and called an ambulance ... It's taken me a while to get myself fit enough for dancing again.

TEST 5

▶▶ **PART 2**

Good morning to you all. Thank you for attending this press conference. My name is David Barns and I'm director of Shopright Contractors, the company that will be constructing the new shopping mall. I'll begin with some practical information. As you know, construction is set to begin next month, so I'd like to start by talking about when we expect building to finish and about the overall costs of the project. I'm going to stick my neck out and say we'll meet the original targets, which is to have the mall open by July next year. I think that's entirely manageable judging by the progress we've been making so far, which is thanks to the builders and design team working closely together.

As for the costs, well, again our estimate was £12 billion, and I'm pretty confident the final cost will not exceed that. I'd be happy to discuss further financial implications later on, if you could save any questions till the end.

I'd like to move on now to our investors. What can they expect to get for the kind of money they're putting into the project?

What is it that's going to make this place special? What will attract customers to the mall? Well, lots of things! <u>For a start, there's a new railway station being built right next door</u>, so people will be able to reach us from the city centre in under 20 minutes.

<u>Of course, we need to provide parking space for those who'll be driving to visit us. The underground car park we've designed has room for 3,000 vehicles</u>, and we're just off the motorway, too, which will mean easy access for customers living up to 100 kilometres from the mall. On top of that, we've put a great deal of thought into how to make shopping easier for families with small children. <u>One excellent idea we have is to provide nurseries – three of them, in fact</u> – so people can leave toddlers in the completely safe hands of qualified staff while they do their shopping. This means the kids are happy and the adults are content in the knowledge that their children are being well looked after.

It goes without saying that we'll have the usual wide range of shopping facilities, from clothing and footwear to furniture and food, but we also intend to offer a range of other attractions in order to persuade customers to shop here.

Indeed, we've put a huge amount into providing those other attractions. <u>There's a fairground in one corner of the mall</u>, which is aimed at providing a bit of fun for visitors. For people who aren't actually shopping, we have some other fun things on offer. For example, <u>we have seven cinemas showing a good range of modern films, including the latest releases</u>. That should suit our younger visitors but we've also come up with an idea for the older generation – in one of the cinemas <u>we'll show classic films – from 40 or 50 years ago – twice a day, morning and afternoon</u>. We're confident that these facilities will make the mall suitable for people of all ages to enjoy together.

As you'll have read in our earlier press statement, we're also planning to make our shopping mall 'greener'. Let me tell you a bit more about what I mean by that. People have become very demanding and prefer malls to have an open, airy atmosphere. <u>So, we're planning to have walkways between the different buildings, with flowers lining the paths</u>, giving the impression that you're actually outdoors. <u>And we're building a Nature Centre, where we'll have a permanent exhibition about the ecology of the area</u>. We're going to have models, photographs and displays to inform people about the wildlife of the local area. So, you see, it isn't simply a mall, but a day out for the whole family.

I'm going to wrap things up there, but before we finish, I'd be happy to answer any questions you might have about the project. Who would like to go first?

▶▶ PART 3

1

I'd always been desperate to work in the film industry but I knew directors' jobs were hard to come by and jobs are rarely advertised. I went to loads of free networking events – with no success. Trying to get through to film companies on the phone was a waste of time, and there was little chance of managing to contact anyone influential directly. As with most things, it's who you know that matters – and <u>I was fortunate enough to meet someone based at a TV studio</u>. In the end he put in a good word for me and I eventually got my first directing role on a low-budget TV film.

2

I work as an insurance sales executive. It's by no means the most glamorous of jobs and is something I never thought I'd end up doing, but anyway, it keeps a roof over my head! After school I applied for anything I saw advertised and I got a job in this insurance company as an office junior, doing all the mundane stuff. <u>I slowly climbed the ladder and got to where I am today – I had a really encouraging manager who saw my potential and pushed me forward</u>. The work's satisfying in its own way and my colleagues are great – I've developed a good social life with them outside work, too.

3

I'm a web developer and design websites for all kinds of businesses in my local area. It can be difficult starting out after school as most employers want experience and most people don't have any – unless they've done a bit of work experience for free or something. That wasn't the case with me – I got my job through simple determination. I used to call companies all the time but I never got through to the manager, <u>until one day she answered herself and offered me the job on the spot</u>. There's little chance of promotion in this line of work, but I'd like to run my own company one day.

4

I've always been creative and did a degree in jewellery design. During my course, I did a work placement in a top design company which I was absolutely thrilled about, even though I didn't get paid. I approached them after I'd finished my studies but there were no vacancies, so I had to start looking elsewhere. I then started selling my creations to my friends who loved my stuff. <u>It was one of them who put me in touch</u> with the creative director of a small jewellery shop, who was looking for new suppliers. Fortunately, my stuff was a huge success with customers and I'm now manager of my own company.

5

It was tough changing careers after a lengthy period as a teacher, and I spent hours on the phone to various marketing companies asking whether they had any openings. I also used social media sites or asked friends if they'd heard of anything. I'd almost given up the idea of working in the field until I remembered about some short-term work I'd done years previously at a small advertising company. So, <u>I drove to see the director and managed to get an appointment with him straightaway</u>. I was pleased I'd taken the chance as they needed someone to start immediately. It was a case of right time, right place.

▶▶ PART 4

Interviewer: Today on *Mind Matters* I'm talking to Dr Ann Winters, an expert on human memory. Ann, welcome to the programme. Now, I suppose the first question everyone would ask is: what exactly is the human memory?

Ann Winters: Well, like so many apparently 'easy' questions, the answer isn't very simple at all! Basically, the human memory is a compartment in our brain, where we store images, rather like the hard drive in a computer – though we can't confirm the brain's limitations yet in terms of available storage space! <u>Like a hard drive, however, our memories can become infected by viruses or even wiped out by accidents</u>. But the comparison breaks down when we consider that we can train our memories to expand and work better – which computers can't manage ... yet!

Interviewer: When you talk about memory being infected, do you mean by a disease?

Ann Winters: Yes. For instance, people suffering from a physiological disease like Alzheimer's forget things that happened in the past and they also forget how to perform straightforward tasks, like tying their shoelaces. This is of course, frustrating for both sufferers and care-givers alike. It can also be extremely difficult for family members who are no longer recognised by patients.

Interviewer: Yes, indeed. But is there anything that can be done for sufferers?

Ann Winters: Well, the good news is that brain exercises can keep the brain young. Research has shown that people who were more successful in education, and have more mentally active jobs, have a lower risk of developing the disease. It's quite a startling discovery, actually, and one that fascinates me.

Interviewer: Yes, that's certainly very interesting. So, how can someone exercise their brain – by thinking a lot?

Ann Winters: In a way, yes! Everyone has times where they feel overwhelmed because there are too many things to remember to do and something inevitably gets forgotten. But you can practise using your memory, which not only exercises your brain but also improves your ability to remember things. Unfortunately, a lot of devices in modern life are designed to make sure we don't forget things, which can make our brain more idle and weaken our memory.

Interviewer: Would you give us examples of how to exercise our memory?

Ann Winters: Sure. There's a very simple technique, although it works better for some people than for others. Whatever you want to remember, think of a physical thing it reminds you of. If I want to remember a date from history – let's say 1066, the date of the Battle of Hastings – I might think that 'battle' reminds me of 'bottle'. So I think of a bottle with the number 1066 written on the label, and I just picture that bottle in detail in my mind.

Interviewer: Why is it easier to remember a physical thing than a sentence such as 'the Battle of Hastings was in 1066'?

Ann Winters: Because our brains are better at recalling pictures than abstract thought. That's why I said it works better for some people than for others; some people are particularly good at seeing pictures in their minds – visualising ideas – and they are the ones that can remember things best using this technique.

Interviewer: Is there anything else we can do to protect our brains?

Ann Winters: You simply have to exercise your brain regularly with new, enjoyable and interesting activities, like learning a new language or playing a new computer game. One of the most successful activities – though it doesn't appeal to everyone – is doing crosswords, which makes the brain more efficient.

Interviewer: I'll bear that in mind! Ann Winters, thanks very much for taking the time to be with us today.

Ann Winters: You're very welcome.

TEST 6

▶▶ **PART 1**

1

I know the film is supposed to be fantastic, but normally I wouldn't bother going to see one like that. I mean, this isn't the kind of film that usually appeals to me. The story is based on a book by Hemingway that we're reading in class this term, and I thought that watching the film would make the book clearer to me, so I think I'll go next weekend. I don't think any of my friends have seen it, so I'll see if any of them would like to come with me.

2

I don't know what the problem was. This wasn't the bottleneck you get when you come off the motorway, and anyway we were travelling towards London, not away from it. I must have been stuck there for over an hour, hardly moving at all, feeling frustrated and anxious that I wouldn't make it in time. I mean it's not as if there was any other way of getting there, so I had to just hope for the best. It took me two hours to reach the airport, although it was only a couple of miles away!

3

It really was a lovely surprise. I thought she was thinking of getting me something else, because she'd asked me what sort of earrings I liked, so I wasn't expecting a dress – and such a lovely one, too! I think the colour really suits me – she's an artist, you know, and she says she's going to paint me in it, and give it to me when she's finished! Isn't that exciting? It was so nice of her to make the effort. It's obvious she'd put a lot of thought into it, you know. And of course, I'm delighted. Let me get it, and you can see for yourself!

4

I thought it was going to be a big mistake, when he got that transfer from Liverpool. They'd been going through a bad patch these last two seasons, but they were a good team and I thought he should have stayed. Anyway, it turns out I was dead wrong! He's been getting better and better since he signed with Arsenal, and he scored a hat-trick in the last match! Now I wonder whether Birmingham will try to sign him next season because I've heard they're very interested in him at the moment.

5

A: Good morning. Do you have any tickets left for this evening's performance?

B: Let me just have a look. Well, the rear stalls and circle are completely sold out. There are a few seats left in the front stalls. How many tickets do you want?

A: Just two.

B: Yes, I can give you two in the third row … they're £39 each.

A: £39? I see. All right, I'll take them.

B: That makes a total of £78. I'll have to ask you to pick them up here by 6.30. And your name is … ?

6

News travels fast in a small village, I suppose, so everyone seemed to know before I got there that I'd be teaching at the local school. Whether that made the villagers more formal in the way they treated me – for the first few months at least – I really don't know. I gathered from the way they spoke that they regarded me as quite foreign because I came from London, and this did startle me for a while. It's different now, however, I'm pleased to say, and I've made quite a few friends …

7

It was an interesting decade, not least as far as music and fashion were concerned. It was a time of wild enthusiasm, but also laid the basis for the future. The 1920s were the dawn of our modern age, when people were still looking back at the previous century. We've recently displayed furniture and paintings from the 1940s and '50s, but you'll see that this is very different. Don't miss the Central Museum's special exhibition. It starts on Monday and will run until after the summer holidays. In fact it will be on until October 15th. Don't miss it!

8

A: I thought the last bit was really great, didn't you?

B: Yes. I'd never have guessed what was going to happen; I mean, everyone thought Molly was miles away on an expedition to Antarctica, and then she walks into the room right at the end, except it's not Molly at all – it's her twin sister!

A: Right! You know, that's what makes some soap operas really great – you just have to watch the next episode to find out how it all works out! My mum's always telling me they're a load of rubbish, and that I should watch things like documentaries instead. And then she'll sit down and watch a quiz show!

▸▸ **PART 2**

Good afternoon, my name's Graham Jones. I'm glad to be here this afternoon and to see so many of you. Thank you for coming. One of the most interesting developments in the toy market has been the revival of interest in that most traditional of toys: train sets. In the 1980s and 1990s, people felt that models of all sorts, and especially railways, were unfashionable, but they have become big business in the last few years.

In Britain there has always been a strong interest in railways, as can be seen from the number of people who go 'train spotting' – collecting information about locomotives and train movements. People are happy to stand outdoors in the cold for hours on end in the hope of seeing an engine or even just a carriage that they haven't seen before, and noting down the serial number. It must be one of the most uncomfortable hobbies in the world! But this interest does help explain why Britain is the largest model railway market in Europe.

Modern train sets are introducing children, who may never have travelled by real train, to the joys of railway modelling. Model trains are more lasting than other toy equipment, their quality is superb and that has added to their popularity with both parents and children. And many parents think model railways are a healthier indoor alternative to computers and videogames.

Market research has been done to see what sort of people the hobby appeals to. Interestingly, the majority of purchasers of model railway equipment today are adults, not children. By that I don't mean that parents buy model railways for their children, although obviously this happens a great deal. I'm talking about people who are willing to spend a lot of money on miniature locomotives and re-live part of their childhood. More detailed analysis into the people who buy this equipment has also proved interesting. Many model trains are bought by middle-aged men, with a large proportion of lawyers, bankers and business executives.

Of course, we need to plan for the future, and make as many predictions as we can based on what we know. It seems reasonable to assume that children will always have a natural interest in models and miniature versions of real-life objects like toy cars and aeroplanes.

Model railway manufacturers are always trying to maximise their sales and come up with new ideas, and they're

experimenting with toy trains aimed directly at girls. But despite their best efforts, one aspect of the market for these items is likely to remain the same: boys will probably continue to find these toys far more appealing than girls do.

Of course manufacturers are also keen to expand outside countries like the UK where there is already a demand for their products. They are investing in new markets in countries in Asia, for example, where there isn't the same traditional interest in railways.

Researchers and marketing specialists believe that there is a lot of potential in these markets, and manufacturers will be taking part in international toy fairs to promote their model trains. It's exciting to think that their products may soon be available – and selling well, we hope – all over the world! There is plenty of work for designers, too, as railway buildings are different all over the world and the models are always incredibly accurate. Many people spend as much money on the miniature stations as they do on the actual trains.

Model railways are becoming more up to date, too. Computer-controlled model railways are available in the toy market now, and of course who knows what the future holds? As long as there are trains, there will be model railways!

▸▸ **PART 3**

1

I went to a private school where it was compulsory to wear a uniform. The school had sent out a list to parents of the items you had to have – school tie, blazer, cap – and the shops where you could find them all before the term started. My mother went on a business trip and didn't manage to go shopping. I was the only one from about 50 11-year-old boys who didn't have a cap or tie. I felt very awkward dressed in a pair of jeans and sweater ...

2

I remember being very nervous as I was walking into the school, because I thought I wouldn't know anyone at all, which might have been a bit frightening. I didn't fancy having to spend the first few days getting used to a new place all on my own. And then I spotted my cousin, Peter, who was two years older than me. I expected that he wouldn't want to have anything to do with me, but unlike some kids that age, he was very nice, showed me round and helped me settle in.

3

When my mother offered to drive me to school, I suppose I should have known that this could be a bad idea because she's always had the most awful sense of direction. And sure enough, she got lost, and it took us ages to find the school. I will never forget how embarrassed I felt when I walked into the first class half an hour after it had started. Awful! After that, things improved. It wasn't a very big school, so I soon found my way around. And I made new friends quite easily, too.

4

I know it may sound unlikely, but I didn't experience any feeling of anxiety. I was confident that everything was going to be fine. I felt optimistic being surrounded by the familiar faces of friends from primary school. My most vivid memory is the warm welcoming speech of Mr Stephens, our headteacher.

I don't recall feeling stressed or lonely. And I was actually pleased there was a uniform, unlike some of my friends who complained about it. I thought it was much easier than having to decide what to wear every morning!

5

My strongest memory from my first day at high school is simply feeling terribly alone and sad. We moved house at just about the time I was due to go to high school, so I ended up going to a new school two weeks after the term had begun. It's not a long time, but it was long enough for all the other new boys to have made friends with each other, so I really had the impression that I was never going to fit in. Of course, I soon made friends and settled down, but the first few days were rather difficult.

TEST 6
FIRST

▶▶ **PART 4**

Interviewer: Hello, Mark, thank you for agreeing to talk to us about your experience of being a student at Gramwell University. I'm sure many of our listeners will be thinking of applying next year, and they'll be very interested in what you have to say!

Mark Stone: Thanks, it's great to be here.

Interviewer: First of all, why did you choose Gramwell University?

Mark Stone: Well, no one in my family had been to university before, and my parents couldn't really help me decide. My mother hoped I'd live at home while I was a student, but I really wanted to go to a different city, and make new friends. And Gramwell is really one of the best places in the country for law, so that's why I went for it.

Interviewer: Was there anything that particularly surprised you when you arrived at Gramwell?

Mark Stone: Yeah, I hadn't actually realised before I came here how different many things would be. It may sound silly, I know, but I hadn't actually spent more than a few hours here – when I came on an open day – before arriving at Gramwell as a student. Of course the buildings are all very modern, but I knew that. I just wasn't prepared for how different everything would feel, you know – most people are my age, so it's all quite exciting. It rains as much as it always did at home, though!

Interviewer: And what's it like, studying law?

Mark Stone: People told me before I started that I'd find it very stressful. It hasn't been too bad, though – I've really enjoyed the challenge. Don't get me wrong, there's a lot of work involved, especially just before a deadline! But the more you put in, the better you do, and as long as you're well organised, which I am – I think I get that from my mother – then it's OK.

Interviewer: Do you have a part-time job?

Mark Stone: Yes, I share a flat with three other students, and I need to pay the rent! It's OK though, it makes a change from the library and the people I work with are cool. It is quite tiring though, especially when I've been studying all day – I'm a waiter in a busy restaurant, so it certainly keeps me fit!

Interviewer: I'm sure it does! And what are your lecturers like? Are they helpful?

Mark Stone: I must admit I was a bit scared of them when I first arrived. You know, I thought 'Why on earth would they want to talk to someone like me?'. In fact most of them are very interested in how their students are getting on. The problem is that students usually don't take advantage of the opportunities they have to talk to them. They have times every week when you can go and see them. Even outside of those hours, it's usually quite easy to find them and they won't mind at all.

Interviewer: Do you mainly mix with other law students?

Mark Stone: I have some very good friends here in the law faculty, but because I lived in a big student residence in my first year, I met people doing all sorts of courses. It was nice not to talk about law for a change! One of my best friends is reading history, and I'm sharing a flat with him, as well as a biologist and a drama student!

Interviewer: Sounds fun! And what's the social life like at Gramwell?

Mark Stone: There are lots of societies, and good sports facilities – there's even a skateboarding club! I've made friends that way too – I'm in the basketball team – and as long as you don't let it take up too much of your time, it's a really good way of unwinding and forgetting about work for a while. And then when I get back to my desk, I'm definitely more focused. I know some people think we just spend all our time at parties, but that's not actually the case.

Interviewer: Well, thanks, Mark, it's been great talking to you. Good luck with your studies!

Mark Stone: Thank you!

TEST 7
FIRST

▶▶ **PART 1**

1

A: Are you looking forward to the music class tomorrow? Remember some professional musicians are coming to do a drumming workshop with us.

B: Oh, yeah, I'd forgotten about that. I've never done any drumming before. It's not that I mind having a go, and I suppose it's not too technical, but aren't we supposed to be giving a performance for the rest of the school at the end of it? I'm not really into getting up on stage in front of everyone – I could totally mess it up.

A: Don't worry! It's new for all of us and no one will expect us to be perfect – it's all about having fun!

2

A: How was your shopping trip?

B: Well, I wasn't looking for anything myself as I'd got that new coat last week, but I'd promised Mum I'd help her find an outfit for the wedding she and Dad are going to. I knew it was a bad idea – not because of Mum, of course, but because I knew I wouldn't be able to resist treating myself once we got into town. Which is why I'd actually given myself a small budget, despite what I spent last time. Anyway, it ended up being a successful trip – Mum got a really nice suit and I came back with a cool pair of earrings!

3

I got a sports car as soon as I could afford it, and it wasn't really very economical, but I decided I could live with that. However, after a few weeks I got a job further away from home, and I realised it was the wrong car for long journeys; it was too noisy, there wasn't enough leg room, the suspension was broken and you could feel every bump in the road. That's why I decided to sell it. I've still got to get from A to B, though, and I've got my eye on something at the car showroom. I'm going to go and test drive it later.

4

Hello, I wonder if you could help me? I'm in room 447 – I just checked in this morning – and there seems to be something wrong with the radiators – they won't come on, so it's very cold in here. I tried turning the control knob, but it simply won't move. Could you send someone to have a look at it, please? Oh, and could you tell me how to operate the TV? I've been trying to follow the instructions for the control but I seem to be doing something wrong. Everything else seems fine – I had a problem with getting the door to lock but I've worked it out!

5

A: So how many kids from your class are going on this trip?
B: Practically everyone's going, Dad! We go on a guided tour of the city, including the Eiffel Tower and a boat trip on the Seine, and then we're back in London by Sunday afternoon, so I'll be home early on Sunday night.
A: Oh, I have no doubt the activities will be worthwhile. Paris is a lovely city and it's not the expense that's bothering me either – I just want to make sure you have enough supervision and won't be spending all day wandering about on your own.
B: You're kidding! Every minute of our time is going to be organised!

6

As soon as we took off, the basket started swaying from side to side, which took a while to get used to, but it was no major concern, really. Apart from the slight creaking that caused, there wasn't a sound to be heard. After doing quite a bit of flying in commercial planes, I think that's what stunned me most about this flight. Drifting along with the wind helped me chill out – I got real peace of mind knowing there was nothing to do but sit back! I think it made one or two of the other passengers a bit nervous, but the operator had everything perfectly in order.

7

A: Have you heard about high intensity training? There was a programme on about it last night.
B: You mean the regime where you just do three minutes of exercise a week and that's supposed to be enough to keep you fit? I can't see how that could possibly work, do you?
A: I had my doubts about it initially – though the scientist on the programme did a good job of explaining things. Cycling as fast as you can for three minutes must be exhausting!
B: Do you really think so? It can't be too challenging to do three minutes a week, can it?
A: I guess it wouldn't be too hard to keep up.

8

I remember the magazine used to come out on Fridays, and every Friday after school I'd race round to the newsagent's and buy a copy, and then spend all evening reading it. It was aimed at girls exactly like me; it gave you ideas how to choose accessories, how to wear make-up and had information about the latest trends in fashion. The only thing it didn't have was interviews with pop stars and free posters! I sent in a story once that I'd written for it – I was convinced it'd get published as I thought it was a great story. I never heard anything back from them, though!

TEST 7

▶▶ **PART 2**

Thank you everyone for attending this presentation about the new college. My name's Linda Brown and I'm the director of the college. I'd like to start with some basic information. We're planning on holding the opening ceremony on April 21st with a view to starting summer classes on June 15th. That gives us enough time in between to make any last-minute improvements and adds a bit of extra time to the schedule, just in case.

It's hard to say at this moment exactly how many students are likely to enrol for the summer school, but there's certainly been a lot of interest, especially after the series of adverts we did on the radio. We were confident those would be more effective than TV promotions as people tend to change channels in the breaks between programmes – less likely on the radio, we thought. So, I would hope we'll have plenty of people signing up for courses through that.

We're hoping to attract some useful publicity at the opening ceremony, and our marketing director has been working very hard on this. We thought it was important to request the services of someone who works within the community to declare the college officially open, and who could be better than the mayor? We're pretty pleased he's agreed as he's proving to be very popular in the town.

We've also invited a number of other local figures to get involved. We're thrilled to announce that the footballer Harry Watson, who comes from the area, has agreed to stand up and give a short talk – we're hoping he'll be a popular draw! We've also asked along a number of business investors and other VIPS from the area.

The aim of the opening is to get local people signing up for courses – we plan to do that by involving them in all sorts of ways. For instance, as far as possible, we're going to have local experts giving classes here instead of academics who have little connection with the area. We'll have the chief accountant from a local business teaching accountancy classes – that kind of thing.

We've decided to place importance on practical subjects at this college, to attract students who may not be interested in a more theoretical kind of course. Basically, we're hoping to get students who are keen on developing their skills – perhaps people who are already working. We've taken a very flexible approach about the students we're going to accept. Many people who don't come out of school with the best grades may well have ended up in jobs they don't really enjoy. These people have a great deal of potential and many of them would relish the opportunity to study – we want them to enjoy the benefits of studying at a higher level, and we're prepared to give them the chance to do so.

Our admissions policy will be to accept students who didn't have the qualifications required for entry into more established colleges. We're pretty sure a lot of young people will be tempted to enrol. We want to attract people who wouldn't normally think about enrolling for higher education.

Something else we believe will boost numbers is our newly-opened applications office right in the middle of the town to create interest. We think it's a great idea to provide visibility for the college, rather than people having to go out of their way to reach the registrations office here at the college itself.

In addition, should members of the public require further information about the college, they can visit our website for a full description of what we do. That's where you can also ask for a brochure with all the details supplied online to be sent directly to your home. I'll give you more information about that a little later on but for now, does anyone have any questions so far?

▶▶ **PART 3**

1
I've only been there a couple of times with my husband, who's a diplomat. I must say the pace of life there is rather hectic. Although it may sound rather trivial, what appeals to me most about the city are the absolutely fantastic department stores! I have to be very careful when I go there not to overspend. I love the green spaces, too – where you can chill out away from the crowds on the street and re-energise yourself after an afternoon of sightseeing before you hit the restaurants later in the evening. Yes, New York is definitely one of my most favourite cities in the world.

2
New York's a dynamic place, full of interesting characters and places to go. I love people-watching and seeing people from every corner of the globe. I guess what really does it for me are the opportunities to try cuisine from all over the world, which I can't get at home as I live in a small village which is pretty traditional. New York caters for every taste and I really look forward to the evening after a day spent walking from one end of the city to another to see the various sights. It's a huge city, but it's a fun place and the people are so friendly.

3
Well, for me the attraction of a city is its inhabitants. In New York the fact that the people there are from such different cultural backgrounds makes it a really exciting place to be. I think you have to have a sense of humour to get by as a tourist in New York. It's a big place to navigate and you're bound to end up heading in the wrong direction away from the museum you wanted to visit and going towards the central shopping district instead! Not that there's anything wrong with shopping – or sitting down for a good meal afterwards in one of the superbly-located restaurants.

4
I'm not so keen on some aspects of big city life, but I do enjoy the facilities that only big cities have to offer. In artistic terms, New York is absolutely splendid, with a wide variety of exhibitions and a very active cultural life. That's the best thing about the city for me. The buildings are magnificent of course and there's a wide range of activities for people of any age, I can see that. There's certainly a lot of life in the streets, though I'm not really a big walker and prefer to use public transport to get around between sights or shops.

5
I love New York. I remember being just stunned by the skyscrapers and that magical view of the Statue of Liberty the first time I visited ... Now I've been there a few times, I think what I like most is the dry wit of the people there. It's that clever type of humour you get in big cities where people live together in a crowded place. Sitting on a bench watching the locals go about their daily routine is fascinating – well, I say locals but there are people in New York from all over the world. I'm not a big shopper, but I find some of the gift shops amusing.

▶▶ **PART 4**

Interviewer: This morning, we've got Ray Garrett in the studio. Ray, how did you become a professional deep-sea diver?

Ray Garrett: Well, when I left school, I got a job in a lawyer's office, and by the time I was 25, I'd worked my way up to the position of office manager. I was good at my job, and it never occurred to me to leave or do something else. When our company was bought out and the local office closed, I started thinking about other jobs. I'd always been interested in scuba-diving, as a hobby, and just about that time I saw an advert in a magazine. A company was looking for people to train as divers, so I put my name down for it.

Interviewer: You were still living at home with your parents at that point. What did they think of your career change?

Ray Garrett: When I told my parents about what I was planning to do, my mother wasn't at all keen; in fact, she and my dad didn't believe I'd last the three months' training! Scuba-diving doesn't take great physical strength or unusual exercise tolerance. All it takes is the desire, plus some basic classroom and in-water instruction.

Interviewer: So, tell us more about the work you do.

Ray Garrett: Well, a qualified diver can safely remain underwater for anywhere from a few minutes to over two hours. Most of the work I do now isn't very dangerous – or very exciting! My job involves working on ships that have to be repaired, so we're not even very deep under water.

Interviewer: What are the risks as far as accidents are concerned in your profession?

Ray Garrett: Working underwater can be dangerous if you don't take the necessary precautions and especially if we need to go right down to the sea bed, perhaps to do some work on a shipwreck. People have accidents when they stop thinking about the dangers facing them in their job, and I never do that. I never exceed the time limit of my dives, which depends on various parameters like depth, rate of air consumption, and the profile of any dives I have done in the previous six to twelve hours.

Interviewer: And what are you working on currently?

Ray Garrett: At the moment we're doing quite an exciting job: exploring an old wreck! We're working off the coast of America, examining a ship on the sea bed that sank almost 150 years ago! I absolutely love this kind of work and I never fail to be amazed not only at the wreck itself but at the sea life around it.

Interviewer: Tell me more about the wreck itself. It was a ship called the SS Union, right?

Ray Garrett: Exactly. She was travelling from the northern states of America to the south in the mid- to late-eighteen hundreds. For a long time, nobody knew where the shipwreck was, but a team from the University of New Orleans found it last year, using some new sonar equipment. The ship is supposed to have a lot of gold on board – although we haven't actually found any yet.

Interviewer: We'll keep our fingers crossed for you! Finally, what are the effects of deep-sea diving on the body?

Ray Garrett: Well, the work itself is absolutely fascinating, but the body can be affected in several ways, For example, problems of diving at such depth include de-compression sickness, air embolism, hypothermia and physical exhaustion. On top of that, the ship can break up at any time, which means that you run the risk of being trapped inside. A couple of days ago I had a lucky escape when part of the shipwreck fell, and that's the sort of thing that can really cause problems for divers. Still, it's a great profession!

Interviewer: Ray Garrett, thank you very much.

 TEST 8

▶▶ **PART 1**

1

A: What would have been your dream job if you hadn't become an accountant?

B: I'd have been a professional musician. I grew up playing the cello and I loved performing. I couldn't think of a more rewarding job when I was at college.

A: So, why didn't you follow your instinct?

B: It was hugely competitive trying to get a place in one of the big orchestras – and to me, if I couldn't play with the best, there was no point. It's not that I think I made the wrong decision, though I wouldn't mind doing something a bit more inspiring. Re-training is so expensive though, and what I do has its rewards.

2

It's odd looking back on the formative experiences of your life. My decision to study French at university was based purely on the fact that I'd been on a school trip to Paris when I was a kid, and I was absolutely enchanted by the city. I'd never previously intended to study French, or become a translator or use the language for work. In fact, my parents were keen for me to follow in my father's footsteps and study economics. But they're proud of my language abilities now, and can see it was the right thing for me to do.

3

Acupressure is an ancient Chinese healing method that involves applying pressure to certain parts of the body to relieve pain. It relaxes muscular tension and balances the vital forces of the body. Acupressure can provide relief from head, neck and shoulder aches, promote healing, and some people say it can even stop you catching colds – though I can't say there's any scientific evidence for that as far as I know. I'll be happy to demonstrate a few techniques in a moment. I just need a couple of volunteers. Thank you, please come and sit here while I …

4

Oh, I think it'll be brilliant playing Marsha! It's a fantastic character part, it really is! You see, my son in the play robs a bank, and the funny part about the whole thing is that his wife is the manager of the bank. He doesn't realise it at first because she's only just been promoted, and she wanted it to be a surprise for him, so she was going to tell him that night. But then he goes in, robs the place and has a taxi waiting for him to get him away from the scene! It's a comedy of course, and I can't wait for the opening night.

5

A: That was a useful class. I've always struggled to remember new words in German.

B: The association technique made a lot of sense – where you write down words you know with similar meanings.

A: It takes ages though.

B: Well, that's a fair point. I still think I'd prefer it to memorisation – just repeating a word until it sticks – totally uninteresting.

A: I've never minded that, but what I found most helpful was the picture technique – where you relate the sound of the new word to something you know in your own language and think of a picture to represent it.

B: That wouldn't work for me – I don't have a good enough imagination!

6

Good evening ladies and gentlemen, this is your captain speaking. I hope you're enjoying the flight. We'll shortly start making our descent into Brussels, where we'll refuel before continuing with the next leg of our journey. The skies are lovely and clear this evening which means that in a few minutes' time you'll be able to see the lights of the port of Rotterdam over to your right if you look out of the window. The bright lights you can currently see to your left are in Amsterdam. No doubt many of you have already enjoyed visiting the city. So, please sit back and enjoy the rest of the flight.

7

I've just started dancing – something I never thought I'd do in a million years! But there've been so many of these dance series on TV, I just thought it might be worth a go. The Latin dances are the ones that really appeal to me, so I booked myself onto a course of salsa lessons. The first class didn't go quite as expected. For some reason, I just thought I'd be a natural, which turned out to be pretty far from the truth. I've got two left feet and my coordination was terrible! I came away feeling slightly disappointed but I'm determined to do better next time. Watch this space!

8

A: Nick, have you read that new book by Zach Park – you know, that brilliant science-fiction writer? I think it really deserves to be called a masterpiece.

B: You mean *Green Apples*? Yes, I have read it, actually, and I enjoyed it a lot. I'm a big fan of Zach Park. I've read all his novels and collections of short stories, and I think this is his best novel so far. Do you know he's also written several film scripts, including *The Track and All About You*?

A: It doesn't surprise me. He's extremely talented.

TEST 8

▶▶ **PART 2**

Hello everybody, my name's Anne England. Thanks for turning up to listen to me talk about my career as a nurse this evening. I hope that some of you will decide to take up nursing in the future, because it really is a fantastic job. First of all, I'll tell you a little bit about how I got started.

I had no idea what I wanted to do, at least that was the case until I was about 14 when I was listening to a family conversation – I was supposed to be doing my homework, but my sister and I always left the door open so we could hear our parents chatting next door. Anyway, my cousin was talking to my dad, and telling him all about how much she enjoyed her work – she was a nurse in a busy hospital – and I thought: yeah, that's exactly what I'd like to do!

When I told my teachers that's what I'd decided, they were very encouraging. But they did say that although I was pretty good at school, and always got good marks in English and biology, I'd have to get a little better at maths or I wouldn't be able to do the job well.

I must say being a student nurse involved a great deal of hard work, and lots of late nights staying up to do my coursework, but I'd known it would be like that. <u>What was a surprise, though, was that there were so many parties</u>, too!

But we did have to study plenty of different subjects – there are so many things that are relevant to nursing, and we covered most of them on our course. Some of the <u>projects</u> we had to do were really demanding, and there were a lot of them. <u>I couldn't have done them all without my friends – some of them gave me a hand when I was stuck</u> and I'll always be grateful for that. My teachers always insisted on everything being handed in on time.

I learned lots of practical things too, of course, and we were taught physiotherapy, which I enjoyed. Actually, <u>the thing that has helped me throughout my career has been knowing how to lift someone without hurting either them or myself</u>. Anyway, I was lucky enough to get my first job in the teaching hospital where I'd trained, so at least I knew my way around. The pay was very low, though, and even though I lived five kilometres away, I couldn't afford to go to work by bus or by tube, so <u>I always had to use my bike</u>, which was tough when it was raining!

I loved working there. My colleagues were lovely and it was all really interesting. I never minded dealing with difficult patients or having to work nights. <u>What wasn't so much fun was all the paperwork</u>, though. I still don't like that much!

Naturally, I've learnt an awful lot since those early days, and I've developed as a person, too, of course. People say I've always been very patient and kind – which is nice of them – but <u>I'm very confident now compared to when I started</u>.

I've looked after some wonderful people over the years, and it's always such a good feeling when people get better and leave the ward smiling and happy. You know you've done a good job then. Patients often give me a hug and a kiss when they go, and <u>I was even given this bracelet</u> by a lady I looked after for six months. I wear it every day.

I think I have one of the best jobs in the world. I can't imagine doing an office job – my sister's an accountant and although she earns far more than I do, I think my job's much more rewarding. <u>One thing I could imagine doing, though, is being an air hostess</u> – you have to look after people and always be cheerful, even when you're feeling tired – and I'd get to do some travelling as well!

 8

▶▶ **PART 3**

1
I think it's vital in this day and age to be well informed about current affairs, which of course isn't difficult now the internet has developed into a news medium. But I also find it's essential to know what intelligent people think about various issues, so <u>you need to get a range of opinions, right across the political spectrum</u>. That's where *Books for All* is so good. It doesn't just review books, you see, it has articles on all sorts of issues related to recent publications and I personally find it fascinating. I wouldn't be without it!

2
I write about style and fashion, and although I have my own ways of finding out what the big fashion houses are doing for the next season, I also want to know what consumers are thinking. I always read *Clothes World* because of what it tells

me about people who buy fashion – about consumers. <u>I think it must be the only magazine that has got articles about the latest trends by very professional fashion editors</u>. That's so important when you do a job like mine and it's always the first thing I read.

3
I've been taking the *International Geographer* for years now. It really is an excellent magazine, with lots of interesting articles about wildlife and the natural world in general. <u>I think the pictures are always first rate. They must have the best photographers in the world working for them, and you can see the results. I spend ages looking at them</u>, and it's very inspiring for me – I just want to get out there and try and do the same sort of thing myself! I never quite manage it, though I'm sure I've improved since I first started.

4
I'm a subscriber of the *Finance Review,* which is a weekly financial magazine. I'm an economist, and reading the *Finance Review* is the best way to keep up with the latest trends. The main reason I get the *Finance Review,* however, is that I don't have time to read a more serious daily newspaper, so <u>the summary it provides, especially of the news in general, is really invaluable for me</u>. I commute to work on the train, and I always have a copy with me. That makes my journey far more interesting. I could download it, I know, but I still like old-fashioned printed paper!

5
I take a monthly magazine called *Railways for All,* which keeps me informed about model railways, which is a great hobby of mine. I'm a collector of antique miniature railways, and <u>I can always find information about auctions or model trains on sale. They also have articles comparing prices of different models and descriptions of new products available</u>. It's something I've done since I was a child, and I hope my children will enjoy it as much in the future – I'm keeping the magazines for them, because they'll probably be collectors' items eventually too.

 8

▶▶ **PART 4**

Interviewer: Today I'm going to be talking to a successful young American singer, Kay Stanley, about a special aspect of her work – one that's not very well known on this side of the Atlantic. And that's the Stanley Trust. Kay, welcome to the programme. Would you start by explaining what the Stanley Trust is?

Kay Stanley: Sure. <u>It's basically an organisation set up by my father to help kids who have problems reading and writing – kids with dyslexia</u>. I'm dyslexic myself, you see, and after I had been diagnosed, my dad realised there weren't many organisations for dyslexic kids, and he decided to set one up himself a few years later.

Interviewer: I believe one of the problems with dyslexia is that it isn't diagnosed in many cases, or not early enough. Was this what happened with you?

Kay Stanley: I used to learn stories off by heart by playing the tapes of them over and over again, and then pretend to read them. In fact, I was so good at it that my <u>mum only guessed there was something wrong when she caught me learning the stories like that</u>! Then my parents got me examined by a doctor, and luckily, he knew something about dyslexia, so he sent me to an expert.

Interviewer: And what did the expert say about your condition?

Kay Stanley: He said I'm pretty fortunate because my condition is less severe, compared to other people with dyslexia. Some people have a great deal of trouble spelling even the most simple, high-frequency words. Other people have difficulty reading very short notices and signs. Of course the experts see all sorts of people so they can build up a picture of the different effects it has.

Interviewer: You must know quite a lot about it yourself by now?

Kay Stanley: I do, yes, but one of the problems with dyslexia is that even the specialists don't really understand it. They know dyslexics think in a different way from other people. They often have distinctive talents and a creative imagination. But whether dyslexia has other effects on the brain or not, nobody really knows. Some people say you use a different sort of logic if you're dyslexic, and it's easier for you to solve problems, but of course it's hard to test that.

Interviewer: And once you were diagnosed, did you start to improve?

Kay Stanley: Not immediately. At first, I was too unhappy about the whole thing, and my parents felt frustrated and confused. I knew at an early age that I wanted to become a singer, and getting school qualifications was not a priority for me. In the end, I did work hard to improve my reading skills just to show my fellow students that I was every bit as clever as they were.

Interviewer: Is it better for children with dyslexia to get special treatment?

Kay Stanley: It depends what you mean by that. I don't think it's a good idea to isolate them and put them in special schools, because that makes them feel awkward. On the other hand, they do need extra teaching in reading and writing, by teachers who understand the problem.

Interviewer: And getting back to the Stanley Trust, how do you feel you can best help the Trust? Will you be giving speeches about dyslexia in public?

Kay Stanley: I doubt it. I think the public would get tired of someone like me talking about the subject all the time. It seems to me the best thing I can do is set a good example of how dyslexics can live a normal, happy life.

Interviewer: Well, I wish you luck with that. And thank you for talking to us today.

Kay Stanley: Thank you.

TEST 1

PAPER 1 Reading and Use of English

▶▶ **PART 1**

1 A   2 C   3 D   4 C   5 B   6 C   7 D   8 D

▶▶ **PART 2**

9 as   10 like   11 It   12 into   13 be   14 when / if
15 with / against   16 off

▶▶ **PART 3**

17 height (adjective to noun)
18 construction (verb to noun)
19 exciting (verb to adjective)
20 imaginative (verb to adjective)
21 drawings (verb to noun, plural form)
22 ideal (noun to adjective)
23 surprisingly (verb to adjective to adverb)
24 recognition (verb to noun)

▶▶ **PART 4**

25 know **I** the cost of
26 should not / shouldn't **I** have deleted
27 due to **I** the bad
28 had better **I** not be
29 has been **I** translated
30 not phone **I** unless she gets

▶▶ **PART 5**

31 A: Incorrect: If he's a three-time world champion, he can't have lost frequently.
31 B: Incorrect: He looks gentle, but he wasn't gentle in the ring.
31 C: Incorrect: He must have fought back to be world champion three times.
31 D: Correct: 'he was just a hulk who knew how to take a hit'.
32 A: Incorrect: After two autobiographies, he has written a novel.
32 B: Incorrect: This is the opposite of what the text says.
32 C: Correct: 'a brilliant first novel ... likely to gain a wide readership'.
32 D: Incorrect: 'there is far more to it than that'.
33 A: Incorrect: The paragraph is about his parents, not about his childhood.
33 B: Correct: 'His father was an athletics director ... his mother a physical education teacher'.
33 C: Incorrect: There's a reference to his parents' educational background, not his.
33 D: Incorrect: If it meant background in athletics, the text would say that he came from this stock.
34 A: Incorrect: They weren't afraid. They thought he would get hurt.
34 B: Incorrect: They insisted on a college education, not training.
34 C: Incorrect: They thought he would quit, not that they wanted him to.
34 D: Correct: 'I am pretty sure they thought I'd get hurt and quit wrestling'.

35 A: Incorrect: He used to resent it, which means that now he doesn't.
35 B: Incorrect: He doesn't say that wrestlers are not good actors.
35 C: Correct: 'I used to really resent the acting label, but it is acting'.
35 D: Incorrect: He means that the acting aspect of wrestling sometimes comes close to being real.
36 A: Correct: 'Wrestling is all about characters'.
36 B: Incorrect: There's no support for this in the text.
36 C: Incorrect: There's no support for this in the text.
36 D: Incorrect: There's no reference to this in the text.

▶▶ **PART 6**

37 D: Link between 'best-selling computer game' in the previous sentence and 'Its success'. Also, link between 'Its success lies in *the use of special effects*' and 'stunning action sequences that rely on fantasy effects'.
38 G: Contrastive link between 'film makers have started to realise that they could set films in similar sci-fi future worlds' and 'However, the difficulty for the producers of Hollywood appears to be ...'.
39 F: Link between the question 'Why do some players feel disappointed by films based on their favourite games?' and the answer 'One reason is technical'.
40 B: Link between 'your favourite thriller', 'You wouldn't be interested in watching the film if you knew the identity of the murderer' and 'In films you are not supposed to have access to all the information'.
41 C: Link between 'Suspense and mystery are essential elements of film-making' in the previous paragraph and '*This* is not true for computer games'.
42 A: Link between 'films and computer games', 'We go to the cinema to let someone else tell us a story' and 'a story and a game'.

▶▶ **PART 7**

43 B: 'And I just don't think it's a very interesting job.'
44 C: 'my mother has always tried to steer me away from taking up the profession.'
45 D: 'but then I began to think of the disadvantages.'
46 A: 'he always tried to push me into taking up the same profession.'
47 D: 'I don't really think my dad's job affected my decision at all.'
48 A: 'My dad is a self-employed builder, like his father and his grandfather.'
49 B: 'there aren't so many jobs available in pure research.'
50 A: 'I do worry that we might have a big fight about this some time in the future.'
51 C: 'very few people get to the top of the profession.'
52 D: 'He also used to tell me about the satisfaction you can get from teaching.'

Questions **1–24** = 1 mark each
Questions **25–42** = 2 marks each
Questions **43–52** = 1 mark each

PAPER 2 Writing

▶▶ PART 1

Question 1

Style: Neutral or semi-formal.

Content: 1 In your introduction state your opinion clearly. Say whether, on the whole, you think learning a foreign language is worth doing or not.

2 Say whether you think it is worth learning a foreign language for work reasons and explain your ideas.

3 Say whether you think it is worth learning a foreign language for travel reasons and explain your ideas.

4 Think of something else that affects your argument, for example, the idea that learning other languages can help you to communicate with friends of other nationalities; or perhaps you think that learning languages is too time-consuming. Explain your ideas.

5 In your conclusion summarise your ideas.

▶▶ PART 2

Question 2

Style: Neutral.

Content: 1 Explain what you are going to write about. Say what your favourite possession is.

2 Now describe the possession. You could include how long you've had it, who gave it to you, what it's like, etc.

3 Explain why it is special to you. For example, is it associated with some special event in your life? What kind of memories are connected with it?

Question 3

Style: Informal.

Content: 1 Thank Maria for her email and say that you are looking forward to the English course, too.

2 Tell Maria whether you think you should choose indoor or outdoor activities and why.

3 Tell Maria which kind of activities you enjoy doing most.

4 Finish by saying you hope to hear from Maria soon. You could also ask Maria whether she agrees with your choice.

Question 4

Style: Neutral or semi-formal.

Content: 1 Write a short introduction and describe the film in general terms. You could say what the film is called, what kind of film it is, who directed it and who acts in it, for example.

2 Describe and comment on the plot and characters.

3 Conclude by saying why you think the film is worth seeing.

Question 5 (*FIRST FOR SCHOOLS* only)

Style: Informal.

Content: Choose the character that is most interesting. He or she does not have to be the main character or the hero in the book. Explain what makes this character interesting. Describe how he or she interacts with the rest of the characters. If this was a film, suggest what sort of actor or actress could play the part best.

The two parts of the Writing Paper have equal marks.

PAPER 3 LISTENING

▶▶ PART 1

1 A 2 A 3 C 4 B 5 C 6 C 7 B 8 A

▶▶ PART 2

9 two	**14** links
10 experience	**15** shopping malls
11 advertising	**16** exhausting
12 active	**17** government
13 education	**18** June

▶▶ PART 3

19 A   20 E   21 H   22 C   23 F

▶▶ PART 4

24 A   25 C   26 C   27 B   28 B   29 A   30 C

Questions **1–30** = 1 mark each

TEST 2

PAPER 1 Reading and Use of English

▶▶ PART 1

1 A   2 C   3 D   4 B   5 C   6 A   7 B   8 C

▶▶ PART 2

9 or   **10** were   **11** of   **12** who   **13** what   **14** To   **15** as
16 It

▶▶ PART 3

17 threatened (noun to verb, past participle)
18 willing (noun to adjective)
19 apparently (adjective to adverb)
20 contents (verb to noun, plural form)
21 possibility (adjective to noun)
22 unexpected (verb to negative adjective)
23 housing (verb to abstract noun)
24 restrictions (verb to noun, plural form)

▶▶ PART 4

25 not **I** as expensive as
26 should have / should've told **I** me
27 came across **I** the photographs
28 were painted **I** by
29 asked him **I** not to stay
30 do not / don't feel like **I** going

PART 5

31 A: Incorrect: She isn't surprised by the fact that she's driving.

31 B: Incorrect: It doesn't surprise her that she has been living in London for so long.

31 C: Correct: 'For a moment the town mouse I have become is being seen by the country mouse I used to be'.

31 D: Incorrect: She would choose to live in the city again 'given a new start'.

32 A: Correct: 'the haunting sound of their wing beats gave way to silence'.

32 B: Incorrect: 'Haunting' here doesn't suggest frightening.

32 C: Incorrect: The sound of the wings beating is not loud.

32 D: Incorrect: The swans don't disturb or worry him.

33 A: Incorrect: The lake itself is not evidence of change.

33 B: Incorrect: Landowners have created lakes in the past as well.

33 C: Correct: 'Formerly, landowners would almost certainly have made such changes for their own benefit, but this time it was done to ...'.

33 D: Incorrect: The need for preservation is not evidence of change.

34 A: Correct: 'second-homers, together with commuters, have come to be accepted as a vital part of the country scene'.

34 B: Incorrect: It doesn't answer the question.

34 C: Incorrect: The text doesn't say where they are from.

34 D: Incorrect: There's no support for this in the text.

35 A: Incorrect: It also depends on your personality and the personality of your neighbours.

35 B: Correct: 'perhaps it was always mainly in their minds'.

35 C: Incorrect: Much depends on the personality of your neighbours.

35 D: Incorrect: There are examples in the text where social life in the country is more exciting than social life in the city ('social life seems dizzying to a Londoner').

36 A: Incorrect: There's no evidence in the text that she had problems adjusting to life in London.

36 B: Incorrect: She says 'I do enjoy my life'.

36 C: Incorrect: There's no reference to the personality of people in her street.

36 D: Correct: 'This is very unlike living in a London street'.

PART 6

37 F: Link between 'extraordinary anatomy' and 'the thumb alone is controlled by nine separate muscles'. Link between 'muscles' and 'Some are connected'.

38 D: Link between 'other species have hands too' and 'the five fingers at the end of an orangutan's arm'. Link between 'No one would doubt' and 'we have to look closer'.

39 A: Link between 'bones' and 'smaller ones'.

40 G: Link between the statement 'Early hands were more exotic' and the examples 'Some species had seven fingers. Others had eight'.

41 E: Link between 'many different types of hands, from dolphin flippers ... hanging hooks of sloths ' and 'By studying *these*'. Link between '*scientists* are beginning to understand' and '*They* can also see'.

42 B: Link between the fact that the differences between a vulture's wing and a lion's paw come down to 'tiny variations' and 'It may just be a little more of one protein here, a little less of another there'.

PART 7

43 A: 'gained a lot of publicity for the school.'

44 D: 'a website that the school had started.'

45 B: 'A leading expert on wild birds was invited.'

46 A: 'and handed over nearly £1000 to the World Wide Fund for Nature.'

47 D: 'took pupils to the coastal marshes of Easton.'

48 C: 'the effects of variations in climatic patterns.'

49 B: 'monitored the progress of species threatened with extinction.'

50 C: 'how pollution can destroy buildings in the region.'

51 C: 'to launch a campaign for the restoration of the medieval square.'

52 D: 'The pupils at this inner-city secondary school.'

PAPER 2 Writing

PART 1

Question 1

Style: Semi-formal or neutral.

Content: 1 In your introduction state your opinion clearly. Say which of the two you think is better.

2 In the body of your essay give reasons for your choice and support them with examples. Make sure you include the points in the notes. Say something about the range of goods available in each and how the prices compare. Also, add a point of your own. For example, you might say something about which type of shop is more convenient, or how friendly the staff are.

3 Make a list of possible disadvantages of your preferred type of shop and give examples. Does it have a wider choice of goods? Are these goods cheaper and / or good value for money?

4 In your conclusion summarise which type of shop you prefer and why.

PART 2

Question 2

Style: Neutral or informal.

Content: 1 Write a brief introduction thanking Fran for his/ her letter and saying you are happy to help.

2 Think of a person who is famous in your country. It could be a historical figure, or someone who is alive now.

3 Give some information about the person, for example what their job is/was.

4 Why is this person famous? What did they do? / What have they done?

5 What do people think about this person? Do people admire them?

6 Conclude by saying what you think about this person.

Question 3

Style: Neutral or semi-formal.

Content: 1 Write a short introduction and give an overview of the TV series. Describe briefly what the theme is. You could also mention who directs it and who acts in it.

2 Outline the storyline briefly and describe the main characters.

3 Explain why people find this series amusing.

4 Conclude by giving your opinion of the series and say if you think it is worth watching.

Question 4

Report (*FIRST only*)

Style: Formal or neutral.

Content: 1 Think of families in your area. What are the most popular spare time activities?

2 What are their favourite hobbies?

3 Are people keen on sports?

4 How often do they go out? What do they do when they go out?

5 Summarise your ideas.

Story (*FIRST FOR SCHOOLS only*)

Style: Neutral.

Content: 1 Read the prompt sentence carefully. Write it down as the first sentence of your story.

2 Think about the rest of your story. Make sure that your story follows on from the prompt sentence and includes TV cameras and a surprise.

3 Why are the TV cameras there? What is happening outside Tim's house? Or are they there to film Tim?

4 What is the surprise?

5 Make sure your story has a clear ending.

Question 5 (*FIRST FOR SCHOOLS only*)

Style: Semi-formal or neutral.

Content: In your introduction explain if the book or story could be performed as a play. Briefly describe the main scenes that you would select and comment on whether the characters are interesting enough for a play. Summarise your ideas and list the main problems of turning the book or story into a play.

PAPER 3 Listening

▶▶ PART 1

1 A   2 C   3 C   4 B   5 A   6 B   7 B   8 A

▶▶ PART 2

9 headteacher

10 60,000 / sixty thousand

11 50,000 / fifty thousand

12 writing

13 all day

14 cultural

15 imaginative

16 optimistic

17 (the) government / governments

18 second / 2nd

▶▶ PART 3

19 D   20 F   21 H   22 C   23 B

▶▶ PART 4

24 A   25 C   26 A   27 A   28 B   29 C   30 A

TEST 3

PAPER 1 Reading and Use of English

▶▶ PART 1

1 C   2 D   3 A   4 B   5 A   6 C   7 A   8 A

▶▶ PART 2

9 in   10 the   11 a   12 for   13 It   14 their   15 were   16 on

▶▶ PART 3

17 happily (adjective to adverb)

18 wealthy (noun to adjective)

19 savings (verb to noun, plural form)

20 departure (verb to noun)

21 luxurious (noun to adjective)

22 disappointment (verb to noun)

23 freedom (adjective to noun)

24 disastrous (noun to adjective)

▶▶ PART 4

25 apologised for **I** being late / apologised **I** because he was late

26 reminds me **I** of

27 to have **I** the kitchen redecorated

28 you mind **I** speaking

29 are advised **I** to buy

30 wish **I** I had / 'd seen

▶▶ PART 5

31 B: This occurred while they were out walking in the Lake District.

32 A: 'It is a living force that feels joy and sadness.'

33 C: 'Wordsworth's home … is now one of the most popular destinations in the Lake District.'

34 D: 'Wordsworth himself was far from keen on tourists.'

35 C: 'they aren't tall yellow trumpets … they're tiny … They're grouped around individual trees rather than collecting together.'

36 B: 'What you're seeing at last is nature transformed by human sight and imagination.'

▶▶ PART 6

37 C: Link between 'the interactive sports games … she enjoyed in her formative years' and 'I've always been sports-minded'.

38 F: Link between 'It's great fun playing against my great-grandma' and 'She's a real pro'.

39 B: Link between 'computer game platforms continue to grow' and 'And as computer game usage amongst older people has risen'; and between 'computer games provide much more than simple entertainment value' and 'Interactive games have been linked to providing'.

40 G: Link between 'isn't just about hitting the treadmill at the gym' and 'Just like traditional forms of exercise'.

41 A: Link between 'finding the right fit can be challenging' and 'Not only are the most successful platforms those with user-friendly controls'.

42 D: Link between 'Games which mimic the movements of the sports they represent' and 'requires users to swing their arms in the same motion as a bowler'.

▶▶ **PART 7**

43 B: 'it's imperative that I stick to certain standards of cleanliness.'

44 D: 'I know that having a sedentary job can cause physical problems.'

45 C: 'the light there makes it almost as good as working in my studio.'

46 A: 'The room's flooded with light which helps me stay really focused when I'm writing.'

47 B: 'without such a lovely space to try things out in, I doubt I'd enjoy what I do even half as much.'

48 A: 'it's important not only to get into the right frame of mind, but the right surroundings, too, in order for the ideas to flow.'

49 C: 'it's fascinating what a calming effect this seems to have on them.'

50 D: 'buying some ergonomic furniture…' and 'it's really increased my performance and output.'

51 C: 'I've noticed recently that the portraits I've produced lately have a real air of serenity about them.'

52 A: 'The benefits extend beyond the walls of the room too – once the door's closed, it means I can totally switch off.'

PAPER 2 Writing

▶▶ **PART 1**

Question 1
  Style: Neutral or semi-formal.
  Content: 1 In your introduction state your opinion clearly. Say whether you think travelling by public transport is better than travelling by car or not.
  2 Discuss the environmental effects of travelling by car or public transport, for example, levels of pollution or noise.
  3 Talk about the cost of travelling by car or public transport for passengers, or for governments, which may subsidise public transport or deal with the cost of road repairs.
  4 Discuss your own idea. You could talk about speed or ease of travel, for example, how easy it is to travel with luggage. You might also talk about the benefits or drawbacks of travelling by car or public transport for people of different ages.
  5 Conclude with a brief summary of your points and your overall opinion.

▶▶ **PART 2**

Question 2
  Style: Formal or neutral.
  Content: 1 Describe your favourite sport. You could say whether it is a team sport or individual sport and why you like it.
  2 Describe the clothes and equipment required for the sport. You could include information such as whether they are expensive and whether they affect the popularity of the sport.
  3 Say what qualities are required for the sport. You could also say how fit you have to be to take it up and describe the kinds of people who enjoy the sport.
  4 You could finish your article by summarising what you have said about the sport, and why you think other people might enjoy playing it.

Question 3
  Style: Informal.
  Content: 1 Begin your letter by thanking Sam for his/her letter and saying you're happy to tell him/her about how your neighbourhood has changed.
  2 Think of two or three things that have changed in your neighbourhood. For example, is the traffic the same? Is the area more densely populated? Are there better facilities?
  3 How has life changed as a result?
  4 Say how you feel about these changes. Are you concerned or positive about the future of the area?

Question 4
  Style: Neutral or semi-formal.
  Content: 1 Write a short introduction. Give the name of the website, and say when or why you used it.
  2 Write one or two paragraphs. Describe the features of the website and say why you think it is better than other websites, for example, is it cheaper to download music? Is the choice of music wider? Is it easier to use?
  3 Conclude by saying who you think would enjoy using the website.

Question 5 (*FIRST FOR SCHOOLS only*)
  Style: Formal or neutral.
  Content: Explain what you feel the message is that the writer wants to convey. Think of two or three sections or scenes that best illustrate the main theme of the book. Describe them in detail and explain why and how these connect to the central theme of the book.

PAPER 3 Listening

▶▶ **PART 1**

1 A **2** B **3** C **4** B **5** A **6** C **7** B **8** A

▶▶ **PART 2**

9 culture
10 economics
11 interviews
12 articles
13 film critic
14 organisation
15 web design
16 football matches
17 research
18 photographer

▶▶ **PART 3**

19 C **20** G **21** F **22** B **23** E

▶▶ **PART 4**

24 C **25** A **26** B **27** A **28** B **29** B **30** C

PAPER 1 Reading and Use of English

▶▶ **PART 1**

1 D **2** A **3** A **4** C **5** C **6** B **7** D **8** A

▶▶ **PART 2**

9 been **10** for **11** has **12** not **13** to **14** on **15** how
16 why

▶▶ **PART 3**

17 popularity (adjective to noun)
18 immediately (adjective to adverb)
19 carefully (noun to adjective to adverb)
20 fitness (adjective to noun)
21 pressure (verb to noun)
22 ability (adjective to noun)
23 competitors (verb to noun, plural form)
24 encourage (noun to verb)

▶▶ **PART 4**

25 will be made **‖** to train
26 provided (that) **‖** I kept
27 I had / I'd told **‖** you
28 succeeded in **‖** getting
29 in spite of **‖** feeling
30 is unlikely **‖** to come

▶▶ **PART 5**

31 D: 'a cord of panic pulls tight around my chest ... It's not anywhere ... Surely I can survive one trip without my supply of foam earplugs?.'
32 B: 'in a cheap hotel ... the deeply discounted hotel room.'
33 A: 'But no traveller can remain in a perfectly controlled sonic bubble ... Not when we're moving through a world in which ... One person's noise is another person's music.'
34 C: 'a non-stop celebration ... It was fabulous.'
35 B: 'we seem to layer noise upon noise. The hotel ... techno music ... retreats into her iPod.'
36 C: 'I'm once again the master of my private sonic world.'

▶▶ **PART 6**

37 F: Link between 'communication equipment, controls, snacks, cameras' and 'We have everything we need for our journey'.
38 D: Link between the idea that few seamounts have been studied: 'We've seen little of these', 'marine biologists have studied only a few hundred' and 'More finely detailed maps of the surface of Mars may exist than of the remotest parts of the ocean floor'.
39 G: 'Some of these' in the gapped sentence refers to 'hard coral, sponges, and sea fans circled by schools of fish'.
40 A: Link between 'deep-sea fishing trawlers drag nets weighted with heavy chains across seamounts' and 'This process'.
41 C: Link between 'We are still in what is called the photic zone, where sunlight penetrates' and 'Then we descend farther, and the ocean around us is completely black'.

42 E: Link between' 'something ... rises' and 'it is the remains of a volcano'.

▶▶ **PART 7**

43 C: 'I didn't pass the test until my fourth attempt.'
44 A: 'I thought because I knew how a car works it would make a difference. That was a big mistake!'
45 D: 'she used to tell me how awful it was, which put me off a lot.'
46 B: 'I was shaking and my knees were trembling.'
47 D: 'I've got a part-time job delivering books ... and I have to use their delivery van.'
48 C: 'my aunt, who owns a farm, let me go into a field and drive around.'
49 B: 'I got there five minutes' late ... they let me go ahead with it.'
50 A: 'I haven't had the chance to drive a car ever since I got my licence.'
51 C: 'in a couple of weeks I'm confident I'll have enough to buy a decent second-hand car.'
52 A: 'I'd been riding a motorbike for six months.'

PAPER 2 Writing

▶▶ **PART 1**

Question 1

Style: Neutral.
Content: 1 Introduce the topic and mention some other ways you can get fit apart from playing sports in a team.
  2 Discuss some advantages of exercising with other people, for example it may be more fun, or you may be more motivated if you don't want to let your team mates down.
  3 Talk about how convenient it is – if you go to a gym instead, for example, you can turn up whenever you like, but in a team, you have to meet at a certain time.
  4 Discuss your own idea – it could be that it's easier to make new friends if you play a team sport so you're more likely to keep doing it. Or it could be that if you exercise alone, you can push yourself harder and improve your fitness faster.
  5 Conclude with a brief summary of your points and your overall opinion.

▶▶ **PART 2**

Question 2

Style: Neutral.
Content: 1 In the introduction say whether music is important in your life or not, and when you usually listen to it.
  2 Write about the sort of music you enjoy and why you like it.
  3 Say who you listen to it with, or say you listen to music on your own. Give reasons.
  4 Conclude by saying (again, but using different words) how important music is to you.

Question 3

Style: Neutral.

Content: 1 In the introduction give the title of the film and briefly mention the historical event it is based on. You could give some basic information such as who directed it and who acted in it.

2 Describe the event as it happened in history and compare it with the film. You could combine this with a description of the real-life people who took part in the event and the way they were portrayed in the film.

3 Comment on the costumes and perhaps also on the film sets, soundtrack and any other features of the film which were important.

4 Conclude by saying whether you think the film was historically accurate, and whether you think people should see it.

Question 4

Report (*FIRST only*)

Style: Neutral or semi-formal.

Content: 1 State the aim of the report.

2 Explain what the young people in your area normally eat and drink. Say what their favourite eating places are.

3 Say what kind of food would be healthier.

4 Suggest how they could be encouraged to try to eat healthier food.

Story (*FIRST FOR SCHOOLS only*)

Style: Neutral.

Content: 1 Read the prompt sentence carefully. Write it down as the first sentence of your story.

2 Decide who Helen and Steve are. Are they friends, colleagues or brother and sister? How old are they? Are they studying or working?

3 Think of what happened before they burst out laughing. Give some background information before you describe the main events of the story. Remember to include a photograph and a computer in your story. Describe the photograph briefly – did they see it on a computer screen, or did they use the computer to email it to someone?

4 Describe Helen and Steve's feelings and reactions to the main event of the story and say how it affected their lives.

Question 5 (*FIRST FOR SCHOOLS only*)

Style: Formal or neutral.

Content: Think of a main event that affects the plot and development of the characters. Give some background information. Say what happens before the main event. Then describe the event. Explain briefly which characters are involved in it and what their involvement is. Now explain why this event is important for the development of the story and how it affects the characters.

PAPER 3 Listening

▶▶ **PART 1**

1 B 2 B 3 A 4 C 5 C 6 C 7 A 8 B

▶▶ **PART 2**

9 18 / eighteen   14 money
10 equipment   15 the government
11 soccer   16 success
12 made redundant   17 reasonable
13 encouragement   18 blue

▶▶ **PART 3**

19 E   20 C   21 G   22 A   23 H

▶▶ **PART 4**

24 C   25 B   26 C   27 A   28 C   29 B   30 A

TEST 5

PAPER 1 Reading and
         Use of English

▶▶ **PART 1**

1 D 2 B 3 A 4 D 5 C 6 B 7 A 8 D

▶▶ **PART 2**

9 a 10 to 11 in 12 is 13 the 14 has 15 not 16 at

▶▶ **PART 3**

17 arrival (verb to noun)
18 beginning (verb to noun)
19 global (noun to adjective)
20 difficulties (adjective to noun, plural form)
21 sharply (adjective to adverb)
22 hunger (adjective to noun)
23 impossible (adjective to negative adjective)
24 observation (verb to noun)

▶▶ **PART 4**

25 never allows us **I** to
26 did not / didn't get home **I** until
27 so that **I** he would
28 advised me **I** not to go
29 should not / shouldn't have **I** left
30 only guest who **I** did not / didn't

▶▶ **PART 5**

31 B: 'Put simply, I'm a better photographer when I'm standing in front of something wonderful like the Grand Canyon in Arizona, USA.'

32 D: 'Example: today my mind is absorbed…' and 'In my head I am getting ready…'.

33 A: 'I'll have a chance once again to ascend the slopes of Skellig Michael. I want to be ready to seize the day.'

34 B: 'Fortunately, it doesn't have to be an either/or decision.'

35 C: 'Knowing what the place looks like in advance is invaluable, so I'll hit several internet photo sites. Besides clueing me in to the photographic possibilities of the location, this…'

36 A: The gist of the whole paragraph gives us the answer. Jim takes care to look for interesting places, and takes its background into account. He also does plenty of preparation before he travels.

▸▸ PART 6

37 C: 'Not really' answers the question at the end of the previous paragraph.

38 F: 'them' refers to 'numbers from one to three' in the previous sentence.

39 E: Contrastive link between 'Humans remember things ... groups or categories' and 'Orangutans, on the other hand, appear to do so according to where they saw them last'.

40 A: Link between 'Orangutans can become very emotional' and 'They feel extremely frustrated' in the next sentence.

41 B: Link between 'animals in captivity' and 'we cannot study ... in their natural environment'.

42 G: Link between 'There are differences ... work' and 'This becomes apparent ... the same task to do'.

▸▸ PART 7

43 C: 'One thing that annoyed me ... was the attitude of people watching.'

44 B: 'asked me to join her a few mornings a week.'

45 B: 'I didn't even get to the end of the course.'

46 A: 'when I started to feel a bit of fatigue kicking in and hit the wall.'

47 D: 'four of us from the office.'

48 C: 'physically I don't think I've got a great deal of talent or ability.'

49 D: 'so I joined the [jogging] club.'

50 D: 'drag myself out of bed on cold winter mornings ... in the pouring rain.'

51 B: 'we watched the news ... he could see my face.'

52 A: 'I can reach the open countryside in just a couple of minutes on foot from my front-door step.'

PAPER 2 Writing

▸▸ PART 1

Question 1

Style: Semi-formal or neutral.

Content: 1 Explain in your introduction that some people agree with this, but others do not. Say, in your own opinion, whether it is better to grow up in a large or small family.

2 Do you think children get enough attention from their parents in large families? Do they get too much attention in smaller ones? Give examples.

3 Talk about the relationships between brothers and sisters. Is it better to have more or fewer brothers and sisters? Give reasons to support your argument.

4 Think of something else that affects the argument. For example, what about sharing things with others? What about financial considerations? Explain what you think and why.

5 Summarise your ideas in your conclusion.

▸▸ PART 2

Question 2

Style: Neutral.

Content: 1 Begin by saying whether you like or dislike traditional music from your country.

2 Say whether you think traditional music is old-fashioned and why/why not.

3 Explain whether you think traditional music has a place in the modern world and why it should/shouldn't continue to be promoted.

4 Say how you think it might be possible to encourage interest in traditional music.

5 Conclude your article by summarising your ideas.

Question 3

Style: Neutral or informal.

Content: 1 Write a brief introduction thanking Kim for his/her email and saying you are happy to tell him/her about your new life.

2 Sum up the differences between life in this small village and your previous life in a city.

3 Explain how you feel about the change in your lifestyle and whether it is a positive or negative change. Illustrate your points with examples.

4 Conclude by saying you hope to hear from Kim soon.

Question 4

Style: Neutral or semi-formal.

Content: 1 Begin by saying whether the TV programme you are going to write about is the best or worst programme you have seen this year.

2 Briefly say what the programme was about.

3 Discuss what it was about the programme that made it so good/bad. Comment on the presenters/actors, the theme/story, or any other features that were important.

4 Finish by saying whether you think another programme on the same theme should be made and why/why not.

Question 5 (*FIRST FOR SCHOOLS only*)

Style: Informal.

Content: Start by recommending this book to your friend. Say what the book is about and what you liked most about it. Give reasons why you think your friend would enjoy reading it during his/her holiday. You may also mention aspects of the book that you think your friend may not particularly like.

PAPER 3 Listening

▸▸ PART 1

1 B **2** A **3** C **4** B **5** C **6** A **7** C **8** A

▸▸ PART 2

9 July
10 12 / twelve
11 railway / train station
12 underground
13 nurseries
14 fairground
15 7 / seven
16 Classic
17 flowers
18 ecology

▶▶ **PART 3**

19 C   20 G   21 E   22 D   23 F

▶▶ **PART 4**

24 A   25 C   26 C   27 B   28 A   29 C   30 C

 TEST 6

PAPER 1   Reading and
Use of English

▶▶ **PART 1**

1 B   2 A   3 B   4 A   5 D   6 C   7 B   8 A

▶▶ **PART 2**

9 between   10 it   11 than   12 front   13 like   14 is
15 to   16 all

▶▶ **PART 3**

17 civilisations (verb to noun, plural form)
18 obsession (verb to noun)
19 traditionally (noun to adjective to adverb)
20 widely (adjective to adverb)
21 responsibility (adjective to noun)
22 regulations (verb to noun, plural form)
23 unable (adjective to negative adjective)
24 profitable (noun to adjective)

▶▶ **PART 4**

25 what I the width
26 wasn't / was not I allowed to
27 has not / hasn't been abroad I since
28 whether I I had read
29 gets on I my
30 took him I three weeks to

▶▶ **PART 5**

31 A: 'what you see first is the kind of thing urban parks
were created to get away from.'
32 C: 'looks ... like some abandoned leftover from the
past', 'Until recently that's precisely what the High
Line was'.
33 B: 'Not the least of the remarkable things about the
High Line is the way, without streets to cross or
traffic lights to wait for, ten blocks pass as quickly as
two.'
34 C: 'I was in love with the steel structure, the rivets, the
ruin. I assumed that some civic group was going
to try and preserve it, and I saw that it was on the
agenda for a community meeting.'
35 D: 'some plans ... which enraged the people who were
trying to get it torn down,' 'we couldn't believe the
degree of rage some of those people had'.
36 A: 'it has been one of the city's major tourist attractions.
Yet it is just as much a neighbourhood park' and
'there seemed to be as many locals treating the area
as the equivalent of their own beach as visitors out
for a promenade'.

▶▶ **PART 6**

37 D: Link between the question 'What is this learning
disability ...?' and 'dyscalculics cannot recognise ...
count them one by one'.
38 A: Link between 'huge problems' and 'Another
problem'.
39 F: Link between 'concept of time' and 'difficulty in
reading schedules and remembering the order in
which things happened'.
40 B: Link between 'end up miles away from their
intended destination' and 'On top of getting lost'.
41 E: Link between 'how much money they have got left'
and 'Dealing with cash ... fear'.
42 G: Contrastive link between the problems listed in
the previous paragraphs and 'On the other hand,
dyscalculics are very good at creative arts'.

▶▶ **PART 7**

43 D: 'I spent half a year writing it.'
44 C: 'I was pretty offended at the time.'
45 D: 'the artistic work on the cover, which I really hated at
first.'
46 B: 'I ... forgot about the book for about ten years.'
47 A: 'I vowed I'd never write a biography again.'
48 B: 'I would write ten pages every morning.'
49 C: 'he wasn't interesting enough.'
50 D: 'I had to be strict about how long I would work for.'
51 C: 'in the short stories I'd had published previously.'
52 A: 'I was awarded the General Haig Memorial Prize for
the book.'

PAPER 2   Writing

▶▶ **PART 1**

Question 1
  Style: Neutral or semi-formal.
  Content: 1 Introduce the topic of fast food, saying some
people disapprove of it.
2 Give reasons why people say fast food is bad
for people's health. Give examples. Think
of examples of fast food that are good for
people's health.
3 Explain how the cost of fast food affects
people's decisions whether or not to eat it.
4 Add your own idea, for example, you could
say that it is convenient/tasty/the restaurants
are pleasant (or not, depending on your point
of view).
5 Conclude by giving your own overall opinion
of fast food.

▶▶ **PART 2**

Question 2
  Style: Neutral.
  Content: 1 Begin by saying that something happened to
you one day that changed your life.
2 Say what it was and describe the experience.
3 Explain in what way it changed your life.

Question 3

Style: Neutral or semi-formal.

Content: 1 Begin by giving some basic information about the play: what play was it, who directed it, who acted in it, where it is/was on.
2 Give a brief outline of the story.
3 Comment on the acting, the sets and costumes.
4 Give your own opinion of the play and say whether you think the play is worth seeing.

Question 4

Report (*FIRST only*)

Style: Neutral.

Content: 1 Describe the job you did and the place where you worked.
2 Give reasons why this was a positive or negative experience for you.
3 Explain what you enjoyed and why. Explain what you didn't enjoy and why.
4 Suggest why this (or a similar summer job) might be a good experience for teenagers.

Story (*FIRST FOR SCHOOLS only*)

Style: Neutral.

Content: 1 Read the prompt sentence carefully. Write it down as the first sentence of your story.
2 Decide why Nola's day was going to be special.
3 Think about the journey – did she make it on foot, on a bicycle, by car, or by another means of transport?
4 Who were the friends? What were their names? Did they go on the journey with her, or did she meet them on the way?
5 Make sure your story progresses logically, with a beginning, a middle and an end.

Question 5 (*FIRST FOR SCHOOLS only*)

Style: Semi-formal or neutral.

Content: Start by saying whether you agree, partly agree or disagree with the statement. For example, the message might help people, but not in everyday life. Then find examples from the book of themes or messages that support your opinion.

PAPER 3 Listening

▶▶ **PART 1**

1 A 2 B 3 A 4 A 5 C 6 C 7 B 8 C

▶▶ **PART 2**

9 unfashionable	14 real-life
10 largest	15 boys
11 healthier	16 Asia
12 adults	17 (toy) fairs
13 bankers	18 controlled

▶▶ **PART 3**

19 F 20 C 21 A 22 H 23 D

▶▶ **PART 4**

24 A 25 C 26 C 27 B 28 A 29 B 30 C

TEST 7

PAPER 1 Reading and Use of English

▶▶ **PART 1**

1 B 2 C 3 B 4 A 5 D 6 D 7 C 8 A

▶▶ **PART 2**

9 for 10 At / By 11 from 12 that 13 could 14 had 15 the 16 as

▶▶ **PART 3**

17 discrimination (verb to noun)
18 practical (noun to adjective)
19 designed (active to passive verb form)
20 inconvenient (adjective to negative adjective)
21 equipment (verb to noun)
22 difficulties (adjective to noun, plural form)
23 development (verb to noun)
24 behaviour (verb to noun)

▶▶ **PART 4**

25 has not / hasn't changed **I** since
26 spent all / the whole afternoon **I** sleeping
27 would not / wouldn't have fainted **I** if
28 would / 'd rather **I** watch football than
29 as soon as **I** you receive
30 has been **I** out of order

▶▶ **PART 5**

31 D: 'I'd always fought shy of doing the adventurous stuff myself' and 'when I was challenged to take part in a mountain climb ... I was unwilling to say the least.'
32 A: 'I set about ... devouring every climbing magazine I could get my hands on.'
33 A: 'he went into great detail about everything to do with the sport. It quickly became apparent that the mechanics of climbing were more complex than I could have imagined.'
34 C: 'Keith made a detailed action plan and I forced myself to stick to it diligently'
35 A: 'My hard-won confidence took a nose dive as the enormity of what I'd let myself in for struck me as suddenly as an avalanche.'
36 B: 'Would I be back for another go? Thankfully not.'

▶▶ **PART 6**

37 F: Contrastive link between 'the government would not allow anyone to operate a private radio station' and 'However, the government's power only extended to the country itself'.
38 C: Link between 'During a period when pop music was extremely popular, the BBC played very little of it' and 'As a result, there were large numbers of young people who wanted to listen ... but couldn't'.
39 E: Link between 'a radio station operating outside Britain' and 'this station'.
40 G: Link between 'the British government decided that some action had to be taken' and 'a new law was passed'.

41 D: Link between the developments at the BBC and 'increasing number of listeners were switching from the pirate stations to the eminent broadcaster'.

42 B: Link between 'Radio Caroline found itself in serious financial difficulties' and 'Its situation became even worse'.

▶▶ PART 7

43 A: 'You've got to be patient and persevere ... That's why they tend to give up before they've even started.'

44 C: 'convinced I was about to become a famous musician.'

45 D: 'there were always loads of other musicians hanging around the house when I was a kid.'

46 A: 'I guess you could apply that same principle to lots of things – you only get out what you put in.'

47 B: 'I've noticed there are some benefits to keeping your mind active in this way.'

48 C: 'he was happy to indulge me in what he thought was just another phase', 'I never went back'.

49 C: 'suddenly realised what I'd let myself in for.'

50 D: 'I'm pretty shy when it comes to getting up on stage and showing people what I can do', 'I've only ever played the drums for my own amusement'.

51 A: 'Everyone just assumes that it's just one of those teenage things – something I'll get bored with or grow out of', 'The reality is that I just love performing'.

52 B: 'I wouldn't say I had any particular desire to learn an instrument, but when I was about eight my parents insisted I give it a go', 'went along to my first lesson just to keep them happy'.

PAPER 2 Writing

▶▶ PART 1

Question 1
Style: Neutral or semi-formal
Content: 1 Explain in your introduction that some people believe this, but others do not. Say whether you agree or disagree with the statement.
2 Give reasons to support your argument. For example, what do you think about the cost of buying new clothes? Are they too expensive or are cheap clothes easily available? Give examples.
3 Say what you think wearing the latest fashions tells people about you. You could include how you feel when you wear the latest fashions and whether or not it is important to you to wear them? Explain your ideas.
4 Think of something else that affects the argument. For example, do you think it is wasteful to keep buying new clothes on a regular basis? What happens to your clothes that are no longer in fashion? Explain your ideas.
5 Conclude by summarising your ideas.

▶▶ PART 2

Question 2
Style: Neutral or informal.
Content: 1 Write a brief introduction thanking Li for his/ her invitation and saying you would like to stay with his/her family for a weekend next month.
2 Say what you would like to do during the weekend and why you would both enjoy that.
3 Tell Li whether there are any types of food that you can't eat and explain why.
4 Conclude by saying you look forward to seeing Li and his/her family soon

Question 3
Style: Neutral or semi-formal.
Content: 1 In the introduction, give some basic information about the film – what it's called and what it's about.
2 How good are the special effects in the film? How heavily does the film rely on them?
3 You could also comment on the other aspects of the film: the story, the acting, the soundtrack, etc.
4 Give your opinion about the film and say whether you think films rely too much on special effects or not.

Question 4
Report (*FIRST only*)
Style: Neutral or semi-formal.
Content: 1 State the aim of the report.
2 Describe the facilities that are available to young people in your local area.
3 Say whether they are suitable for young people's needs or not. Explain why/why not.
4 Suggest other facilities that young people might enjoy and say why.

Story (*FIRST FOR SCHOOLS only*)
Style: Neutral.
Content: 1 Read the prompt sentence carefully. Write it down as the first sentence of your story.
2 Decide what the phone call was about and what happened as a consequence of making it.
3 Think about who you talked to on the phone and why you had to make a bus journey. Give some background information before you describe the main events of the story.
4 Who was the stranger you met? What influence did they have on the events of the story?
5 Describe your feelings and reactions to the main event of the story and say why you wish you hadn't made the phone call.

Question 5 (*FIRST FOR SCHOOLS only*)
Style: Neutral or formal.
Content: Start by saying whether you agree or disagree with the statement. Is the setting important? Does the time and place make any difference to whether you like it or not? Think of the book or short story you have read. Do you think it has universal appeal? Do you think that because of when and where it is set it will appeal to a specific group of readers? Give reasons and support your views with examples from the book.

PAPER 3 Listening

▶▶ PART 1
1 C **2** A **3** C **4** A **5** B **6** A **7** B **8** A

▶▶ PART 2
9 June 15th
10 ads / adverts / advertisements
11 mayor
12 footballer
13 experts
14 practical
15 flexible
16 qualifications
17 applications
18 website

▶▶ PART 3
19 C **20** G **21** B **22** H **23** D

▶▶ PART 4
24 A **25** B **26** C **27** C **28** B **29** B **30** A

TEST 8

PAPER 1 Reading and Use of English

▶▶ PART 1
1 B **2** D **3** B **4** A **5** C **6** D **7** C **8** A

▶▶ PART 2
9 to **10** what **11** who **12** how **13** nothing **14** any
15 these / they **16** at

▶▶ PART 3
17 unknown (verb to negative adjective)
18 professional (noun to adjective)
19 directors (verb to noun, plural form)
20 Generally (adjective to adverb)
21 rejection (verb to noun)
22 notify (noun to verb)
23 typically (adjective to adverb)
24 creativity (verb to noun)

▶▶ PART 4
25 time **I** you decided
26 has / gets **I** his hair cut
27 should not have **I** insulted
28 can't have **I** forgotten
29 only **I** we had
30 to cut down **I** on

▶▶ PART 5
31 B: The first paragraph is a list of all Irving's achievements. Giving his age at the end highlights how young he is to have done all this already.
32 B: 'The secret, he believes, is having a dream in the first place.'
33 C: 'I told him I didn't think I was smart enough.'
34 A: 'Then another dream took hold.'
35 D: '... it wasn't all the fanfare that changed my life. It was seeing so many young people watching and listening.'

36 C: Various ways in which people are being educated are described, then the writer tells us what the strongest and most effective one is: what Irving himself has done and his attitude to life.

▶▶ PART 6
37 B: Link between 'the two large display windows' and 'The display on the right'.
38 D: Link between 'the total you have to pay', 'For security reasons, you have to do this' and 'you can only collect the goods after you've paid'.
39 G: Link between 'one of the biggest problems', 'The challenge is to create a piece of machinery which will be delicate enough ... but at the same time strong enough to ...'.
40 C: Link between 'every new invention has been regarded with some suspicion at first' and 'The real question is whether ... enough people will overcome their doubts'.
41 E: Link between 'the small shopkeeper in inner-city areas' and 'Many shops like these'.
42 F: Link between 'considerable advantages' and 'Machines do not take lunch breaks ... Isn't this the sort of efficiency people want from a shop these days?'.

▶▶ PART 7
43 A: 'sports can teach children the importance of teamwork. ... sports are about working together towards a common goal.'
44 B: 'sports can teach you how to be humble and realistic.'
45 D: 'Sports can teach you ... how to remain focused.'
46 A: 'To do well in almost everything else at school ... individual effort.'
47 D: 'the Olympic spirit ... which nowadays is more important than ever before.'
48 A: 'give children who are not high achievers a chance to excel at something.'
49 C: 'learn the importance of fair play.'
50 C: 'from the most popular ones ... to the less popular ones.'
51 B: 'obesity ... nutritional value of food, etc. should be included in sports lessons.'
52 D: 'Taking part in a sports lesson can be a major source of embarrassment for less athletic children.'

PAPER 2 Writing

▶▶ PART 1
Question 1
Style: Neutral or semi-formal
Content: 1 Explain in your introduction that some people believe this, but others do not.
2 Say whether or not, in your opinion, people spend too much or too little time at work or studying. Give reasons to support your arguments.
3 Do you think people have enough free time to spend with family and friends? Give examples.

4 Think of something else that affects the argument. For example, people need time off just to relax and do nothing, to pursue hobbies, to clean their homes. Say whether or not you think people have enough time to do this. Explain why you think this.

5 Say what your opinion is, on balance.

▶▶ PART 2

Question 2

Style: Neutral or semi-formal.

Content: 1 In the introduction, give some information about the shop – what it's called, what it sells, when it opened.

2 Describe the shop. Is it large or small? What is the atmosphere in the shop? Is there any background music?

3 Give more detailed information about what the shop sells. Is there a range of goods on offer? Is there anything you think they should add to the range?

4 Explain whether you would recommend the shop to other people your age and why you would/wouldn't.

Question 3

Style: Neutral or semi-formal.

Content: 1 Explain whether you think local traditions are important.

2 Give reasons and examples why they are or are not important to small communities.

3 Discuss whether forgetting local traditions is a problem or not.

4 Give examples of any traditions that you think are important and why you think they should be preserved.

Question 4

Letter of application (*FIRST only*)

Style: Neutral or semi-formal.

Content: 1 Address your letter to Mr Green.

2 Say who you are and what your interest in photography is.

3 Think of reasons why you would benefit from the course, and how it might help you in the future.

4 Say you hope Mr Green will consider your application.

5 Finish the letter with 'Yours sincerely' and your full name.

Story (*FIRST FOR SCHOOLS only*)

Style: Neutral.

Content: 1 Read the prompt sentence carefully. Write it down as the first sentence of your story.

2 Decide who Dan is and what the text says or is about. Why was it not a good idea for Dan to reply to the text? Why did he do it anyway? What happened as a result?

3 Remember you must include the points in the notes. Was someone else driving the car, or was it Dan? Who was the present for?

4 Make sure your story progresses logically with a beginning, a middle and an end.

Question 5 (*FIRST FOR SCHOOLS only*)

Style: Neutral or semi-formal

Content: Decide which of the characters in the book or short story you have read made an important decision. Describe the character and explain in detail the decision he or she had to make. Explain how this decision affected the life of the character and the lives of the rest of the characters. Say whether you would have made the same decision if you had found yourself in a similar situation.

PAPER 3 Listening

▶▶ PART 1

1 A   2 B   3 A   4 B   5 B   6 C   7 C   8 B

▶▶ PART 2

9 cousin

10 maths / Maths / mathematics / Mathematics

11 parties

12 friends

13 lift

14 bike / bicycle

15 paperwork

16 confident

17 bracelet

18 air hostess

▶▶ PART 3

19 C   20 H   21 D   22 B   23 F

▶▶ PART 4

24 C   25 B   26 A   27 A   28 B   29 B   30 C

Introduction to the DVD-ROM

This edition of *Exam Essentials* Practice Tests for students of Cambridge English: First (FCE) includes a brand new DVD-ROM which focuses on the Speaking test component of the Cambridge English: First examination. The DVD-ROM includes two videos:

• a complete Cambridge English: First Speaking test based on Test 3 of the Practice tests.
• a short clip giving valuable advice about the Cambridge English: First Speaking test.

To maximise learning from the complete Cambridge English: First Speaking test, the following PDFs are also available on the DVD-ROM:

• a worksheet for individual or class use
• an answer key for the worksheet
• the complete script of the Speaking test.

A complete Speaking test

A full Cambridge English: First Speaking test interview is approximately 14 minutes in length. Please note that the interview shown on this DVD-ROM is a slightly extended version of the Speaking test. This allows for a wide range of language and types of response to be included. This interview also features high-level candidates whose performance would achieve a good pass in the exam. The video therefore provides a good model to follow. Don't worry if you feel you may not perform to this high standard in every area of the test. You will need to demonstrate a good level, but you will not need to use every structure or item of vocabulary perfectly in order to pass the test. Please see page 64 and pages 165–167 in the Practice Tests for the material used in this interview.

The video clearly details:

• the role of the examiners
• the timings of the test
• the four parts of the test and what is involved in each one.

Tips and advice

Following the Speaking test, there is a short clip to supplement the speaking tips given in the book. In this section, which is about five minutes long, an examiner gives some tips and advice about how to do well in the Cambridge English: First Speaking test.

The worksheet

This printable worksheet accompanies the complete Cambridge English: First Speaking test. Although primarily designed for self-study, the worksheet can also be used in the classroom. It provides in-depth information about the Speaking test and focuses on the language each candidate uses in the video.

The worksheet is divided into four sections, which relate to each part of the Speaking test. It includes activities which:

• draw students' attention to key features of the candidate's response
• relate these features to the marking criteria used by the examiners
• give the student practice in developing their own answers for similar questions.

A separate answer key and a full video script are also provided.